D0148598

EDUCATION IN THE THIRD WORLD

Education in the Third World

EDITED BY KEITH WATSON

CROOM HELM
London & Canberra

© 1982 J.K.P. Watson
Croom Helm Ltd, Provident House, Burrell Row,
Beckenham, Kent BR3 1AT

British Library Cataloguing in Publication Data

Education in the Third World.
  1. Underdeveloped areas – Education
  I. Watson, Keith
  370'.9172'4   LC2605

  ISBN 0-7099-2749-5

Printed and bound in Great Britain by
Billing and Sons Limited Worcester

CONTENTS

Colonialism - and all its facets, most of all those
facets of policy which have had a direct bearing on educational
development, never ceases to fascinate. Colonialism is still
a vitally important part of the heritage of most Third World
countries and, in many instances, influences relations
between these countries and the Western powers. But in
spite of its importance, remarkably little has been written
on the subject that has not been either eulogistic or down-
right critical.

Many of the early writings tended to be laudatory, being
written by apologists of colonial rule, people deeply
involved in or actively committed to the colonial process,
and believing deeply in the civilising mission of the
European powers. Arthur Mayhew's Education in the Colonial
Empire (1938) would have fitted into this category and while
Lord Lugard might have periodically criticised educational
policies and practice, he nevertheless had a firm belief in
the colonial relationship as his Dual Mandate in British
Tropical Africa (1929) shows. There were critics of
colonialism who were not necessarily Marxists - Hobson's
Imperialism (1900) and Furnivall's Colonial Education Policy
and Practice (1943) immediately spring to mind - but there
has been a tendency during the past fifteen to twenty years,
for writers to take a highly critical and political, usually
Marxist or neo-Marxist position, e.g. Carnoy (1974); Fanon
(1967); Mannoni (1964); Memmi (1965). How valid is such an
approach? How much of their attack is based on evidence,
how much on political polemic? Are their criticisms
universally applicable or only applicable to certain
countries or regions (e.g. Latin America)? It is in an
attempt to examine some of the evidence, and where
necessary, to redress the balance, at least partially, that
this volume of essays is offered.

It is based on papers that were given at the Annual
Conference of the Education in Developing Countries Study
Group of the Development Studies Association held at the

University of Reading, during 21-22 September 1979. This was
partly inspired by Altbach and Kelly's volume, <u>Education and
Colonialism</u>, which appeared in 1978. It was however,
recognised that there were a number of omissions in that
volume and that most of the authors wrote from an American
perspective. The present volume of essays therefore, should
be seen as complementary to and not in competition with
Altbach and Kelly's book. It was however, much more a concern
for the need to reassess the role education played in the
colonial policy of the metropolitan powers, as well as the
impact of colonial policy on educational development in many
Third World countries that led a group of us to meet together,
at the Reading Conference to thrash out some of our views.
Other contributions have been added to the conference papers
subsequently.

All the contributors have either lived and worked in
Third World countries strongly influenced by colonial control,
either as officials of colonial governments or as public
officials in government agencies in the post-colonial period.
They hold no brief for colonialism: nor have they any anti-
colonial axe to grind. Their desire is to examine the
colonial relationship with regard to education and to high-
light the positive aspects of this relationship as well as to
identify its weaknesses. In some cases, this relationship has
been viewed from a macro-perspective of a region or a country:
in others from micro-studies of individual projects or educational schemes. In all cases, it is hoped that some new
light has been thrown on to the colonial relationship. It
must be pointed out at the outset, however, that the topic of
education and colonialism is so vast and controversial, that
the following essays can be little more than an offering in
the debate. Moreover, they can in no way be considered
definitive, if for no other reason than that they concentrate
mainly on British colonial policies. They do, however, try to
cover the policy issues and the application of these policies
during the colonial era, as well as trying to show how the
colonial relationship is an ongoing process.

I should like to thank all those who have given so
generously of their time and effort: all the contributors -
without whom there would have been no symposium, let alone
a book; the Executive Committee of the Development Studies
Association, which organised the conference; the Warden of
St. Patrick's Hall of Residence at the University of Reading;
to Ray Davies for his helpful advice; and to Christine
Hargreaves, Christine Bland and Hellen Barnes for their
patience in de-cyphering and typing the script.

BEATRICE AVALOS   was born and taught in Chile. She came
                         to this country after the fall of the
                         Allende regime and was until 1981 a
                         lecturer in the Education Department of
                         the University College of Wales at Cardiff.
                         She is the author of 'Educational Change
                         in Latin America: The Case of Peru' and
                         is currently at the Ontario Institute for
                         Studies into Education in Developing
                         Countries in Canada.

COLIN BROCK   has taught in schools and teacher training
                         institutions in Britain and in St. Lucia,
                         British West Indies. He has also taught
                         in the Overseas Education Unit at Leeds
                         University and is currently a lecturer in
                         Education at Hull University. He is co-
                         author of 'The Changing Nature of
                         Educational Politics in the 1970s' and has
                         produced several textbooks for use in the
                         Caribbean.

BRIAN GARVEY   has taught in England and Zambia, where
                         he worked closely with the British Ministry
                         of Overseas Development and the World Bank
                         and did his doctoral field work. He took
                         his doctorate at the University of London
                         Institute of Education Department of
                         Education in Developing Countries where he
                         also taught for a time. He is currently
                         at the Overseas Education Unit at the
                         University of Leeds.

DUDLEY HICK
originally taught in England and Europe before going out to Australia. He has travelled in South East Asia and has made a study of educational change in Vietnam. He is currently a Senior Lecturer in Education at the University of Sydney and is editing a book on 'Schooling in Asia'.

TONY HOPKIN
has taught in Wales, New Zealand and Fiji where he did his doctoral work. He is currently a lecturer in the Education Deparment of the University College of Wales at Cardiff.

KEITH WATSON
has taught in England, Poland, Bangladesh and Thailand where he was an Education Officer with the British Council. Part of his work was responsibility for administering some of Britain's Educational aid. As a British Council Officer he also visited the Middle East and Indian Sub-continent for different periods of time. He took his doctorate at the University of Reading where he is currently a lecturer in Comparative Education. He is the author of 'Educational Development in Thailand'.

CLIVE WHITEHEAD
began his career in England and took his doctorate at the University of London Institute of Education before going to Australia. He is at present a Lecturer in Education in the University of Western Australia. His research work has centred on educational policy in Fiji, Malaya and Singapore.

Chapter One

COLONIALISM AND EDUCATIONAL DEVELOPMENT

Keith Watson

1. INTRODUCTION

     Colonial involvement in the development of education
systems in so much of what is today known as the Third World
is still a matter of heated debate amongst historians,
educationists and development economists alike. It is both a
fascinating and complex topic. As Coleman (1965) has said
'one of the major indictments made by critics of Western
colonialism has been its alleged neglect of education' both
quantitatively in the numbers enrolled in schools and
qualitatively in the type of education offered which has been
blamed for being inappropriate, being too dominated by
colonial culture or because it spoilt the indigenous culture.
The result is that the term 'colonialism' is as likely to
bring about a glow of pride and self-congratulation amongst
former colonial administrators as it is to bring about anger
and cynicism amongst liberal intellectuals and Marxists in
the Western and Third Worlds.
     The earliest writers on the topic of education and
colonialism were mainly apologists of colonial rule, convinced
that the European powers' civilising mission could only be
beneficial for the native peoples of Africa or Asia, the West
Indies or the islands of the Pacific region. (Raffles 1830;
Lugard 1929; Mayhew 1938; Scott 1937). During the 1920s and
1930s with the Phelps-Stokes Commissions examining education
first in West Africa and then in East Africa (Berman 1971;
Jones 1922, 1925; Lewis 1962) and with missionary societies
re-examining their policies at conferences in Jerusalem (1928)
and Madras (1938) serious doubts began to be expressed about
the direction of colonial educational policies. Inevitably
some of the severest criticism was to come not from colonial
governments but from neutral observers (e.g. Furnivall 1943,
1956). During the period of transition from colonial
dependency to independent nationhood, especially during the
late 1950s and 1960s, it became fashionable to denounce the
colonial powers while at the same time arguing that the

1

colonial educational legacy should be built upon for the purposes of national development.

More recently it has become fashionable, especially from radicals, to attack all forms of colonialism, especially their impact on educational development (Carnoy 1974; Fanon 1969; Freire 1971; Mamouni 1963; Memmi 1965; Reimer 1971). Missionaries have been accused of being 'the lackeys of imperialism'. The colonial education systems have been accused of being little more than tools used by capitalists to exploit the underdeveloped world and to keep their peoples in subjection. The colonial powers have been accused of pursuing educational policies that have led to misshapen development or even to underdevelopment while at the same time they have been accused of neglecting education. The following aspects of policy are used to sustain the argument. There was an uneven distribution of school provision throughout the colonies. Dual standards were encouraged because on the one hand there were urban colonial schools for the indigenous elites, usually conducted in the language of the colonial rulers (e.g. English, French and Dutch), while on the other hand there were poor, rural, vernacular schools for those peasants who could avail themselves of the opportunities so provided. Much of what was taught was irrelevant for the real social, psychological or employment needs of the pupils who attended. There was an excessive concentration on diplomas and examinations which originated in and were designed for the metropolitan powers but the achievement of which was in time to become the major purpose of much of colonial schooling. (Dore 1976). There was too little concern for developing mass education, adult literacy, vocational education and certainly higher education. Many of the current educational development problems faced in countries of the Third World can be directly attributable to the policies of the colonial powers.

On the other hand some recent attempts have even been made to show that colonial involvement, especially in Asia, was little more than a passing phenomenon which in a long historical timescale has had little impact on the course of events or on traditional relationships between different groups in the region. (Romain 1962; Eisenstadt 1978). Such a view would not be held by most observers of the Third World scene especially in the African context and particularly by those development economists who subscribe to 'dependency theory', which argues that most poor countries of the world are in a state of greater dependency on the Western powers today than they ever were at the height of colonial control. (Frank 1967; Chilcote 1974; Galtung 1972). Indeed Beatrice Avalos' paper in this collection shows that this is the situation in the modern Latin American context. Because the industrialised nations of the world control the terms of trade they have a greater influence on the economies of the

Colonialism and Educational Development

Third World than they ever did as colonial rulers. Because
the industrial nations of the world control the purse strings,
they can dictate the shape of educational developments. Far
from being a dead issue, therefore, colonialism is active
and well in a more subtle form - what Altbach has called
'the highest form of colonialism' - namely that of neocolonialism. (Altbach 1971, 1977; Dumont 1966; Hayter 1971;
Mende 1973).

How valid are these criticisms? Is it possible to draw
up a balance sheet on colonialism and educational development
free from political overtones and bias? Is it possible to
talk about 'colonialism' and 'colonial educational policies'
in blanket terms when there were so many variations depending
on the colonial power, the territory involved, and the time
being referred to? Can all the problems of educational
underdevelopment be laid at the feet of the colonial powers
when countries like Afghanistan, Iran, Liberia, Nepal and
Thailand, which were never directly colonised, share so many
of these problems?

From the hindsight of the 1980s it is an easy thing to
criticise. Our attitudes to education have changed; our
understanding of the complexities of education's role in the
development process have become better formulated. (D'aeth
1978; Simmons 1980; World Bank 1980). It is perhaps easier
to be critical of policies in certain countries, rather than
in others, and it is all too easy to blame current
educational problems on to the policies of colonial powers.
However, what is frequently overlooked and ignored in the
criticisms is that many colonial administrators, in many
different parts of the world, acted from the highest motives
according to their own educational experience and upbringing
and acted according to the conventional educational wisdom
of the time (e.g. that education equalled schooling with a
neo-classical academic curriculum, that grants-in-aid were
only permissible if examination results were satisfactory
and inspection was allowed). Colonial administrators may
have been patronising but many of them had to develop an
ad hoc policy on the spot with the best of intentions and
without any guidance from the colonial government back at
home. This was undoubtedly more true of English administrators
than French ones but it applied across the board. (e.g.
Jayasuriya 1978; Stevenson 1975; Woodruff 1963).

What is also frequently forgotten is that many of the
early 'colonists', whether missionaries or servants of
governments or trading companies (e.g. Raffles of Singapore;
Macaulay of the East India Company; Lugard of Nigeria) were
pioneers in developing the written forms of the vernacular
languages, in the development of printing and the means of
disseminating knowledge other than through the oral tradition,
in the education of women and in the development of
vocational and technical education. The fact that colonial

policies, let alone colonial educational policies, often
evolved only slowly and haltingly, is often glossed over by
writers who can only see the evils of the colonial relationship. Nor should it be forgotten that universal secondary
education did not become a feature of Western Europe until
after the Second World War. Another feature that is all too
readily glossed over by American writers especially is that
the United States has had a profound and lasting colonial
relationship with the Philippines, Thailand (theoretically
never colonised) the Lebanon and even Japan, while the
Marxists gloss over the fact that the present day influence
- or control - of the Soviet Union on education in Eastern
Europe and certain Third World countries (Angola, Cuba,
Ethiopia, etc.) is just as great, if not greater, than that
exercised during the period of high classical colonialism.

     It is hoped that the essays included in this book, while
neither definitive nor unduly polemical, may add something of
value to the debate about the colonial influence on educational
development. As they seek to give a balanced reassessment
of some colonial policies and practices, and as they seek to
examine the evidence it is hoped that some of the more
extreme criticisms of colonialism may be countered.

2. THE ACQUISITION OF EMPIRE AND THE COLONISING PROCESS

     While an impression is often given that the European
colonial idea formed a coherent and social philosophy which
in practice aimed at the conquest of the poorer parts of the
world, the evidence is often very far from this. Indeed it
has frequently been argued that the British acquired their
empire as much by accident as by design (Cross 1970). The
European expansion which began in the sixteenth and seventeenth centuries was not part of some carefully worked out
scheme. In fact as empires rose - and fell - attitudes to
imperialism and motives for expansion differed quite
markedly. Few of those who first planted the European flags
on foreign soils three to four hundred years ago could have
envisaged the far reaching effects of their actions, let
alone appreciated the conflicting views over colonial
responsibilities aired by politicians and administrators
during the early and mid-twentieth century.
     It must be recognised that European colonialism was but
a passing phase in the timescale of history. Many parts of
the world not only had a pre-colonial history (conveniently
forgotten in most Western textbooks) but they have also had
a post-colonial history. Although the Spanish conquistadores
destroyed the empires of the Incas and Aztecs in Latin
America, in other parts of the world early European expansion
was as much concerned with securing trading posts as with
territorial conquest and the defeat of indigenous political

4

Colonialism and Educational Development

systems. Until the nineteenth century at least, when
capitalism and industrialisation began to change attitudes,
European contacts with different civilisations were ones of
equality, not superiority. Members of the East India Company
in the eighteenth century, recognised the differences of
Indian civilisation but they did not necessarily despise
these differences. European observers in seventeenth century
Thailand recognised in the court at Ayuthia, the then capital,
a civilisation as advanced, sophisticated and colourful as
anything that could be offered by Louis XIV at Versailles.
Traders in West Africa recognised the richness of the
Ashanti Kingdom of the Gold Coast, while traders in South
East Asia, the Middle East and North Africa likewise
recognised that there were deeply established civilisations
in those parts.

Nevertheless it is possible to identify certain phases
of European expansion that were to lead from trading relation
-ships to colonial ones. During the sixteenth, seventeenth
and eighteenth centuries a series of chartered trading
companies established outposts in different parts of the world
with the express intention of carrying on trade, making
profits and providing their shareholders with dividends.
They had no interest in the social welfare or education of
the people with whom they came into contact. Missionaries
followed the flag, partly to care for the souls of the
traders, partly to convert the natives to Christianity. In
the context of Latin America especially this was to lead to
the establishment of schools and colleges and seminaries.
As the nineteenth century progressed and European power
rivalry increased, annexation of land became a feature of
colonial policy but with economic and trading motives for so
doing being paramount. By the time of the First World War
there was growing discussion about and concern for the
social welfare of native peoples under colonial rule. This
led to more positive action being taken on the part of
colonial governemtns regarding health, education, social
welfare and the development of the economy during the inter
war years. In the aftermath of the Second World War the
European powers gradually relinquished their colonies,
frequently after armed struggle. The most recent phase of
colonialism has been the attempts to establish special
relationships between the former colonial power and the ex-
colonies, which can be seen in Commonwealth preferences and
special agreements between the French and their former
territories. As will be seen in a later section, educational
policy evolved in similar stages as the colonial relationship
changed.

The growth of empire and attitudes to imperialism have
thus differed according to the historical timescale and
according to the colonial power concerned. The sixteenth
and seventeenth centuries saw the first waves of overseas

expansion largely from Roman Catholic Spain and Portugal to
Latin America, though it also saw French missionary endeavour
into Asia and British moves towards establishing trading posts
in North America, India and the Caribbean. The main thrust of
Iberian expansion was for the exploitation of natural resources
- gold, silver and spices - for the treasuries of Spain and
Portugal. The conversion of the indigenous peoples to
Christianity was a secondary aspect of the imperial thrust
though the work of the Jesuits in establishing secondary and
tertiary level institutions(1) was to have a profound effect
on the future shape of educational systems and attitudes towards the education of elites and the rejection of education
for the masses in Latin America. Imperial control waned as
the power of Spain and Portugal gradually declined in the
face of challenges from the Dutch, the French and the British,
but the impact on Latin American societies has been profound.
This can be seen in the Language (Portuguese in Brazil,
Spanish elsewhere in South and Central America except for the
few Dutch and British settlements). It can also be seen in
the forms of government, intermarriage between Europeans and
the peoples of Latin America, the dominance of the Roman
Catholic Church and church influence in secondary and higher
education. The development of higher education from such an
early period sets Latin America apart from other colonised
parts of the Third World where higher education was not
established until the twentieth century. India was the one
exception to this since higher education was begun there
during the last century. The patterns of Latin America are
also substantially different from other Iberian colonies, the
Philippines (Spanish), Timor, Goa, Macao and later Mozambique
and Angola (Portuguese) where educational investment was low
and enrolments were correspondingly low. Even as late as
1960 only 21% of the age group was enrolled at primary level
in Angola and 48% in Mozambique, though these figures compared
favourably with enrolments in French West Africa.

    Dutch expansion began in earnest during the seventeenth
and eighteenth centuries into the East Indies (Indonesia),
Malacca, and parts of the Caribbean. This coincided with the
Dutch merchant fleets' control of the spice trade and of the
high seas. Again the main motive was economic exploitation
and the plantation system - imposed in Java - was to destroy
the existing social and economic patterns and was to have a
profound impact of population growth. Nevertheless by the
latter part of the nineteenth century concern was being
expressed for the development of an education system and
there was a combination of colonial government and mission
schools spread unevenly throughout the major islands of the
archipelago.

    The late seventeenth/early eighteenth centuries saw
British and French expansion into the imperial world, initially
to North America, the West Indies and the Indian subcontinent,

but it was not until the nineteenth and twentieth centuries
when the real scramble for empire began as territories in
Africa, Asia and the Middle East became annexed. This period
can truly be called 'the age of imperialism'. Belgium,
Germany, Italy all became involved and different territories
were carved up to suit the needs, pride and convenience of the
metropolitan powers. During the twentieth century we have
seen the USA, Japan, Australia and the Soviet Union all enter
the colonial race, and although since 1946 there has been a
gradual unscrambling of colonial control in the Pacific, Asia,
Africa, the Middle East and the Caribbean we have also
witnessed the growth of colonial control in a more obvious
form in Eastern Europe and in those territories strongly tied
to the Soviet economic and defence systems (e.g. Cuba, Angola,
Ethiopia and Afghanistan), and in more subtle forms in the
continuing links between the metropolitan colonial powers and
their former dependencies.

Thus on a historical timescale colonialism has differed
from one geographic area to another, depending on which powers
have been involved. Nevertheless by World War II most of what
is now known as the Third World was under some form of colonial
domination. South America was largely independent but the
rest was under French, British, Dutch, Italian, Belgian,
Portuguese or American control. It was being exploited or
being brought the benefits (or evils) of Western civilisation
according to one's personal or political perspective. Even
those countries not directly under colonial control - e.g.
Thailand, Nepal, Afghanistan, Iran, Saudi Arabia - were
nevertheless strongly influenced by the Western powers and
their manifestations of colonialism.

It was inevitable that policies differed according to
the political convictions of the colonising nation. Thus
from the very beginning Spain and Portugal sought economic
domination, accepted assimilation and intermarriage between
races, imposed Roman Catholic beliefs and encouraged the
Catholic church to establish hospitals, schools and clinics.
The French likewise sought economic domination, but they also
had a strong sense of mission civilisatrice, initially and
intellectually believing that they could create black, brown
and yellow Frenchmen with the same views and outlooks as the
metropolitan Frenchman. That this position became increasingly
untenable did not in any way detract from the myth that it
was possible (Marshall 1973). The French politicians and
administrators believed in the superiority of French culture,
the French language, literature and administrative structures;
and the French language was used as a means of colonial
domination and control while the indigenous languages were
scorned. (Asiwaju 1975; Knight 1965). Gradually they came
to see that colonies in French West Africa, North Africa
(especially Algeria) and the West Indies, designated the
Department d'Outre Mer, should become not only extensions of

7

metropolitan France but that Guineans, Algerians, Senegalese, Cambodians and Guadaloupese should develop the same views and values as Frenchmen and that they should send deputies to the National Assembly in Paris. Following the first World War many future leaders of these territories, including Ho-Chi Minh and Pol Pot(2) were educated in French universities. During the inter war years the belief in 'the assimilation' of colonial territories and peoples defined by Clignet and Foster (1964) as 'the elimination of parochial cultures and the creation of men who are peers and culturally undifferentiated', gradually yielded to the concept of 'association' which legitimised the French colonial bureaucracy, especially in black Africa, but which allowed the educated elite in colonial territories a share in power and at the same time granted them citizenship rights. (Hargreaves 1976). Following the Second World War there developed a belief in a loose 'union' with France, with voting rights for colonial citizens rather than independence, though in 1958/9 under De Gaulle French West Africa was given the option of independence or of becoming an extension of metropolitan France. Guinea opted for independence, but Dahomey (Benin), Chad and Senegal opted for 'links' with the French community. Ever since 'independence' French advisers have continued to play key roles in the economies of former French colonies and 90% of French aid and technical assistance is channelled into former French colonies.
    The British, often called 'the reluctant colonisers', certainly acquired many territories not so much in a fit of absentmindedness as in an attempt either to protect their own citizens, as for example in the case of the Federated Malay States, or as a means of preventing others from getting control, as for example in India, Singapore, the Pacific Islands and some of the Caribbean territories. In central and southern Africa there was a much more deliberate policy, especially under the inspiration of Cecil Rhodes of 'getting there first' and 'of civilising the natives'. There was certainly no common colonial policy. This was largely due to the way the Indian Civil Service and the Colonial Service were kept separate, but it was also due to the regionalisation of policy making in London. Thus policy varied from colony to colony according to the strength of personality of the governor and according to the different racial and ethnic groups involved. Frequently concern was expressed that certain groups (e.g. Muslims in northern Nigeria or Hindus or Malays) should not be corrupted by contact with Western civilisation and should be allowed to live a relatively sheltered existence. Thus while the French sought to win the allegiance of all ethnic groups and to bring about cultural assimilation and imposed the French language on their colonies to this end, the British treated different groups differently, fostered indigenous institutions and also encouraged indigenous languages. In Malaya for example, while

a clear cut policy towards the Malays had been formulated by the beginning of the twentieth century, no such policy towards Indian and Chinese settlers was agreed upon until the 1920s/1930s. Likewise in Ceylon the Singhalese and Tamils were treated differently, in Kenya and Mauritius the Africans and Asians were also treated differently.

British colonial policy changed therefore over a period of time. From a belief in trusteeship and moral responsibility in the nineteenth century policy progressed towards a sense of obligation to subject peoples and to the eventual recognition that the colonial purpose was to modernise societies and to hand over power to the local peoples. By 1917 in India at least the goal of British policy was already accepted as the handover of power to the Indians. The question was when? That the colonial rulers still thought in terms of centuries rather than in decades or years can be seen from the classic exposition of British Colonial policy given in the House of Commons in December 1938 by the then Colonial Secretary, Malcolm MacDonald:

> The great purpose of the British Empire is the gradual spread of freedom among all His Majesty's subjects in whatever part of the world they live. That spread of freedom is a slow, evolutionary process. In some countries it is more rapid than in others. In some parts of the empire, in the Dominions, that evolutionary process has been completed, it is finished. Inside the Colonial Empire the evolutionary process is going on all the time. In some colonies like Ceylon the gaining of freedom has already gone very far. In others it is necessarily a much slower process. It may take generations, or even centuries, for the peoples in some parts of the Colonial Empire to achieve self-government.

3. THE EVOLUTION OF EDUCATIONAL POLICY

Just as colonial policy changed and evolved over a period of time so did educational policy. We need to remember that while there is widespread criticism that the European powers did not develop adequate education systems in their colonies before World War II compulsory state primary education was only introduced in England in the 1870s, in France in the 1880s, and that in no European country was universal secondary education made available until well after the Second World War. It would be fairer to recognise that there were educational policies, but that they reflected policies accepted in the metropolitan power at the time. Thus if a policy of laissez-faire was pursued in most British colonies in the nineteenth century this

9

reflected the prevailing pattern in England. The 1870
Education Act only encouraged local authorities to establish
primary schools where the churches had failed to do so.
Payment by results as a measure for receiving grants in aid
was introduced in England in the 1860s and was also
introduced into India, Malaya, Ceylon and East Africa in the
1880s and 1890s. Primary extension schools followed by
restricted entry academic secondary schools became a feature
in English education following the 1902 Education Act and
were likewise introduced into many colonies. Vocational
education which became fashionable in England immediately
prior to and following the first World War (e.g. the Fisher
Act of 1918) became a feature of policy in West and East
Africa, India and Malaya, though interestingly enough in the
French colonial context it was the other way round.
Vocational education tried in the French West African
territories was later introduced into metropolitan France
(Clignet and Foster). French insistence on centralised
control, academic standards and secularisation of education
was likewise translated into the colonial scene. It is
generally true to say that policies that existed in the
colonial situation largely reflected developments in the
metropolitan power and that the importance of education was
not acknowledged by most West European governments until the
1930s and 1940s and changes were not actually implemented
until the 1950s. As Sutton (1965 p.60) has pointed out,
'The fact that the great Western spread in the world took
place at a time when western societies still had much of
their modern educational development ahead is an important
historical fact'.
    Thus, in spite of scathing critics such as Carnoy (1974)
who has argued that 'the primary purpose of (colonial)
schooling was control' and '...the primary purpose was to
build a cultural dependency among the educated and ruling
classes so that revolutionary overthrow would never be a
likely alternative', and Furnivall (1956) who argued that
colonial educational policy sought to transform society to
a westernised viewpoint, the truth is that there was no
coherent policy before the 1920s, at least in Britain, as
Clive Whitehead shows in his paper in this volume. As
Scott (1937) observed, '...no steps to formulate an educational
policy, or at least to make it public, appear to have been
taken before the (First World) War'. In fact Lord Lugard
was particularly critical about the confusion and lack of
co-ordination in educational policy especially in West
Africa (Lugard 1925) while Beck (1966) has described developments in British East Africa as 'sporadic and unorganised'.
    Not only were there differences in French, English and
Dutch rule in South East Asia (Furnivall 1943) and French
and English rule in West Africa (Asiwaju 1975; Clignet and
Foster 1964), but individual national policies differed

from one part of the colonial empire to another. For example
British policies in the Pacific region, the West Indies,
India and Malaya, often called 'Further India', differed
quite markedly from policies in West Africa which differed
in their turn from those in East Africa. In both Malaya and
India for example the government provided vernacular primary
education for certain groups, leaving English medium secondary
education in the hands of missionaries. In many African
territories, however, the arrangement was often though not
always the other way round. Moreover policies towards
different ethnic groups differed quite markedly even within
the same territory, as the chapter on Malaysia in this
volume well illustrates. In that instance colonial treatment
of Malays differed markedly from the treatment meted out to
other groups like the Tamils and Chinese. Only after World
War II was any real attempt made to redress the situation.

The truth of the matter is that colonial educational
policy was not clearly thought out and Carnoy's observation
that 'there was no general re-thinking of education in the
British Colonial Office between 1847 and 1925' (Carnoy p.139)
is essentially correct. It was often a hasty response to an
immediate crisis as was sometimes the case for the French in
Indo China and the British in Ceylon. It was often
inconsistent and was frequently changed, depending upon the
findings and recommendations of different royal commissions,
and each colony evolved its own system independently. There
was no blueprint for all the colonies. Too often analysis
of colonial educational policy has been based on policy
statements and documents issued in London, Paris or the
Hague, when the reality of what happened in practice was
often very different from official policy statements,
because local situations demanded local responses and because,
as Stevenson (1975) has shown, the character and temperament
of individual officers in the field were so variable. Some
were interested in education; others were not. Some carried
out official policy as far as possible; others sought to
make their own or sought to interpret official policy in
their own lights. There were also those like Lord Curzon
in India who as early as 1904 bemoaned that educational
policies were misguided, because they were too academic and
too European.

Nevertheless it has been suggested that in the case of
the British (Scott 1937; Lewis 1954; Furnivall 1956) there
were four phases in the evolution of colonial education
policy: (1) the period of _laissez-faire_ on the part of
governments, when education was largely left in the hands
of missionaries; (2) the period of growing government
interest as missionaries and governments worked alongside
each other; (3) the period of change as policies were
questioned and reformulated during the inter war years; and
(4) the period of growing state control and direction.

Colonialism and Educational Development

(a) The role of missionary societies
While the French might have had a strong sense of
mission civilisatrice and a desire to spread le culture
générale, which led to strong government control of missionary
activities, British governments in the early stages of
colonisation largely ignored education, being more concerned
with the maintenance of law and order, defence and economic
development (exploitation). There was 'an absence of any
clear educational ideas on the government's part as well as
a lack of belief in education ...' (Mayhew 1938) with the
result that the colonial governors were quite prepared
either to leave any local or indigenous methods of education
largely untouched or to leave educational developments in
the hands of missionaries, who, in the absence of others,
were in many cases the only people offering any formal
schooling. As such they were often the spearhead of modern
educational developments. As Lewis has commented 'what
distinguished the effort of the Christian Missions was its
persistent and expanding nature' (1954 p.10). In many
British and Dutch colonies especially, the impact of
missionaries on educational developments in the early years
especially was often far greater than that of the colonial
government as Watson's paper on South East Asia illustrates.
It has been frequently suggested by African and Asian
nationalists amongst others that missionary societies and
colonial governments worked hand in hand 'to convert
Africans from barbarians into civilised humans, to prepare
them to fill the role of agricultural producers instead of
slaves in the European run world economic system' (Carnoy
1974 p.81). Even Mao Tse-Tung blamed many of China's
problems on 'the cultural imperialism' of the missionary
movement which he saw as an arm of European colonialism.
The truth is frequently somewhat different. Many missionary
societies (e.g. in the Caribbean and India) began educational
work before the colonial governments took over from merchants
and trading companies, and were only allowed on sufferance
to continue their work after the territory had changed
status. Their work was not always welcomed by colonial
governors and there were occasional conflicts between
missions and the colonial authorities as Brian Garvey's
chapter on African educational development clearly shows.
Moreover many of the missionaries were not themselves of the
same nationality as that of the colonial power. The De La
Salle Brothers in Malaysia and Singapore were largely Irish,
Belgian and French; the Roman Catholic Brothers in Bengal
were mainly French or French Canadian; the Don Bosco groups
in India often had Irish or Italian priests; while in Ghana
a number of schools were operated by Swiss Basel missionaries. Lauwerys has aptly pointed out that 'Missionaries
were never entirely free to do as they wanted: the British
authorities supported them when it suited their purpose and

12

placed restrictions on them when this seemed necessary in the
light of their own aims'. (Lauwerys 1967, ix).

The reasons are not difficult to find. The main purpose
of missionary education was proselytisation - the conversion
of indigenous peoples to Christianity - and emphasis on
standards of behaviour and morality characteristic of
Christian Europe. To achieve this purpose required them to
teach basic literacy so that pupils could read the Bible and
memorise the catechism. This often resulted in pioneering
instruction in vernacular languages and translating the
Word of God into these same languages. In many cases (e.g.
Rhodesia and Southern Sudan) missionaries opened up schools
in inaccessible rural areas or in tribal areas in which the
colonial government had little interest. In other cases
they pioneered education for women or amongst different
ethnic groups ignored by the colonial administration (e.g.
Tamils in Ceylon, Tamils and Chinese in Malaya and Singapore).
In all territories, whether the Gold Coast, Nigeria, the
East African states or Ceylon, the main purpose of teacher
training institutions was also to train native ministers who
could further the cause of Christianity. On the other hand
colonial administrators were as concerned that pupils should
acquire vocational skills, numeracy, practical training and
English that could be used in clerical or commercial posts,
as in the development of moral or religious education. No
group was beyond the pale as far as missionary evangelism
was concerned. As far as colonial governments were concerned,
however, there were very definitely certain religious groups
who should not be proselytised. Thus while missionaries
were given a free hand in the West Indies and Ceylon in both
Malaya and Nigeria they were expressly forbidden from
working amongst Muslims with the intention of conversion.
The attitude of some colonial authorities towards missionary
societies was such as to provoke Lord Lugard into commenting
that 'in Africa the schoolboy came to the conclusion that
the government looked on religion with contempt'. (Lugard
1925).

Again missionary societies and their school systems are
frequently denigrated for destroying indigenous and traditional
education such as the Buddhist monastic schools, the Hindu
temple schools and the Koranic schools. Not everyone takes
the extreme view expressed by Jayasuriya when he says of the
situation in Ceylon 'Vicious onslaughts on the indigenous
religions were made through the religious tracts that were
profusely turned out by the printing presses established by
the missionary societies, operating through the patronage of
the government. School children were being subjected to
brain washing in the schools'. (1978 p.223). It is more
generally suggested that while missions did not set out with
a deliberate policy of destroying traditional/religious
schools nevertheless as a result of changing attitudes towards

life and as realisation dawned that missionary education
could lead to a new life in the European-controlled economy
the value of indigenous education faded and missionary
education increased. This view was certainly expressed most
forcefully by Furnivall (1943, 1956) in his classic comparison
of British and Dutch rule in South East Asia and is brought
out by Brock, Garvey and Watson in their papers in this
volume. However there is evidence to show that while
missionary education might have superceded local education
in importance the latter did not die out entirely. (Brown
and Heskett 1975; Kelly 1978). There is also evidence to
show that far from destroying existing religious schools the
impact of Christian mission schools was to lead to a resurgence of Buddhist and Hindu schools. This was certainly the
case in Ceylon and in Vietnam it was the strength and revival
of traditional education that was to be the 'major mobilising
link in the anti-French resistance', that was to force the
French colonial government to take an interest in education
and that forced the government to take drastic measures to
suppress opposition. (Kelly). Undoubtedly the impact of
Christian missions was to lead to a resurgence in Hinduism,
Buddhism and Islam as these great religions sought to come
to terms with the western impact in the different colonial
territories. (Pannikar 1959).

That there were limitations to missionary education
needs to be clearly recognised. Policies were not always
easily arrived at nor clearly worked out. There were
conflicts over whether or not conversion was more important
than education; whether the language of instruction should
be English or the vernacular - (the French did not have this
problem: the colonial government strictly controlled
missionary education and the medium of instruction was
French); whether schooling should be selective or for all-
comers. There was unnecessary rivalry between different
missionary societies and between Roman Catholic and
different Protestant missions, a problem that is still to be
seen in Malawi, Nigeria, Ghana, Kenya and some of the
Carribbean islands, an aspect that created confusion amongst
many Africans (Beck), and one that negates the view that
missionaries were the spearhead of the policy of colonial
governments to suppress and subjugate the native peoples.

The quality and training of many of the missionary
teachers also left much to be desired, though what was
lacking in qualification was frequently made up for in zeal.
One reason for the lack of qualified staff was financial
constraint, especially as school systems grew and pupil
demands increased. It was this financial shortage that
restricted educational provision for a small minority and
that also affected the narrowness of the curriculum and the
textbooks used. The emphasis on primary education, especially
in Africa, largely accounted for why at the time of independence

secondary and tertiary levels of education were so underdeveloped. The emphasis on a literary and academic education
as opposed to practical/vocational training, in spite of
efforts to change this, was to have a profound effect on
attitudes towards formal education and rejection of non
formal skill training, and was to lead to the problem of so
much education being unrelated to the needs of peasant
farmers working in the bush.

While Lugard might claim that 'the educational activities
of the missions have left much to be desired' and Dr. Jones,
chairman of the Phelps-Stokes Commissions might have
criticised them for their lack of teaching practical skills
and for their concern for teaching Bible knowledge, it is
probably fair to say that while many missionaries may have
been misguided, bigoted, short sighted, obstinate or simply
wrong, they operated in the light of their own consciences
and understanding and usually with highly altruistic motives.
At the least the mission schools were no worse and were
frequently much better than government schools. As the
Phelps-Stokes Report on East Africa (Jones 1924 p.88)
commented,

> Careful perusal of the evidence will show that
> missions have committed about the same proportion
> of errors as the governments and the economic
> organisations that have been compelled to deal
> with Africa on the basis of European or American
> experience. The three European parties have
> suffered from the conceits of language, nation-
> ality and colour. Each has brought the best
> they knew in their home country. This has been
> the strength and weakness of their methods and
> objectives.

Support for mission schools generally came from families
of the ruling classes, though not usually in the first
instance; merchants; those aspiring to upward social or
political mobility because for many people mission schools
provided the avenue for such mobility; poorer groups in
society such as the lower castes and untouchables in India
who sought protection through English medium education and
the acceptance of Christianity, the Tamils in Ceylon,
Singapore and Malaya. As a result mission schools had a
profound effect on certain groups in society out of all
proportion to their numbers. Conversely those groups that
sought to avoid mission schools (e.g. Muslims in India)
found themselves at a severe disadvantage.

The success or otherwise of mission schools is often
difficult to assess, especially since following independence
in many territories they have been taken over by governments,
the language media has occasionally been changed and the

religious/proselytisation aspects have been played down. Yet
their achievements should be recognised and acknowledged. In
terms of converts, at least outside Africa and the Carribbean,
they cannot be said to have been very successful. In their
influence over future leaders of independent territories,
however, they were extremely successful. The ideas of freedom,
nationalism and democracy discussed in mission schools were a
heady mixture for young Africans and Asians who aspired for
independence from colonial rule. Mission schools were also
often unifying institutions for different ethnic and linguistic
groups in society since they were all treated as equals in
these institutions. This situation was clearly recognised in
multi-racial Malaya and the Education Report of the Federation
of Malaya (1954) said that 'the mission schools everywhere
co-operated to create that feeling of cohesion between the
different races of the country which is the best hope for the
emergence of one nation'. Such views were echoed in the
Razak Report of 1956.

Missionary schools frequently pioneered vernacular
education, the education of women, a point recognised by the
Straits Settlements Annual Report on Education for 1926 which
said that 'while missionary bodies have done so much for boys'
education they have done almost everything for girls' education.
A few years ago there was no demand for the education of
girls; that the attitude has changed is due among other
causes to the work of the converts and other missionary
schools'. Similar recognition comes from numerous annual
reports from East Africa. Missionaries also pioneered
technical and vocational education (e.g. the Don Bosco
schools, especially in India) and agricultural education,
though as Foster (1965) and Cameron and Dodd (1970) have shown
demand from parents was for intellectual/academic schooling,
not for second-class vocational education. It is perhaps not
surprising that the highest rates of literacy were in areas
of greatest missionary activity (Holmes 1967).

However perhaps the greatest success of missionary
societies lay in the recognition between 1910 and 1920 that
they had to reappraise their position; that they had to
rethink the kind of curricula offered to rural children
unlikely to have more than a few years of primary education;
that they needed to force governments to take a more intell-
igent interest in the education of their colonial peoples;
and if necessary that they needed to co-operate with these
governments. The fact that the British government began to
consider developing a policy towards education in the
colonies during the inter-war years is largely due to the
pressures from missionary organisations.

Before turning to these changes in policy, however, it
is worth looking briefly at some of the other developments
that took place during the period of laissez-faire.

(b) Individual experiments/administrators

It is important to remember that while missions were numerically the most influential in early educational develop -ments there were other agents - merchants, traders, philan- thropists, humanitarians - who were also active in promoting education. In the seventeenth century for example, the Bermuda Company paid the salaries of teachers to teach the basic 3 Rs; in the mid-eighteenth century the Royal African Company requested the Society for the Propagation of the Gospel in London to send out a teacher to begin a school in the Gold Coast. Accordingly in 1765 the Rev. Thomas Thompson was sent out, and in 1820 the Ashanti Treaty recognised the need to establish schools and if necessary to raise taxes for them. At the beginning of the nineteenth century the East India Company appointed Anglican chaplains in Penang (1805) and in Singapore (1826) with the intention of ministering to the spiritual needs of company servants and of establishing schools. The first school was founded in Penang in 1816 by the Rev. E.S. Hutchings and it is claimed that 'he lighted a torch that was to be carried throughout the peninsula' (Wong Hoy Kee and Ee Tiang Hong 1971 p.14), though it was in fact Sir Stamford Raffles in Singapore who had the greatest educational vision of any of his contemporaries. He wished to develop vernacular as well as English medium education and vocational and technical as well as academic education. His grandiose schemes came to very little but the inspiration he gave to future Singaporeans has remained very much alive.(3)

It is ironical that it was not until its dying days that the East India Company in India took any great interest in education but in 1854, following a debate on education in India held in the British parliament the previous year, the Court of Directors issued a directive and policy statement on education. The Company Directors saw education as a blessing to 'the native peoples' and the British government had a sacred duty to provide it. The curriculum should consist of that European knowledge most likely to benefit the people locally and the medium of instruction should be in both English and the vernacular. Education should be made available for the mass of the people and schools should be provided in every district. Teachers should be found who had a knowledge of both English and vernacular languages. Since the costs of providing an extensive network of schools was too great for the company or the government, voluntary bodies, missionary societies and individuals should be encouraged to provide schools. Grants in aid would be made available. It is interesting to note that this approach to educational provision was pursued in Malaya as well as in other colonies.

In fact Stevenson (1975) has shown that the extension of education in the Malay states during the latter part of the nineteenth and early twentieth centuries was due not to any

coherent policy on the part of the British government but was
due to the efforts and the commitment of certain individual
officers working in the field. A similar picture emerges
from many other territories, e.g. Ceylon, Rhodesia, Gold
Coast - since the man on the spot, not the politicians and
civil servants in London, had to make local decisions and
had to see what could/would work on the spot.

        The most interesting experiments however came from
individuals who were concerned that European education as
introduced by missions was divorcing indigenous peoples from
their own traditions and cultures and who felt that a different
approach should be pursued. Two of the most famous experiments,
Melangali in Tanganyika and Omu in Nigeria, were both
concerned that schooling should reflect local culture and
traditions. In describing the Melangali experiment Mumford,
its founder, wrote that the school should be built on native
tradition but that it should at the same time train pupils to
be leaders in social and economic progress. In other words
there should be a judicious blending of European syllabuses
with the practical needs required for agriculture and cattle
rearing in a particular society. Because the experiment
deviated from the European pattern it was widely criticised
but it is difficult to assess it fairly because Mumford was
not there long enough to see it through to a successful
conclusion. In hindsight and sifting the evidence one can
only conclude that too many of the ideas were only half
thought through and that without official, and popular,
support the pressures for Melangali to conform to a more
normal pattern of colonial school were overwhelming.

        The Omu experiment in Nigeria (Clarke 1937) was 'an
attempt to combat the subversive tendencies which were
troubling the minds of the older men and to guide the
inevitable changes so that they might benefit the people'.
Like Melangali, though, it also suffered from being an
experiment never seen through to fruition. In the curriculum
there was a strong emphasis on moral and religious education,
a bias towards agricultural and manual work, the use of the
local environment for study, and the use of local materials
and design for the school. In both cases however, 'an
attempt was made to pattern the life and activities of a
school upon lines which reflected local conditions'. (Lewis
1953 pp.58-9). This was also what the new policies developed
by the government and missionaries during the 1920s were
designed to do.

(c) Policy changes during the 1920s
        Until the 1920s there was neither a coherent policy nor
a co-ordinated effort between colonial governments and
missionary societies but by then both the British government
and the mission societies were ready for a new approach to
education and a recognition of a role of trusteeship, as

Clive Whitehead points out in his chapter in this book.
There had been growing concern amongst missionary groups
since the Edinburgh Conference of 1910 that educational
practice, especially in Africa, was out of tune with local
environments and with the needs of students attending schools,
but that a large injection of cash was needed if anything
adequate was to be done. Colonial government officials were
also beginning to share these concerns. There was also
mounting pressure from public opinion for closer co-ordination
and Lord Lugard summed up the sense of frustration that was
frequently felt at the lack of co-ordination and even interest
in education on the part of colonial governments when he
urged that 'it is an opportune moment for establishing that
close co-operation which has been so signally lacking in the
past'. (Lugard 1925).

Pressures for change came from several quarters over a
period of years. In 1914 a British missionary group began
urging a review of educational provision in Africa, but the
Colonial Office declined to support it. (Berman 1971). In
1918 a local commission of inquiry instigated by J.R. Orr,
the Education Officer in Nairobi, was appointed to study
every aspect of education in East Africa - physical, moral,
intellectual and commercial. In 1919 under pressure from
the American Baptist Missionary Society and the Foreign
Missionary Conference of North America the Phelps-Stokes Fund
supported a study to determine the educational needs of West
Africans. The findings of the Phelps-Stokes Commission on
education in West Africa (1919) and in East Africa (1924)
with its detailed study of education in colonial territories,
its strong recommendations for education systems more suited
to the needs of the Africans, its criticisms of the scant
sources of money allocated for African education and its
recommendations for increased funding were to have a profound
effect on thinking about education in the colonial territories.
(Jones 1922, 1925; Lewis 1960; Berman 1971; Beck 1965).

A few years later the American Methodist Mission Society
carried out an inquiry into the place of mission schools in
Malaya with the express intention of examining whether they
should be funded if they were not specifically proselytising.
The inquiry concluded that if there was no government school
provision then missionaries had a responsibility to step in
whether or not there was proselytisation.

In 1921 the First Secretary of the International
Missionary Council, J.H. Oldham, organised a petition in the
form of a memorandum entitled 'Labour in Africa and Principles
of Trusteeship' which was signed by many well known personal-
ities with and without missionary connections and which he
presented to Alfred Milner at the Colonial Office asking for
a Royal Commission of Investigation. The request was granted
and in East Africa a commission was appointed in 1924. It
reported in 1925. In addition, under pressure from the

Education Committee of the Conference of Missionary Societies of Britain and Ireland (1923) requesting that the Colonial Office establish a permanent Education Advisory Committee to explore possible avenues of closer co-operation between government and mission societies, the government established the British Advisory Committee on Education (1923). This was made up of interested parties with both domestic and colonial experience. The Advisory Committee was initially concerned with education in Africa but on 1st January 1929 its title was changed to the Advisory Committee on Education in the Colonies. While some countries (e.g. Ceylon) were to refuse to make use of the committee, others (e.g. Nigeria) were to make great use of it.

The Advisory Committee's first report, the famous 1925 Memorandum on Educational Policy in British Tropical Africa (HMSO 1925) marks a watershed in colonial educational policy because it laid down principles for education systems in the colonial dependencies and also recognised that the metropolitan government had a responsibility for providing some funds though it firmly believed that the colonies should finance health and education as far as possible from their own economic resources and revenues. It recognised that while the government should guide educational policy and supervise institutions it should collaborate with voluntary and religious agencies; it should provide grants in aid; it should recognise voluntary schools as equals to government schools. Religious education and moral education sould be regarded as fundamental aspects of education which should as far as possible be adapted to local needs. There should be greater emphasis placed on vernacular education and on the provision of vernacular textbooks at primary level, and teachers should be trained with African life, needs and society in mind. Funding for education should be increased. The hope was that this would encourage local developments and initiatives, and local languages and culture rather than an aping of European attitudes and standards. The education of women, regardless of social or religious opposition and technical and vocational education should also be encouraged. Manual occupations should be placed on the curriculum. While primary education should be co-educational there should be greater variety and selection at secondary level and at tertiary level, some of which institutions might ultimately become universities.

In 1933 a further memorandum was issued, which agreed to provide grants in aid where necessary to boost the salaries of missionaries and to provide schools where missionary efforts were inadequate, ineffective or simply not there. In this way there was a very clear divergence from French colonial policy which provided no financial help for missions.

The 1935 Memoradum on Education in the African Communities restated earlier policy outlined by the Advisory Committee as follows:

> The first task of education is to raise the standard alike of character and efficiency of the bulk of the people, but provision must also be made for the training of those who are required to fill posts in the administrative and technical services as well as of those who, as chiefs, will occupy positions of exceptional trust and responsibility.
>
> As resources permit, the door of advancement through higher education must be increasingly opened for those who by character, ability and temperament show themselves fitted to profit by such education.
> (HMSO 1935, Col. 103 #1).

The memorandum was also concerned with rural areas and recommended a study of community development, linking schools with their communities and economic environment and using teachers as community leaders, as well as the development of mass education and adult literacy programmes. This is interesting thinking in the light of later recommendations advocated by the international agencies in the 1960s and 1970s. The memorandum visualised closer co-operation between government and voluntary agencies. Although this principle of co-operation through grants in aid worked in England and Wales according to Beck (1965), co-operation between missionaries and colonial governments was not always very easy especially as in certain instances religious education as an examinable subject was not allowed.

Although it must be acknowledged that a colonial education policy of sorts evolved during the 1920s and 1930s it was far too generalised to cover the specific needs of individual territories in such a diverse colonial empire. Policy decisions therefore still continued to be made on an ad hoc basis in many of the colonies. There was almost constant discussion between colonial governments and missionary societies regarding policy and the practical aspects of educational provision during this period. For example both the Jerusalem Conference of 1928 and the Madras Conference of 1938 considered a whole range of educational issues ranging from textbooks, grants, languages and examinations to vocational and technical education and teacher training. The policy of economic independence of the colonies as far as possible hampered the growth of educational provision because, with the exceptions of Singapore and Hong Kong which were commercially thriving, most colonies had great difficulties in raising sufficient revenues for even basic school provision. While the 1929 Colonial Development Act had made available £1 million for economic development schemes throughout the British colonies it was not until the 1940 Colonial

Welfare and Development Bill that funds were made available
for the social services, including education as well. Even
so only £5 million for all the colonies were made available.

(d) French policies
The French approach was markedly different, though
according to Clignet and Foster (1964) the actual working out
in practice, especially in French West Africa, was not so
strikingly different. In fact they argue that 'in spite of
apparent formidable differences in colonial ideology, it
would seem that French and British practices were less unlike
than their underlying philosophies'. (p.132). Certainly
French policy never underwent the heart searching that
characterised British policy in the inter war years.
Although initially French administrators believed that when
their mission civilisatrice was complete there would be black,
brown and yellow Frenchmen who would at least be 'culturally
assimilated' and who would think and behave like Frenchmen,
it quickly became apparent that their real concern was to
train and educate indigenous leaders who could 'co-operate'
and 'associate' with French colonial officials in administering
the colonial territory. Cessation of French control was
never seriously considered, and although during the inter
war years this view was challenged it was not until after the
Second World War had changed the situation and the colonial
relationship that French policy began to change. (Marshall
1973).
French policy allowed the development of dual societies,
those that were French educated and those that were educated
in the traditional school systems, especially in the Koranic
schools of north and west Africa. (Capelle 1949; Knight 1955).
Needless to say the latter were regarded with considerable
disdain by Frenchmen and women of all walks of life. (Knight).
Furthermore within the urban areas the policy was to provide
one type of French school for French citizens (who in Algeria,
Morocco, Senegal and Ivory Coast numbered several thousands),
which was based on the syllabus and curricula laid down for
metropolitan schools by the Ministry of Public Instruction
and Overseas Education, and another type of French school
thought fit for the Arabs and Africans who sought a watered-
down classical French education.
Unlike the British approach which allowed laissez-faire
and encouraged mission schools the French government initiated
educational developments and insisted, as in France, on strict
centralised control of what was taught, how many schools were
opened, who could teach in them, and the use of the French
language as opposed to vernaculars. Thus none of the debate
of the 1920s/30s in England really troubled the French. There
were critics of the principle of colonial control, but there
were no critics arguing in favour of closer co-operation
between mission schools and colonial governments, of the need

to expand school provision to the masses, or of the need to
develop vernacular languages and local, practical curricula.
Mission schools were very tightly controlled. They received
no government subsidies and there was little question of
collaboration. Not until after World War II did the Roman
Catholic mission schools find themselves being encouraged to
expand.

An interesting comparison has been made of French and
British rule in the Yoruba speaking area of Dahomey and
Nigeria which argues that in post-colonial terms French
policies in Dahomey left the Yorubas in a far worse position
than did British policies in Nigeria. (Asiwaju 1975). The
French restricted entry to secondary schools and to Western-
type education. Because of the belief in centralised (i.e.
metropolitan) control they destroyed any sense of local
initiative. Because they would not encourage mission schools
and insisted on strict control of those schools that were
available, not only was there no competition but far fewer
educational opportunities were available, a situation that
was true throughout French West Africa. (Mamouni 1969).
Yet bebause money was not made available for education the
result of these policies was that schools were few, of low
grade and of poor quality. Perhaps this situation could be
excused on the grounds that there was no sense of urgency.
Not until 1945 was a fifty year plan drawn up anticipating
full attendance at primary school in French West Africa by
1995!! The implications of these low levels of enrolment
can be seen from the following figures. In 1951 only 2% of
the age group was enrolled at primary level in Upper Volta
and French Equatorial Africa; barely 6% in Ivory Coast; 10%
in Chad; 15% in Danomey; 18% in Senegal; and 27% in Gabon.
(Kitchen 1962 pp.8/9).

Another aspect of French policy of sticking rigidly to
the letter of the law was that a child who had reached the
age of fifteen was expected to leave school regardless of
educational attainments. This is in marked contrast with the
situation in some English colonies. In Tanganyika for
example adults were encouraged to come to school. Parents
in French West Africa were positively discouraged from
seeking education for their children since, in addition to
a school fee, they were expected to pay a tax for children
over the age of ten. The long term results in West Africa
were that the educated elite was far smaller than in the
British colonies. Moreover because they had been educated
almost entirely in the French language they had lost contact
with the vernacular languages and with the needs of people
in the rural areas. In fact the barriers were even greater.
Because they had succeeded at school many Africans could
speak and think in French to such an extent that they
psychologically often had more in common with metropolitan
Frenchmen than with their fellow countrymen. As Asiwaju

23

argues, 'French education with its emphasis on cultural assimilation tended to weaken the educated Africans' sense of attachment to their home areas'. (Asiwaju 1975 p.447).

Moreover whereas English policy was concerned with developing local schools with local teachers using local skills and crafts the French insisted on building replicas of French schools, complete with all the trappings of French academic grades and standards. As Jean Capelle (1949) has observed, 'The French colonial formula was: shape the natives in such a way that they may be efficient and devoted auxiliaries to the Europeans'. It is perhaps little wonder that the French suffered from very high levels of absenteeism: for most African children the value of a French education that divorced them from their environment was highly questionable.

For those who did manage to jump the various educational obstacles successfully and who were capable of benefitting from higher education the only openings were in France itself, but it was frequently difficult, if not impossible, for West Africans, Moroccans and Tunisians to obtain permits to study in France. It is easy therefore to understand why so many felt frustrated and resented their treatment as inferior.

Another interesting contrast is that while female education was greatly encouraged in British colonies, both by missionaries and as a result of government encouragement, in the French colonies, especially in the Muslim countries of north and west Africa, girls' education was deliberately discouraged. Facilities that were available were poor and the curriculum was largely concerned with craftwork, domestic science and allied subjects. Academic skill training was frowned upon.

Frustration with the lack of educational provision in French colonies led many groups to establish écoles libres (free schools), independent of French administrative control, using vernacular languages and teaching skills required in the local environment. Such schools were opened in Tunisia, Morocco, Vietnam, Laos and even Algeria, at one point regarded as a French département and not as a protectorate. In time these schools were to breed 'subversive elements', namely freedom fighters.

One last feature of French education that needs to be mentioned, however, was the attempt to develop écoles rurales, schools adapted to rural conditions in Africa as perceived by French administrators. The result was a curriculum that was markedly different from that pursued in metropolitan France, and one which was supposedly linked to economic realities. Ironically it was not until after World War II and the Langevin-Wallon reform proposals in France (1947) that French education began to move towards linkages with the economy. In this instance policies tried in the colonies were modified for metropolitan use.

(e) The Second World War
   The Second World War marked a watershed for colonialism,
especially in Asia, since the supremacy of Europe had been
shown to be short-lived. However, although some colonial
governments tried to restore the status quo ante bellum, in
many countries this was simply not possible: there was a
changed relationship between rulers and ruled. The war also
led to the recognition that colonial governments had a
responsibility to provide assistance for economic and social
development. Thus in Britain the Colonial Development and
Welfare Fund was increased from £5 million to £17.5 million
while in France in 1946 the government established the Fonds
d'investissement pour le développement economique et social
(FIDES) to provide funding from the French exchequer for
social and economic development in the colonies.
   Even so the concept of handing over power to the colonies
varied considerably. While the USA granted independence to
the Philippines and Britain granted independence to Burma,
India, Pakistan and Ceylon, though hoping to retain links
through what came to be known as the British Commonwealth, it
did not show the same eagerness to grant independence to
Africa. The Elliott Commission set up to examine the role of
African University Colleges (1945) for example, saw them as
providing future leaders on a time scale of between fifty and
one hundred years. The French, Dutch and Belgians had no
plans to abandon their African and Asian colonies and were
prepared, by force if necessary, to retain control and to
re-establish their position as it had been before the Second
World War. What was to lead to the eventual and, in the end,
surprisingly rapid colonial withdrawal during the 1960s and
1970s, was the upsurge of nationalist movements demanding
independence.
   This was undoubtedly a direct consequence of the colonial
educational legacy since in the post war period, depending on
the position of the territory, much greater emphasis was
placed on the reassessment of the goals of education and on
the need to build up a cadre of adequately trained secondary
school leavers. There was a gradual expansion of school
systems, the introduction of tertiary level institutions,
including universities, and inspired by the 1944 Education
Act in England and Wales, there were attempts to improve basic
education. In territories like Hong Kong, Malaya and Singapore,
devastated as a result of Japanese occupation, the initial
emphasis was on rebuilding the school system, but it was also
recognised that education needed to be used to weld together
diverse ethnic groups with a sense of common identity.
(Mason 1959; Watson 1973a, 1979). The latter views came to be
expressed increasingly in a number of African territories as
well, and within a few years the momentum of change could not
be halted.

4. COLONIAL SCHOOL SYSTEMS

The school systems that developed under the colonial powers were essentially alien creations. They reflected the philosophy of their founders, whether the metropolitan power, the voluntary agency or the missionary society, and they were designed to serve the needs and interests of these groups as perceived by them. Thus, as we have seen, missionaries saw schools as a means of proselytisation and conversion to Christianity. As a general rule they preferred to stress moral and general education rather than vocational or practical courses, though there were exceptions to this rule. They were not specifically concerned with education for employment except for a career in the church or in teaching, though many of the students who attended them saw the European language and the examination qualifications as a route to employment in government service or in business and commerce. They believed that literacy would lead to new ideas, to a new awareness of the needs of society, to a new appreciation of the need for hygiene and cleanliness, or, in modern parlance, to social and economic development. Standards were generally high, as were the levels of integrity and dedication of the staff and many have need to be grateful that they were educated in mission schools.

Most missionaries viewed education philanthropically. Trading companies, voluntary agencies and colonial governments, however, were far less concerned about the philanthropic aspects of education. In fact education was often so low down the list of priorities that few, if any, funds were made available. They saw education in functional terms, as a means of providing literate and numerate clerks for the civil service or commercial houses, though there was considerable disagreement amongst certain colonial adminis-trators as to the role of schools. (Stevenson). Some believed the education of indigenous peoples would be a mistake because they believed it would lead to rising expectations and aspirations which could not be filled. This was especially true in Malaya (Watson 1973b) where early colonial administrators did their utmost to prevent rural Malays from becoming 'contaminated' with Western ideas and culture. Others however, e.g. Macaulay in India and many French colonial administrators, believed that the spread of Western schools would further the cause of colonial develop-ment and would lead to greater co-operation with and respect for the colonial power on the part of the colonised peoples.

Although missionaries and colonial administrators did not necessarily see eye to eye over the place and purpose of schooling - e.g. missionaries often opened schools in rural areas and amongst different ethnic and linguistic groups such as the Karens and Shans in Burma, the Chinese and Tamils in Malaya, the tribal groups in Gnana, Nigeria,

Uganda and Kenya, and the Montagnards of Vietnam, whom the
colonial powers did not necessarily see as their prime
responsibility - nevertheless neither group consulted the
colonised people about the scope or content of schooling. As
a result schools opened and policies were adopted without the
consent of and often against the wishes of the colonised
people, as Berman (1971) shows happened as a result of the
peregrinations of the Phelps-Stokes Commissions in Africa.
There are many examples of missionaries going out to exhort
parents to send their children to school, of offering inducements or even of physically conveying children (especially
girls) to school because they positively believed in the
virtues of modern education. After compulsory education laws
were passed and the value of Western schooling as a passport
to a job came to be recognised of course, demand frequently
outstripped supply.
        As colonial school systems developed the existing
patterns of traditional schooling began to lose their
importance. Because of the power of the colonial rulers,
because of new economic structures, because of the growth of
urban centres and because most well paid jobs in colonial
government or commercial service required a secondary level
of education together with a knowledge and understanding of
the colonial language new attitudes developed towards social
mobility. There was growing scorn for the existing patterns
of schooling. Sometimes this attitude of mind came from
colonial officials, but more often than not opposition came
from the newly educated classes. Thus gradually monastic
schools in Buddhist countries, maktabs and koranic schools in
Muslim countries and Hindu temple schools in the Indian sub-
continent, while not ceasing to exist became less important
to those who sought to ally themselves with the new rulers.
Thus education ceased to be linked to the traditional values
of society and schooling was seen as an avenue towards earning
a living. Interestingly in many countries, especially in
Africa, there has been a reaction against the alienation of
Western schooling from traditional values and the local
community and there have been attempts to combine the best of
both worlds. (Nyerere 1967; Watson 1973b, 1973c). Many of
the views currently being expressed by the World Bank (1980)
and other international agencies recognise the necessity of
having school systems linked with the local community and
advocate using some of the traditional patterns more
effectively. In Thailand for example 20% of primary schools
are still based in Buddhist monasteries while in Ethiopia
traditional church and koranic education institutions are
being used as part of the expansion of nonformal education
programmes.
        Closely linked with the decline of traditional education
is the fact that the gulf between traditional schools and
European colonial schools gradually widened. The philosophy,

assumptions and methods of teaching of the colonial school
differed enormously from those of indigenous schools.
Colonial schools were deliberately set apart from the
indigenous culture with the result that those who attended
them gradually grew away from their original roots, a trend
that was lamented by many missionaries by the 1920s but one
that was by then very difficult to reverse. Because there
was a lack of clarity regarding which society and what place
in society students were being prepared for colonial schools
did not necessarily prepare for leadership in the indigenous
society nor for leadership in the colonial society. They
were designed to fit people into a world different from that
with which they were born and in which their parents lived
and worked.

Many schools were boarding institutions so that at
secondary level at least there was actual _physical_ separation
from family and friends, but because of the curriculum and
method of teaching students would also have a different
outlook on the world, one conditioned by European teaching
and culture rather than by indigenous teaching and culture.
Whereas outwardly at least these institutions resembled
their European counterparts in terms of philosophy and
curriculum, though not necessarily of syllabus, they were in
fact very different, and not simply because they were in
exotic settings or out in the bush. This was as true of the
French schools of Indo-China as of the British schools in
the Caribbean or in West and East Africa. Even the Melangali
and Jeanes Schools of East Africa (which originated in the
United States) were dissimilar from any European counterpart
and the craft and vocational courses taught, such as spear
throwing, herding of sheep, goats or cattle and basket
weaving, were quite different from the normal vocational
skills taught. Colonial schools were thus neither part of
the colonial culture and society nor part of the indigenous
colonised culture and society. They were distinctive.

The hallmark of education in most countries was one of
dualism: dualism between urban and rural schools, and dualism
between schools for Europeans and schools for indigenous
peoples. Thus in most colonies there were three strands
of education: (1) There were European schools in urban
settlements for children of colonial civil servants. These
were generally for whites only, followed a European
curriculum and eventually prepared their pupils either for
entry to secondary schools in Europe or for the same
examinations as would be undertaken by their contemporaries
back 'at home'. (2) There was indigenous education, already
mentioned, in the form of traditional schools or preparation
for religious rites in society. Because they were usually
outside government control and because the language of
instruction was unknown to many government officials they
were frequently feared as subversive, which in many instances

they were. The Chinese schools of South East Asia for example disseminated anti-European propaganda, especially after 1919 (Purcell 1966; Watson 1973a) and the Arabic schools of French North Africa had a decidedly anti-colonialist flavour. (3) The third strand of education in colonial times was the colonial schools run by the government or missionaries for colonial peoples, as opposed to Europeans, and which, especially in the French colonies. superficially resembled European schools.

Organisationally the colonial schools were very like their European counterparts until World War II, in so far as progress up the educational ladder was by way of a series of obstacles that had to be overcome if a student was to proceed up the ladder. Primary level lasted for two, four, or even six years. This was followed by upper primary school or 'primary top', as was the situation in Kenya, or by a competitive entrance examination to the fee paying academic secondary schools or vocational/technical schools where these were available. The majority of colonial schools were situated in or near urban settlements, though there were a number of mission schools stuck out in the rural areas. Many, especially in French colonies, prepared students for secondary or even tertiary level education in the metro- politan country, a not unnatural situation given the French view of its colonies as an extension of metropolitan France. Even in some British colonies however there were special scholarships available for the most able children to be educated in England.

The major hurdles in all colonies were costs and exam- inations. These are still major hurdles in many Third World countries. Not only were (are) there the intangible costs such as loss of help in the family or on the landholding, but there were (are) costs of uniform and/or slates, books and pencils, and at secondary level of fees and of boarding. The costs of the latter were often quite considerable. In Kenya for example boarding fees in the European schools were 2250 shillings per pupil per year, compared with 60 shillings per pupil in African schools. Examinations were also a problem, particularly in French colonial schools where grade repetition was quite normal. Unless a pupil had a good command of the colonial language, however, there was very little chance of progressing beyond primary school because all secondary education was conducted in a European language.

The majority of colonial school systems were primary level only. Some had upper primary or lower secondary levels attached. The few secondary schools, usually fee paying and invariably in urban areas, only benefitted those who lived in the towns and had access to them. Until the 1930s there were no universities, except in India and Indo- China, and most reports, French and British, on tertiary education in Africa did not foresee university development until later in the century. The colonial schools have thus been rightly criticised as leading to nowhere and because they did not adequately prepare students for any role in society. This was especially true of Tamil and rural Malay schools in Malaya. They have also been rightly criticised because being selective only a small percentage of the population attended them and because as a result at the time of independence levels of literacy were very low. For example India had a 16% literacy rate in 1947 and most of French West Africa had a literacy rate of less than 10% at the time of independence. It must be borne in mind however that in the European countries by the end of the Second World War barely 10% of pupils went on to secondary level and only about 3% went on to tertiary level.

The weakness that too little emphasis was placed on developing the secondary sector was to have long term implications, especially in the shortage of trained middle-level manpower after independence. Where there were secondary schools in British territories the medium of instruction was generally English and the schools themselves were modelled on the pattern of grammar schools or public schools then existing in England, with an emphasis on academic and literary curricula leading to examinations. In many cases Latin and English history were studied in preference to vernacular languages or local history and geography, though there were undoubtedly exceptions to this. (Jones 1965). Generally both in principle and in practice, schools were designed for an elite who had mental ability and whose parents could afford the fees. The majority were deliberately modelled on English (or French) boarding schools. In 1831 the Colebrook Commission urged the colonial government in Ceylon to develop English, rather than vernacular schools, while in 1844 the Maharaja of Kerala in India announced that he would offer public positions only to those with an English education. Raffles' Girls School in Singapore was modelled on an English high school for girls. In Malaya, for example, Malay College at Kuala Kangsar; in parts of India, for example, Aitcheson College at Lahore, Lawrence College at Abbotabad; as well as numerous other colleges both there and in many parts of Africa (e.g. Kenya, Uganda, Nigeria) and even in Latin America many schools were modelled on English public schools, while Jamaican boys' secondary schools were patterned on English grammar schools. Frequently they were Christian foundations with a clergyman as principal and with many Christians on the staff. Their syllabuses and courses were linked to the Cambridge Overseas Examinations Syndicate. In French colonies, although there were mission schools unsupported by the government, there were also other boarding schools which were run on lines more like an English boarding school than those of a French lycée.

The effects of this 'modelling' can be seen from two
reports from two very different colonies. In 1942 the Report
of the Gold Coast Education Committee pointed out that 'the
chief danger is not the creation of unemployment, but the
production by the examination ridden secondary school of a
class of unemployables who over estimate their own achievement
and worth'. (Gold Coast 1942). Even more damning was the
Jamaican Education Department's Report of 1950 which said
that 'secondary education has failed to serve adequately the
peculiar needs of the country because of its bondage to
overseas examinations, those of the Cambridge Examinations
Syndicate'. (Jamaica 1952). Similar views were echoed
periodically in Ceylon, Malaya, Nigeria, Kenya and India. In
defence of the policy, however, it must be pointed out that
secondary education in Europe at this time was also bookish,
academic, and was linked to an examination structure and
competitive entry to university.
        The sphere of technical/vocational, trade and agricultural
schools varied enormously - it was probably most well developed
in Penang in Malaya - but until after World War II little
emphasis was placed on developing universities, partly because
it was thought that there were insufficient students of high
calibre, partly because the school systems were incapable of
providing adequate numbers. The latter is one reason why
when universities were developed they were often seen as
regional institutions (e.g. the University of the West Indies,
the University of the Pacific, the University of East Africa)
while the French University of Dakar in Senegal was expected
to serve the whole of French West Africa. There were however
a series of reports on the establishment of tertiary level
institutions produced during the 1930s - (East Africa 1937;
Gold Coast 1939; Sierre Leone 1939; Malaya 1939) - but
progress was interrupted by the World War. Following the
War there was a greater sense of urgency in creating
universities, modelled on British counterparts and invariably
linked with the University of London, but their very smallness
meant that they were inadequate for producing enough national
leaders for when independence came.
        Where colonial school systems differed markedly from
European school systems, however, was in their disjointedness,
the lack of coherence of school structure and in the curriculum.
In many cases there were parallel school systems in different
vernaculars with no linkage at primary level and leading only
to secondary school if students passed through a special
Remove or Transition class to bring their English up to
scratch. In most cases the child in the rural area therefore
might begin his schooling in his native tongue and learn
(orally) the rudiments of what the colonisers thought was
most important for his way of life in the way of the three
Rs, and knowledge of crafts and hygiene, etc. For the
majority of children this is all that formal education would

consist of and they would then return to village life. If a
child was talented or his parents were wealthy he might move
to a primary school in an urban area where he would learn
through the medium of a European language about European
culture and about his own culture or society as viewed through
European eyes. If successful the child might move on to post
primary or secondary school, often a boarding institution.
At the end of schooling, whether or not it had been completed
successfully, students would go into clerical posts in the
civil service or in European firms, would go into small scale
business, or would set themselves up as lawyers. In speech,
dress, mannerisms many of them aped the Europeans, yet at the
same time (e.g. the Indian 'babu') they were despised by the
Europeans.

   Control over school systems and the approach to the
school curriculum reflected the attitudes of the colonial
power and the local colonial rulers. This varied from one
colonial power to another and from one territory to another.
In Dutch Indonesia there was central control over textbooks
and materials for use in colonial schools while French
colonies reflected the traditional pattern of centralised
direction and control. After 1903 especially there was central
control of textbooks, teacher training, certification and
degrees in the French colonies. In Algeria, Morocco, the
French West African states and Indo-China an Office of Public
Instruction was created which commissioned textbooks and drew
up lists of texts permissible for classroom use, issued public
curriculum guidelines, supervised the hiring of teachers and
their performance in the classroom in public schools, inspected
private schools and set examinations. As in metropolitan
France private schools, including mission schools until after
1951, were expected to operate without any form of subsidy
or grant in aid.

   In the British colonies there was no such degree of central
control. As has been seen much of school provision was left
in the hands of voluntary agencies and missionaries, many of
whom were not English. Provided they did not interfere with
or upset the colonial order they were largely left to get on
with things in their own way. Thus in the Federated Malay
States much of the education provided for the Chinese and some
of the education provided for the Tamils was left in the hands
of missionaries while in many African colonies the majority
of rural schools were mission controlled. Colonial control,
where it was exercised, was through grants in aid, payment
by results and inspection: there was no direction over textbooks, curricula or syllabi.

   It could be argued that the most effective form of
control was exercised through the language used as the
medium of instruction but here again policy varied. Thus
while in some French colonies indigenous languages were used
for the first three years of schooling all urban and most

rural schools, especially in French West Africa taught through the medium of French. A policy statement for the whole of French West Africa, issued in 1921, justified the use of French unequivocally.

> Education proposes above all to spread the
> French language among the population in order
> to establish their nationality. It should
> then try to endow the native with enough
> general knowledge to assure him of better
> living conditions and open his mind to French
> culture and Western civilisation.

Such a policy fitted well with the belief in the superiority of la langue francaise and of French civilisation and with the belief that French colonies were an extension of France itself. It also fitted the argument that it was too expensive and too big a drain on limited resources to develop textbooks and teaching materials in local languages.

In British colonies urban schools invariably taught through the medium of English at both primary and secondary levels. In Asia English was also used in most rural schools since Macaulay's famous Minute of 1835, which dismissed vernacular languages as poor and rude, devoid of any literary or scientific knowledge and as decidedly inferior to English, was to have a profound effect on developments in India, Burma, the Straits Settlements, the Federated Malay States and Ceylon. In the African colonies on the other hand, indigenous languages were frequently encouraged in the rural areas for at least the first three years, with 'bridging classes' for any children moving to urban schools to catch up on English.

Even where indigenous languages were taught, however, they were only seen as a preliminary to real education through the medium of a European language. Although the language was European, however, the culture taught was not necessarily so. In some territories (e.g. Nigeria, Indo-China) pupils were taught about their own culture as viewed and understood by European teachers. On the other hand much of the history and literature that was taught in East Africa, India and parts of West Africa was related to England and to the benefits of European civilisation. This information was necessary because it was examined in the externally set examination papers.

Religious education was taught in English schools; moral education in French schools. In most colonial schools there were also gardens, farms and craft courses, even though these were frequently unsuccessful. The school curriculum was generally not based on the society from which the child came, except marginally. It did not teach him about the traditions in his own society nor did it develop skills which would be

useful in that society. As a result many were alienated from
their own society but were not at the same time fitted for the
colonial society. For many pupils therefore the curriculum
imposed a great strain, partly because of instruction through
the medium of a foreign language but largely because of the
unreality of much of the content to the local situation.
Emphasis therefore was on literature, history (French/English),
mathematics, language. There was little emphasis on commercial,
agricultural or manual skills. On the other hand not only was
there little demand for this type of course until after World
War II, but the economies of most colonies were not geared to
absorbing many skilled manual workers.

The response to colonial schools varied from open
hostility and opposition through apathy to eager support.
Considerable opposition was shown towards the education of
women and girls because of suspicion and because it was
feared that their help would be lost in the family small-
holding or in helping with the upbringing of younger members
of the family. Hostility and opposition were frequently
shown by Muslim groups, especially over girls' education and
in India the Muslim elite established its own schools and even
its own university at Aligarh. In Vietnam and Morocco and
Algeria there was considerable opposition to French education
in all its manifestations. Some traditional elites (e.g. the
tribal chiefs of West Africa, the Malay sultans and the
Indian princes) welcomed European elite education because
they saw it as a means of preserving and sustaining their own
elite status. In some cases (e.g. in India and Malaya) certain
schools and places at secondary schools were set aside for the
children of indigenous ruling elites.

Other groups quite simply viewed colonial education as a
means of rising either to aspired indigenous elite status or
of upward social mobility away from the rural areas to the
urban areas. This was particularly true of Nigeria and
Ghana where families were prepared to take a gamble of seeing
one or more of their sons pass through colonial education in
the hope that they would get white-collar employment at the
end of the process, even though there were never enough
clerical jobs available for those finishing school. It is
perhaps as well therefore that 95% dropped out before
completing the primary level since only a few could ever hope
to achieve upward social mobility.

In many territories, however, in spite of various
inducements used by the authorities to encourage parents to
send their children to school, such as offering free places
in secondary schools for Malays who had completed four years
of Malay vernacular education, reaction was one of apathy and
indifference to something that was regarded as alied and
irrelevant to their needs. The Report of Education in the
Federated Malay States for 1905 pointed out that a major
problem was to win the co-operation of parents who were

'apathetic, jealous of the loss of their children's services
and distrustful of secular teaching'. At least that is how
education was viewed until the mid 1930s when a new attitude
became apparent. Many who had passed through school, as well
as many who had not, began to see in European education,
science and technology, the keys to the revitalisation of
their own societies and the means of achieving autonomy and
independence from the colonial yoke. Thus as independence
became a possibility following the Second World War the demand
for education increased as a means of upward social mobility
and as a means of access to white collar jobs in the urban
sector.

One group of schools with a particular curriculum emphasis
that was never successful were the agricultural/technical
schools. These schools which missionaries and colonial
educators, with the best motives in the world, tried to relate
to local conditions and needs by emphasising agriculture and
the manual arts, were rejected as inferior by indigenous
peoples. Foster's (1965) work in Ghana has shown that the
demand from parents - and pupils - was for academic, literary
education which was perceived as the route to success and
secure employment in the bureaucracy or business. The result
was that the colonial powers bowed to the inevitable pressures
and provided academic education; and most well intentioned
attempts at modifying syllabuses to local conditions were
discarded because of local opposition. To blame European
educators for education that was, in hindsight, 'irrelevant'
to local needs is not therefore entirely fair. The most
telling aspect of this can be seen from the Ashanti Survey
following the Second World War which showed that 95% of boys
who had had primary education went on to seek work in the
towns and not in the rural areas.

5. THE CONSEQUENCES OF COLONIAL EDUCATION

The introduction of Western education systems into
colonial territories was to have far-reaching effects on the
socio-economic developments in those territories. Ironically
Western education was to hasten the end of colonial rule.
In the first place it led to the training and education of
indigenous elites based on educational qualifications rather
than on traditional political or economic status. These
elites were to become the future leaders of independent
societies. The training of individuals who would co-operate
with and who would eventually take over was part of deliberate
policy as a French document on education in West Africa shows:

The duties of colonialism and political and economic
necessities have imposed a twofold task on our work
in education. On the one hand we must train
indigenous cadres to become our auxiliaries in every

area, and assure ourselves of a meticulously
chosen elite. We must also educate the masses,
to bring them closer to us and transform their
way of living ...

This attitude applied to Senegal, Ivory Coast and Niger.
It also prevailed in British schools in India for the sons
of the nobility modelled on British public schools (e.g.
Aitcheson College, Lahore; Lawrence College, Lucknow College)
and in Malaya where the Malay College at Kuala Kangsar was
established in 1910 for the sons of Malay sultans. The
students trained in these institutions, men like Nehru,
Nkrumah, Tungku Abdul Rahman, were to become the spearhead
of indigenous leadership, who, using the arguments of political
values of the Western liberal tradition or the ethical values
of Christianity were to demand a transfer of power from the
colonial rulers.

At the same time these elites became divorced, as a
result of their education, from the real needs, feelings and
aspirations of the rural hinterland. They became Westernised
in manners, behaviour, outlook, dress, interests, style of
living and as a result, once in the seat of power, became
more colonial in their attitudes than was the white man. In
Africa especially, a number of these leaders developed a
sense of inferiority towards anything African. The view that
anything European is bound to be superior is particularly
prevalent in French West Africa, where the links with
European (i.e. French) civilisation have died hard, and many
present day rulers seek every opportunity to visit Europe -
some, like the former Emperor Bokasse of the Central African
Empire, even have appartements and villas in France - or to
invite European 'experts' to their countries. As long as
these views are held by rulers of independent nations it is
hard to see how Western influences and ideas can be reduced.

Psychological barriers are not only to be found amongst
the leaders, however. Many ordinary citizens of former
colonial territories find themselves caught between two
cultures, the Western educated, urbanised culture and the
traditional, indigenous deep-rooted culture of their home-
land. Many find it very hard to come to terms with this
situation and live uneasy lives, unsure of their real
identity. (Clignet 1971, 1980).

A second consequence of the colonial educational legacy
has been the creation of a bureaucratic machinery. Because
the purpose of colonial education at secondary level was to
train clerks, administrators, teachers, doctors who could
work within the colonial sphere, when the colonial rulers
left those they had trained continued to run the administrative
machinery and in many cases to plan the economy. At the time
of independence many moved into politics and many of the
teachers, because they were amongst the best educated people

in the country, moved into bureaucratic posts to replace
European colonial civil servants. As civil servants they
have continued to enjoy all the trappings, traditions, working
procedures, grades, salary scales, promotion procedures and
prestige that they believe their European predecessors had.
One only needs to become involved in some bureaucratic
wrangle in a Third World country to appreciate how so often
the original model has become an unchanging and unchangeable
part of the social and political fabric. Civil servants, at
least in the higher grades, seek to emulate Europeans in
dress, housing and taste. Where they do not emulate their
predecessors, however, is in the level of corruption. They
find themselves so pressurised by relatives and contacts in
the traditional extended family context that it is hard not
to succumb to bribery and corruption. Their power, position
and prestige, however, like their European predecessors, set
them apart from the ordinary mass of citizens.

A third consequence of colonialism and Western education
has been double-edged. As a result of colonial conquest many
societies found themselves becoming multi-racial communities,
'plural societies with different sections of the community
living side by side, but separately, within the same political
unit' (Furnivall 1956), either because colonial governments
brought in indentured labour, especially from Southern India,
or because certain groups, especially Chinese, saw trading
advantages in the stability of territories under European
control. Thus colonies from as far apart as Guyana and
Jamaica, to Kenya, Uganda, the Seychelles, Ceylon, Malaya,
Singapore and Fiji became in a very real sense multi-racial
and multi-cultural. At the same time Western education
systems were to help unleash a sense of nationalism amongst
different groups. Discussion in the curriculum, often
incidentally, of issues like democracy, nationalism, liberalism,
elected governments, justice, was to lead not only to a
recognition of the incongruous relationship between coloniser
and colonised, but to the desire for independence and national
identity.

While there were those in the colonial hierarchy who
were concerned about the discovery and preservation of
archaeological sites (e.g. Dutch work in Indonesia and
French work on the ruins of Angkor in Cambodia, British
work on Taxila and Mohenjodaro in what is today Pakistan);
while there were colonial officials who were interested in
the history, culture and religion of different peoples; and
while there were missionaries who sought to transcribe
vernacular languages, much of the curriculum in colonial
schools dismissed indigenous languages and culture as
inferior while stressing the superiority of European civilisation. The combination of these factors was to lead many
nationalist leaders to stress the past glories of their
people and to revive a national culture, history and language.

Above all, however, these nationalist leaders have sought to use language (e.g. Swahili, Behasa Indonesia, Bahasa Malaysia or Hindi) as a unifying force wherever possible. (Wong Hoy Kee 1971). Where an indigenous language has proved unsuitable a European language - e.g. French or English - together with the school system have been used to create a sense of national unity amongst diverse ethnic, linguistic and tribal groups.

A fourth consequence of colonial involvement in education has been the high valuation placed on schooling throughout the Third World and the legacy of formal, linear school systems complete with the appropriate administrative network. Education (i.e. schooling) came to be seen not only as an avenue to up-ward social mobility but as an instrument for social change and progress and as a means of welding different ethnic and linguistic groups together. Leaders of newly independent nations without exception voiced confidence in the role educ-ation should play in the socio-economic development of their country. The most interesting aspect, however, is how few countries, (until Mozambique, Angola, Guinea-Bissau and Cambodia tried in the 1970s), tinkered with their education systems or experimented with alternative forms of education. Even Nyerere's Education for Self-Reliance in the late 1960s was not particularly revolutionary and made great use of experiments tried earlier by colonial rulers. (Cameron 1975). Most developing countries simply expanded educational provision, especially at the base line of primary education, developed a few more secondary schools, and expanded higher education where feasible, but the trappings of these school systems, their ethos, methods of instruction, buildings, grade promotion, examinations, certificates, diplomas and degrees, and at tertiary level all the paraphernalia of faculties, administ-rative structures and academic dress owe much to their colonial/European creators.

The most telling indictment against colonial powers can be seen from the following table 1.1 which shows the enrolments and literacy rates of selected French and British territories in 1960 on the eve of independence for many territories, and again in 1977. At the time of independence in much of French Africa only about 10% of the age group was enrolled at primary level, about 4% proceeded to secondary level and only about 13% of those had any form of higher tertiary level education. Illiteracy rates were in the region of 92/93%. Only in Indo-China was the picture more optimistic. Generally the British territories were better educated and more literate. Even so the achievements of most of these countries in terms of enrol-ments and reduction of illiteracy since independence are nothing short of dramatic, especially if one considers the population growth rate, though the figures conceal another aspect of the colonial legacy, namely the uneven distribution of schools between urban and rural areas and between different ethnic/tribal groups.

Table 1.1 Enrolments and Literacy Rates in Selected Colonial Territories in 1960 and 1977 as a Percentage

| | Primary Level | | | | | | Secondary Level | | Tertiary Level | | Literacy Level | |
	Total		Male		Female							
	1960	1977	1960	1977	1960	1977	1960	1977	1960	1977	1960	1977
(French)												
Cambodia	64	-	82	-	46	-	3	-	-	?	36	-
Laos	25	92	34	99	16	84	1	14	-	-	28	-
Mali	10	28	14	36	6	20	1	7	-	1	3	10
Chad	16	41	29	61	4	21	-	3	-	-		
Upper Volta	8	16	12	20	5	12	-	2	-	-		5
Niger	5	23	7	29	3	16	(-)	3	-	-	2	8
Benin (Dahomey)	26	58	38	80	15	37	2	11	-	1	1	11
Mauritania	8	31	14	40	3	21	-	4	-	-	8	17
Senegal	27	47	36	57	17	37	3	11	1	2	5	10
Cameroon	65	119	87	132	43	106	2	17	-	1	6	-
Morocco*	47	68	67	86	27	50	5	17	1	4	19	28
Tunisia	66	100	88	118	43	81	12	22	1	5	14	55
(British)												
Bangladesh*	47	81	66	103	26	58	8	23	1	2	22	26
India*	61	80	80	95	40	64	20	28	3	6	28	36
Malawi	63	62	81	75	45	50	1	4	-	-	-	25
Sierra Leone	23	37	30	45	15	29	2	11	-	1	-	15
Tanzania	25	70	33	79	18	60	2	3	-	-	10	66
Uganda	49	53	65	63	32	44	3	7	-	1	35	-
Kenya	47	104	64	110	30	98	2	17	-	1	20	40
Ghana	38	74	52	84	25	64	5	29	-	1	27	30
Zambia	42	95	51	104	34	87	2	16	-	2	-	39

(Source: World Bank; World Development Report 1980). *Already independent for some years

The _fifth_ and one of the most disturbing consequences
of the impact of Western education on Third World development
has been on the attitudes of mind of pupils and parents alike.
Furnivall pointed out in 1943 that 'formerly the child learned
in school how to live; now he learns how to make a living',
because so many of the skills, crafts, techniques and knowledge which had a direct bearing on everyday life ceased to
matter or to be taught. Unfortunately Western administrators
and educators mistook schooling and academic instruction for
education because this was how it was understood in Europe,
with the result that there has been scorn for manual work or
for work in the rural areas. At the turn of the century
education in Malaya was criticised as 'unpractical, to make
the people litigious, to inspire a distaste for manual and
technical work and to create a class of literary malcontents,
useless to their communities and a source of trouble to the
Empire'. (Wilkinson 1902). This picture could have been
repeated in most other colonies and in spite of changes on
the part of colonial governments in the 1920s/30s it was to
persist. In fact this legacy was to have a profound effect
on attitudes to work and development and even those socialist
societies that have deliberately sought to foster a healthy
respect for manual work such as Tanzania and Mozambique have
found themselves faced with an uphill struggle.
        Yet ironically one of the most lasting consequences of
the impact of colonialism on education has been the effect on
thought patterns as a result of the scientific knowledge
taught through schools and later through the universities.
This was especially true in Asia where wisdom and knowledge
tended to be seen in religious terms and as something that
resided in the past. 'The structure of Asiatic society,
precise in its pattern, allotted to each man his due place in
society, while the comprehensiveness of Asiatic religion
embracing as it did the past, the present and the future,
enabled him to come to terms with his environment. The
individual expressed himself as part of the group, and the
economic activity of the one was the complement of the economic
activity of all'. (Attygale 1961). The impact of Western
thought, and science especially, which separated the real
world from the metaphysical, was to have a profound effect on
the thinking of certain groups, who saw through science,
education and industry a means of modernisation and development. This was to lead to a dichotomy in societies between
urban educated, Westernised thinkers who accepted scientific
progress and the majority of rural peasants, scarcely affected
by education, let alone scientific thinking, a situation that
is all too familiar today.
        The result of Western thought, science and industrial-
isation in the Asian context, and to a lesser extent the
African one, therefore, has been the most far reaching under-
mining of old established traditional civilisations that has

ever occurred in history (Eisenstadt), the breakdown of the
traditional and legitimate power of rulers, the creation of
a sense of change and modernisation, the creation of economies
- and wealth - based on trade of export crops and industrial
development, and to a belief that power could rest with a
different kind of leader. Thus nationalism and socialism,
frequently interlinked, can be directly attributed to the
Western impact. It has even been argued that socialism is as
much a product of and a protest against the West - as a belief
in a new dynamic for future change.

The most lasting legacy of colonial control, however, is
seen in what has come to be known as neocolonialism, the
domination of the rich world over the poorer countries of the
Third World, even though the latter are officially independent.
(Mende 1973; Altbach 1971, 1977, 1978; Brandt 1980). In
educational terms as is to some extent shown by Brock, Avalos
and Watson in this volume, control may take place through
foreign aid programmes, capital aid for buildings, technical
assistance training, publishing firms, newspaper publishing,
the media, recognition of examinations and diplomas, research
links between universities in the Third World and in the North.
As Altbach has pointed out 'Neocolonialism is partly a planned
policy of advanced nations to maintain their influence in
developing countries, but it is also simply a continuation of
past practices' (Altbach 1971). The point is that important
elements and structures built up under colonialism continue
to operate and have a continuing impact throughout the
developing countries. These structures and elements may
include school systems, universities, languages of instruction,
textbooks, curricula and examinations.

Western dominance continues because of economic control
of trade and access to raw materials (Brandt; Mende; Hayter)
but also because the majority of educational and research
centres, especially in science and technology, are in the
Western world (or the Soviet bloc) and have an international
reputation. There are a few exceptions with UNESCO/FAO
Research Centres in the Philippines, Mexico, Bangkok, but
these are small in number and influence in comparison. The
leading journals, publishing houses, universities, are in
Europe, the USA, Japan and the USSR thus ensuring that Third
World countries look to these for leadership, expertise,
guidance. Where developing countries aspire to emulate it
is inevitable that they will copy Western models.

Not all neocolonialism is the fault of the industrial
countries, however. Some results from the policies of the
developing countries themselves. Universities and polytechnics
are generally modelled on those in the West - in Europe or
North America - in design, ethos and administration. Even in
non colonial countries such as Thailand and Iran, Western
models have been copied and because of the international scope
of university research and links with universities elsewhere

they find themselves trapped into an international network.
Although models vary they are essentially European or North
American and where change has been attempted, as for example
in China, it has not proved acceptable in the longer term
because of falling standards. The cost of changing the medium
of instruction is high, time consuming and frequently resented
because of the shortage of textbooks. Indonesia, Malaysia
and India have been reasonably successful, but because the
majority of research - and textbooks and journals - are
produced in English and other European languages and because
these languages provide access to research and publication
many academics prefer to work in international languages.

The costs of changing the pattern of teacher education,
developing rural areas, and establishing models of nonformal
education for rual development are likewise costly in terms
of cash and administrative reorganisation. (Coombs and
Ahmed 1974; Paulston 1976; World Bank 1980). Thus inertia
and cost are often major internal constraints against change.
Frequently though discretion is the better part of valour.
Pressures from the electorate for educational expansion (e.g.
in Nigeria, Indonesia, India) rather than for change and the
adaptation of new approaches are often so great that few
governments find they can resist these pressures.

Levels of overseas aid to the Third World also help to
ensure neocolonial involvement. 80% of British aid goes to
former British colonies, while 90% of French aid goes to
former French colonies. Aid in the form of equipment,
personnel, scholarships, technical assistance, oversight of
examinations, reinforces this dependency.

The legal and administrative structures inherited from
the colonial powers have often been left intact or only
marginally changed. Only in a few cases - Bangladesh, India,
Indonesia, Malaysia, Pakistan and Tanzania - have there been
serious attempts to replace the European languages as the
language of administration and/or of education. Many
countries positively use a European language as a means of
unification and control as can be seen in Ghana, Kenya and
French West Africa as well, of course, as Latin America. In
India for example thirty years after Independence over 50%
of the books and slightly under 50% of the newspapers published
are in English yet only 2% of the population are literate in
English compared with 35% literate in other languages.
(Altbach 1971). This is a remarkable hold. Interestingly
enough recent attempts by the Marxist government of West
Bengal to replace English with Bengali as the State language
have met with considerable opposition.(4) The fact that
the majority of international journals are also published in
European languages means that aspiring intellectuals use
these languages. As a result intellectual, academic and often
legal and administrative life is orientated away from indigenous
culture and society towards European or North American society.

Closely linked with linguistic control of the system by
Western influence academics is the fact that 90% of all
research takes place in the industrial world and the bulk of
the world's scholars and universities are to be found in the
rich world, with the result that not only are problems and
research funds seen through the perspective of the advanced
countries, but many research programmes are geared to Western
national - and individual - needs rather than to Third World
country needs. Where 'experts' are provided they are
invariably provided by the rich world. The 'brain drain', in
spite of local government efforts to retain people's services,
favours the rich world. (Mende). There is thus constant
dependence on the part of the Third World on the industrialised
nations, especially on the USA.

As Altbach and Kelly observe 'under neocolonialism foreign
control of education is far more subtle (than under traditional
colonialism). It is not exerted through direct political
occupation of a country but rather through international
inequalities in wealth and power and the legacy of classical
colonialism that contributes to the development of not only
inequalities, but expectations of the uses to which education
could be put'. (1978 p.41). The legacy of colonialism in
terms of education is thus far from over. It continues in a
different form but with many far reaching implications for
reform, change, modernisation and development. It accounts
for why the World Bank and UNESCO policies towards non-formal
education and rural development are taken so seriously and
yet are resisted because of fear that they will lead to
further inferiority. It also explains why many of the current
Third World leaders seek not to change things radically, but
rather to emulate developments in the West.

6. THE THEORETICAL FRAMEWORK OF THIS VOLUME

All the aspects touched upon above - the evolution of
policy, the role of missionary societies, the development of
school systems, the curriculum, experimental projects, the
colonial legacy and forms of neocolonial control - are to some
extent looked at in the following chapters. The first part
of the book is more concerned with policy issues and colonial
practice in historical perspective; the second part is concerned with the continuing impact of this legacy.

Clive Whitehead surveys the changing nature of British
educational policies in the colonial dependencies between
the two World Wars and shows how, far from pursuing a uniform
policy such as that pursued by the French or the Portuguese,
decisions were largely left to men on the spot in individual
territories, a point also highlighted by Brock and Watson.
Whitehead illustrates the paternalistic approach of most
colonial officials as well as the degree of confusion that
took place at this time in the debates about indirect rule,

the length of time that could be expected to pass before
colonial peoples were ready for a degree of independence, how
far Malays, Fijians and Africans should be isolated from
Western culture and values and how far they sould be Westernised. Not surprisingly he points out 'that no one knew with
certainty what to do with the many millions of people living
in the colonies' and highlights the dilemma that was never
satisfactorily resolved: how to provide adequate schooling
without funds, because of the low economic base of most
territories, and with insufficiently trained teachers.

Brian Garvey examines British colonial policies in
Africa, seeking to meet the specific criticisms levelled
against them, namely that there was inadequate provision of
places and that colonialism led to underdevelopment. He
traces some of the problems and insecurities facing the
early missionaries and colonial officers and highlights the
inadequate financial base of most colonial education. While
not denying that there were socio-economic changes brought
about as a result of colonial education he argues that some
of these were deliberately welcomed by African groups.

While much of early Western education in Africa revolved
around the missions, Keith Watson shows how this was also the
case in South East Asia, and how even in 'non-colonised'
countries like Thailand Western mission penetration was
considerable. In the context of multi-racial Malaysia the
colonial legacy left many problems that have still not been
resolved adequately largely because internal colonialism has
exacerbated racial disharmony and because neocolonial influences on structures, syllabuses and examinations have prevented radical solutions.

Vietnam has experienced every form of colonial control,
military, political, linguistic and ideological, and Dudley
Hick traces the different colonial influences on Vietnam from
the earliest contacts with China to the withdrawal of US
forces in the mid-twentieth century. Particularly interesting
in the Vietnamese context are the different cultural and
educational strands from China and India that had a deep
impact long before the French ever arrived on the scene.
Hick also shows that while 80/85% of the population were
literate when the French arrived in the mid-nineteenth
century only 15/20% were literate when they left in 1954
largely because the French failed to replace the existing
administrative and educational structure with a viable alternative. Because the French never came to terms with the
traditions of the past and because they tried to impose their
own elite system they alienated the masses and enabled dis-
affected groups to rise up and eventually overthrow the
French - and later the Americans. Interestingly enough the
anti-colonial struggle continues, not so much against the
neocolonial influence of France and the U.S.A., but against
ideological influences from Moscow.

Colonialism and Educational Development

The theme of neocolonialism is taken up by both Colin
Brock and Beatrice Avalos. Brock unravels the levels of
colonial control that still pervade the West Indies and that
lead to inertia. He shows how education only really mattered
after the emancipation of slavery but because it looked to
the various colonial powers as a focal point it distorted
future developments and the attitudes of indigenous leaders
towards their island homes. Avalos takes a historical as
well as political and economic approach to the place of
colonialism in Latin America; and shows how after one or even
two centuries of political independence the Latin American
countries are yoked under a different colonial umbrella, that
of dependency in their relations to the U.S.A. and the multinational corporations to such an extent that 'the general
picture of Latin America is still one of cultural control'.
This is clearly borne out in the conflict between Freire's
incrementalist approach to development and the US structuralist-
functionalist approach. Thus where international aid agencies
sense that educational programmes are revolutionary or subversive they refuse to support them.

Tony Hopkin provides an interesting account of the
co-operation scheme between New Zealand and Fiji which raises
a number of interesting questions about centre-periphery
relationships, racial positions in schools, the place of
examinations, the values inculcated and the difficulties of
recognising qualifications. Even if a scheme is a co-operative
venture it can nevertheless result in a colonial relationship.
As the aid relationship changes to one of mutual respect and
co-operation it is worth considering that it can so easily
change into a different, but subtle, form of neocolonial
control.

Finally Keith Watson brings together the various facets
touched upon and shows that far from being over the colonial
relationship continues in a different form.

NOTES

1. See Hans, N. (1964): _Comparative Education_. London:
Routledge and Kegan Paul for a discussion of the role of the
Jesuits in the early colonial education of Latin America.
2. See Osborne, M. (1971): _Region of Revolt, Focus on
South East Asia_. Harmondsworth, Penguin for a discussion of
Ho Chi Minh's education in Paris.
3. There is an analysis of Raffles' work in the development of education in Singapore in Watson, J.K.P. (1973):
Educational development in South East Asia: a historical and
comparative analysis of the growth of education in Thailand,
Malaya and Singapore. Unpublished Ph.D. thesis, University
of Reading.
4. Bulletin Education en A.O.F., No. 45, February-March
1921. Imprimerie du Government Général, Dakar.

    5.   Bulletin de l'Enseignement en A.O.F., No. 74, p.3.,
1923. Imprimerie du Government General, Dakar.
    6.   This was pointed out in an article in the Observer,
22 February 1981.

Chapter Two

EDUCATION IN BRITISH COLONIAL DEPENDENCIES 1919-1939
A RE-APPRAISAL

Clive Whitehead

British colonial education policy has been subjected to
frequent criticism since the end of the Second World War.
Nevertheless, a few years ago Margery Perham (1974) suggested
that the time was probably not far off when there would be
an increasing interest in reassessing the imperial record.
Now, when the colonial empire is little more than 'a curiosity
of history' (Cox 1965 p.125), seems an appropriate time to
initiate a re-examination of the principal criticism levelled
at British colonial education policy during the past thirty
years.
        This chapter deals with the period between the two
world wars when the British Empire was seemingly at its
zenith. Imperial expansion was no longer a major issue and
the problems of de-colonisation still lay over the horizon.
Public interest lay not in whether to have an empire but how
best to govern it and in whose interests. These concerns
were given added impetus by the establishment of the Mandates
Commission after the First World War and the trusteeship
requirement that Britain be accountable internationally for
the welfare and progress of several former German colonies.
The inter-war years also saw the Colonial Office and local
colonial governments adopt a more positive role in the
promotion of schooling, especially in Africa, where it had
hitherto been the almost exclusive preserve of the Christian
missions. Increased state involvement necessitated the
formulation of an education policy which, in turn, led to
the establishment in 1923 of the Colonial Office Advisory
Committee on Native Education in Tropical Africa.
        The limited opportunities available for schooling
constitute the fundamental criticism levelled at Britain's
colonial education policy before 1939. Although there is
no single study devoted to this theme it was a persistent
criticism voiced in the local press and in legislative
assemblies after 1945. Provision for schooling varied from
one territory to another but nowhere did more than a minority
of children attend school regularly. Moreover, the distributio

of schools within a colony was often very uneven, with children
living in or near to towns having a much better chance of
attending school than their rural counterparts. The
proportion of girls in attendance was also very low, especially
in the African territories, and only a tiny minority of
children who went to school completed the six or more years
of basic primary instruction. Opportunities for secondary
schooling were very limited, often expensive, and confined
mainly to urban areas, while university education was unavailable in most colonies until after the Second World War.

The British have also been criticised for condoning, if
not actively encouraging communal or racially-segregated
schooling. The practice, common in multi-racial communities
like those found in Kenya, Tanganyika, Malaya and Fiji, has
been condemned on the grounds that it exacerbated racial
distinctions and animosities and was inimical to the development of a sense of national identity. Some writers (e.g.
Chai Hon-Chan 1964 p.279-280) have even suggested that communal
schools were part of a deliberate policy to 'divide and rule'.
Further criticism has been focussed on the literary curriculum
that prevailed in most colonial schools by the late 1930s,
and the seemingly slavish adherence to English school syllabi
and examinations; what W.G.A. Ormsby-Gore (1924), Parliamentary
Under-Secretary of State for the Colonies, once referred to
as 'the cult of the certificate'. Academic schooling has
been blamed for the excessive demand for white-collar jobs
which led to urban migration and the consequent breakdown of
traditional society. Critics have also accused the British
of placing insufficient emphasis on the promotion of technical
education and trade training. Even the motives for state
intervention in education have been questioned. For example,
it is frequently asserted that the British encouraged the
establishment of schools in the colonies to ensure an
adequate supply of clerks and minor officials to run the
administration of the empire at minimum cost. (Ikejiani 1964).
Finally, some critics even claim that the content of schooling,
with its heavy emphasis on European civilisation and knowledge,
was deliberately designed to promote a sense of inferiority
and inadequacy in the minds of colonial peoples. (Carnoy
1974; Mannoui 1956; Menni 1965; Fanon 1968).

Many of these criticisms clearly stem from the framework
of a broader ideological commitment which reflects the strong
wave of anti-colonial sentiment of the past thirty years.
Detailed studies of educational development in specific
dependencies(1) cast serious doubts on the validity of many
of the criticisms outlined above. A more objective assessment
of British colonial education policy seemingly calls for a
deeper appreciation of the nature and limitations of colonial
government, the difficulties associated with interpreting the
trusteeship principle, and the influence of local conditions
in determining educational policy and practice.

After the First World War the colonial empire, excluding
India and the self-governing dominions, consisted of more
than sixty diverse territories spread over three million
square miles with a total population of about fifty-five
million(2). The African colonies, comprising two-thirds of
the land area and three-quarters of the population, were the
chief source of concern. Theoretically, the colonies were
administered from the Colonial Office but the far-flung
nature of the empire and the slowness of communication during
the preceding century had necessitated a substantial decent-
ralisation of responsibility for the daily running of affairs.
Consequently, each colony was administered as a separate
fiscal and legislative entity, responsible via the governor
to the Colonial Office, but able to act with a considerable
degree of independence. Unlike the French, the British had
no uniform colonial policy. Such policy as there was
originated less in clear strategic directives from Whitehall
than from empirical decisions made locally. Each territorial
administration was expected to determine its own rate of
development in accordance with local resources. The heavy
reliance placed on the advice and judgement of 'men on the
spot' left governors and their senior advisers with a high
degree of initiative if they chose to exercise it. At best,
the Colonial Office kept a paternal eye on what went on in
each territory supplemented by the occasional visit of an
official or adviser from London. The development of
education was a prime example.
     After the First World War, the Colonial Office was
confronted with the perplexing problem of defining the
function of trusteeship as enshrined in the mandated
territories, the full implications of which were only slowly
recognised. Should Britain promote the transformation of
colonial society into a modern western type of civilisation,
and if so at what speed? Or should traditional society be
preserved, purged of its grosser abuses such as cannibalism
or slavery, so that it might survive until the native people
were able to rule themselves? The theoretical issue was
linked to an urgent practical consideration. Was it humanly
possible, and if so, by what means, to ensure that the
impact of European civilisation whether by administration or
by white settlement or both, was gradual and evolutionary in
its effects, not cataclysmic and disintegrating? Throughout
the inter-war years the Colonial Office endorsed the principle
of indirect rule which incorporated the use of traditional
institutions in local government. The policy, traditionally
associated with Lord Lugard's administration in Northern
Nigeria, was designed to assist colonial peoples to adapt to
the needs of a changing society by a gradual blending of old
ways and new without attempting to prescribe in advance what
character the mixture should ultimately attain. What had to
be avoided at all costs was the rapid disintegration of

traditional society.

Lugard outlined his ideas in The Dual Mandate (1929), unquestionably the most influential book on colonial policy in the 1920s. He advocated the simultaneous development of the colonies in the interests of both the native peoples and the world at large, but placed primary emphasis on the protection of native society and culture. The traditional way of life would inevitably change but every effort should be made to ensure that the change was gradual.

In the 1920s Lugard's theory of adaptation was accorded the status of canon law amongst most colonial officials. This was unfortunate because the practice of indirect rule was never meant to provide a formula for colonial development. The use of native rulers in local administration was originally viewed as a progressive policy subject to constant modification as circumstances dictated. It also presupposed a leisurely pace of political and administrative evolution in what were essentially rural communities. The quickening pace of economic and social change in the 1930s resulted in mounting criticism of the policy from native and European spokesmen alike. Moreover, the theory of cultural adaptation, in which the best of the old and the new are fused together, proved to be fallacious. It rested on what Philip Foster (1965 p.165) calls 'a jig-saw puzzle' theory of culture which doesn't work. Experience in Africa and elsewhere indicates that the effects of social change cannot be controlled in such a way as to avoid major disruptions and dysfunctionalities occurring in other areas of social life. Indeed, Foster suggests that social change is almost synonymous with upheaval and dislocation. (Foster 1965). Once set in motion, it is impossible to control or halt the process. The best that can be hoped for is to mitigate some of the less desirable aspects.

The nebulous nature of the theory of adaptation inevitably left many colonial officials unsure of themselves and high-lighted an essential truth about British colonial rule between the two world wars; that no one really knew with any certainty what to do with the many millions of people living in the colonies. Julian Huxley was made very much aware of the uncertainty underlying the general aims of colonial policy when he toured through East Africa in 1929 at the request of the Advisory Committee on Native Education. It was evident to him that the objectives and even the vocabulary of 'social progress' had not been rigorously thought out and that colonial administrators had little or no idea of what they thought or hoped their territories would be like in fifty or a hundred years time. (Huxley 1932 p.374). J.M. Lee has said much the same about colonial policy after 1945, when it seemed that the ideas encouraged by the Colonial Office were based on hunches about the kind of society that would develop in the colonies rather than on any concrete objectives. (Lee 1967 p.159).

Colonial officials did their best to moderate the socially

disruptive effects of social change but attempts to preserve
traditional cultural elements while simultaneously introducing
Christianity and western civilisation inevitably set up
tensions. Often an overly protective policy was adopted -
what Sir Andrew Cohen referred to as the 'woad policy' (Cohen
1959 p.19) - with the result that Africans, Malays and Fijians
alike were embalmed in cultural cocoons isolated as far as
possible from the worst features of western civilisation.
Huxley emphasised the novelty and complexity of administering
native races in a comparatively 'primitive' state of culture
but saw no simple solutions to the numerous practical
difficulties confronting colonial officials. He could only
warn against adopting policies which might precipitate unforseen social changes or worse, tribal disintegration; 'The
watchword of those responsible for the experiment of Indirect
Rule should be gradualness...' (Huxley 1932 p.132). The
advice was of little practical value to men on the spot and
supported Cohen's belief that the Colonial Office was more
concerned with safeguarding African society than with helping
Africans to develop. (Cohen 1959 p.19).
     Huxley endorsed the paternal approach adopted by most
Europeans in their dealings with colonial peoples. Men like
Sir Gordon Guggisberg, governor of the Gold Coast in the early
1920s, and Norman Keys, an outspoken critic of British rule
in Kenya, were the exceptions rather than the rule in expressing
an optimistic view of native potential for development. Most
Europeans believed the native peoples to be different by
nature from whites and therefore inferior. By virtue of their
superior knowledge, whites considered themselves entitled to
prescribe how blacks should live. Native peoples were to
develop along their own lines, which meant in practice
acquiring manual skills useful to the Europeans but such that
they did not constitute any threat to the political, social
or intellectual superiority of the whites. Many colonial
officials likened the Africans to children who must be raised
slowly in the scale of civilisation. District Officers in
particular, often felt strongly the need to protect them from
low-class Europeans, traders and farmers who had little respect
for traditional society and culture. Nowadays such 'racist'
attitudes are roundly condemned but at the time they were
sincerely held, and it is necessary to appreciate this fact
in order to understand both the conceptual and practical
difficulties associated with colonial development. Amongst
even the most liberal and humane of colonial officials there
were few who could genuinely envisage the time when the native
peoples would run their own affairs, and even the harshest of
colonial critics in the inter-war years drew back from the
idea that Britain should abandon its colonial responsibilities.
     The motives behind the acquisition of the colonies were
varied but it was generally agreed that Britain had a moral
responsibility to prepare and eventually to grant each territory

its independence. While this sense of altruism was heightened with the establishment of the trusteeship principle after the First World War, the years that followed hardly indicated any urgency in the way in which Britain discharged this aspect of its imperial responsibility. In retrospect, the main feature of British colonial policy that stood out during the inter- war years was the tranquil assumption of the long-term character of colonial rule. At no stage did the British Government appear to conceive it to be part of its duty 'officiously to strive' (Robinson 1965 p.7) to bring self- government into existence. This attitude was in marked contrast to that which prevailed after 1945, when the concept of empire became both outmoded and embarrassing to sustain.

The cautious, even leisurely manner in which the Colonial Office went about its business was due mainly to the lack of any electorate to which it was accountable. The Secretary of State for the Colonies was answerable to the House of Commons but colonial affairs rarely aroused more than passing interest in Britain, and few subjects emptied the House as readily as the annual colonial estimates. Most people in the United Kingdom were abysmally ignorant of life and conditions in the colonies and few had any wish to be better informed. Why should they? In theory, the colonies were self-supporting. It was nice to see lots of red on the map of the world but the British people had little or no concept of social responsibility for the colonial peoples. After the First World War the British Government felt obligated towards those who had contributed to the war effort. It was no longer enough merely to keep the lines of trade and communication open and to preserve law and order but how best to promote colonial development was a contentious issue best left to men on the spot.

It is hardly surprising to find that colonial education policy reflected the vacillating and indecisive nature of colonial policy in general. The absence of any clear strategy for the long-term future of the colonial empire and the often chronic shortage of funds and personnel frequently forced colonial educators to adopt measures in which expediency rather than principle was the guiding motive. The policy of cultural adaptation was reflected in education by widespread emphasis on a type of schooling fitted to the 'mentality and needs of the natives' within their traditional rural setting. The rapid spread of western-style academic schooling was feared by most colonial officials because of its potential political repercussions. The disastrous example of what had occurred in India in the nineteenth century was not readily forgotten.

The progress of education in any colony was dependent on several often inter-related factors. These included the influence of the governor and other senior officials in the administration, the nature of the relationship between the

government and the missions, the strength of the local
economy, and the attitude of the local population towards
schooling. In the early stages of colonial rule government
officials were concerned mainly to establish law and order,
organise an efficient administration and develop a viable
source of revenue. Most governors knew little about the
problems of educational administration and were content to
leave them to lesser government officers and the missions.
An outstanding exception was Guggisberg, who promoted ambitious
plans for the development of education in the Gold Coast.
Philip Mitchell was another who placed a high priority on the
development of education when he served as governor in
Uganda and Fiji, but such men were exceptions rather than the
rule. Governors and their senior officials were generally
preoccupied with ensuring that the colony functioned smoothly
and did not prove a financial embarrassment to the British
Government. Native policy, the promotion of the economy, and
where applicable, the handling of disputes between white
settlers and the local population were their primary concerns.
Moreover, within the limits of British Treasury doctrine the
promotion of development could never be other than marginal
activity. The Colonial Office was concerned primarily to
preserve a framework in which the natives would develop at
their own pace and expatriate commercial enterprise could
operate in conditions of security. In a pre-Keynesian era,
the provision of social services was not considered essential
to economic well-being. Schools and hospitals were desirable
if they could be afforded but low on the list of priorities
for the supply of scarce development capital as illustrated
by the first colonial development act of 1929.

The progress of education was also affected adversely by
the requirement of economic self-sufficiency. Colonial
officials were acutely aware that the spread of schooling
could be ruinously expensive if social demand was allowed to
grow unchecked. Hence, it was prudent to proceed cautiously
in extending grant-in-aid to the missions or in establishing
government institutions. The rate at which schools expanded
was closely related to the resources of the missions.
Colonial governments provided aid but the initiative remained
with the missions to start schools in the first place.
During the inter-war years the strain on mission resources
increased as social demand for schools intensified and
traditional sources of finance and personnel became less
forthcoming. It was the growing inability of the missions to
cope with the rising demand for schooling which was primarily
responsible for colonial governments taking an increasing
share of the financial burden. The rising local demand for
education was most apparent in the 1930s when many self-help
or 'bush' schools appeared. Unfortunately the prolonged
economic depression of the 1930s dealt a crippling blow to
all colonial revenues and in many instances the growth of

schools dwindled almost to a standstill. By then, there was
widespread recognition of the need for more and better schools
and no lack of interest at official level, as numerous
reports of investigating committees testify, but governments
and missions alike lacked resources to implement their
recommendations.

In retrospect, the British appear to have adopted an
equivocal attitude towards education in the colonies in the
period under review. The expansion of schooling was recognised
as an essential preparation for self-government but its
implementation was left to men on the spot with the proviso
that all social development should be financed from local
sources. Given the reticence of many colonial officials to
depart from a gradualist policy, the preference for economic
rather than social projects in capital funding, and the
debilitating effects of the long economic depression, it is
not altogether surprising that educational progress seemed
slow before 1939.

From the outset, a fundamental feature of colonial
education was the free scope given to private or voluntary
enterprise. It was this, coupled with the problem arising
from local demographic factors and various practical
difficulties associated with running individual schools which
gave rise to the preponderance of communal schooling in
British colonies. Arthur Mayhew described the principle of
voluntaryism as 'a fundamental feature of English (educational)
policy at all times and in all places'. (Mayhew 1938 p.44).
It was clearly financially expedient from a government viewpoint. Unlike the missions, colonial administrators could
not call on divine assistance when raising revenue.
Voluntaryism was also justified on the grounds that it safe-
guarded moral education and ensured a variety of aims and
methods, thereby offsetting the possibility of official
standardisation and rigid uniformity. Colonial governments
were expected to exercise a supervisory role and to fill
obvious gaps in the provision of schooling if and when funds
permitted.

Limited financial resources made it impossible for any
colonial government to establish a solely public system of
schools. Moreover, to have done so would have run counter to
metropolitan practice which enshrined the idea of a dual
system of private and public schools. It was also highly
unlikely that local communities would have worked as hard to
raise funds to support public schools as they did their own
schools, nor could one have been sure that they would have
supported government schools by sending their children to
them. The Chinese in Malaya, for example, zealously defended
the independence of their schools in the 1930s.

Multi-racial communities like those found in East Africa
and South East Asia also encouraged communal schooling.
Cultural attitudes often differed on such important matters

as religion, the place of women in society, economic values, standards of hygiene, eating habits, and the value placed on European as opposed to traditional education. Consequently, multi-racial schooling was interpreted by many communities as a threat to their cultural identity, especially if the language of instruction in the school was foreign and the teachers were of another race. The Chinese and Indians in particular, made concerted efforts in the face of numerous difficulties to establish and maintain their own schools. Only in English-medium schools, invariably located in urban areas, did racial segregation break down as all races sought the advantages of a European type of education. The natural tendency to maintain racial distinctions was often reinforced by the geographical separation of the races. Malays and Fijians, for example, lived in the rural hinterlands whereas the immigrant Chinese and Indians were found in or near to towns, sugar or rubber-growing districts or in mining centres.

Various practical problems also made it difficult to establish multi-racial schools. The most obvious was the language of instruction. Unlike the French who conducted all schooling in their own tongue, the British thought it preferable to commence schooling in the child's native language and to delay the introduction of English as a medium of instruction until about the fourth year. To implement this principle it was necessary to have schools catering for different language groups. In practice, multi-racial schools were only effective if they used English as the medium of instruction but the supply of competent teachers was totally inadequate to contemplate universalising the idea. The lack of comparable educational standards amongst differing races also posed serious problems. Expatriate Europeans expected their children to be taught in English-medium schools geared to the curricula and examinations of the English education system. Few schools catering for non-Europeans could satisfy such requirements. There was also a severe shortage of staff qualified to teach at that level and the salaries they could have commanded would have been beyond the resources of most school committees. Major organisational problems would also have arisen in multi-racial schools. For example, the age of entry varied depending on race, proximity to schools, and the importance attached to schooling by the local population. It would have been necessary to provide for smaller class groupings and appropriate streaming procedures if pupils from very diverse backgrounds were to have been taught under the same roof but the extra teachers and classrooms required were not available.

Cultural attitudes also created serious practical problems. Moslems especially, disliked sending their children to mission schools for fear of proselytism. They also objected on moral grounds to co-education and the teaching of young girls by male teachers. Some Europeans opposed multi-racial schools for health reasons. Unfortunately, in some colonies the incidence of tuberculosis and other contagious diseases amongst non-Europeans was too frequent not to be taken seriously. Europeans were also critical of the standards of personal hygiene of some races. Cultural attitudes also influenced the curriculum. In Malaya and Singapore, for example, the Chinese adhered staunchly to the traditional curriculum and pattern of schooling of mainland China.

English-medium schools were almost invariably multi-racial because people of all races recognised the economic value of an English education, but there were relatively few of them and the high cost of fees ensured that all but the wealthy and those fortunate enough to win scholarships were excluded. Most children attended communal schools but the arrangement was not a deliberate act of policy by the British. To suggest that racially-segregated schooling was part of a strategy to divide and rule is not supported by the facts. During the 1930s, the British would have welcomed the chance to close Chinese schools in Malaya because they were a source of political unrest but this was not possible because of a lack of resources to provide alternative schooling. Moreover, it was the management committees of communal schools who were often primarily responsible for maintaining racial segregation. In Fiji, for example, they frequently refused entry to children of other races for fear of antagonising parents of existing pupils.

The British could have enforced multi-racial schooling throughout the colonial empire only if they had been prepared to establish systems of state schools open to all pupils. They had no wish to do so for reasons of principle nor did they have the necessary manpower and financial resources if they had so wished. Nor was it feasible to bully local management committees into accepting pupils of all races when they bore the brunt of the cost of running the schools. This does not necessarily mean that all colonial officials approved of communal schools. Mitchell strongly opposed the system in Fiji when he went there in 1942, but as the Director of Education remarked at the time, to have opened all schools to all pupils would have met with strong resentment, especially from Europeans. (Fiji 1943). Communal schools appear to have been the logical outcome of applying the voluntaryist principle in multi-racial societies. The underlying motive was a belief in the right of people to select the school of their choice rather than some sinister political calculation.

The low level of enrolment and poor school attendance of girls in colonial territories is also explained by cultural attitudes and practical considerations rather than by any deliberate policy of neglect. The early age of marriage constituted the main obstacle. (Harvey 1929). Allied to this was the lack of any economic motivation. (Broomfield 1927

When girls left school there were no jobs available for them
in the modern economic sector. Women in all traditional
societies were tied to child-bearing and domestic duties and
it was not possible to alter this pattern until social
attitudes changed, but this took time. The British were also
reluctant to exert undue pressure to encourage more girls to
attend school for fear of triggering off unforseen and maybe
grave social consequences. For example, women fulfilled a
vital role in food production in many African tribal societies
and the rapid introduction of schooling might have put that
function at risk. Children at school would have been unable
to mind the younger siblings while the mother worked. A
more favourable attitude towards female education was dependent
on a growth in the proportion of educated males. As the latter
sought educated wives so they became more sympathetic to
schooling for girls but the major breakthrough in this respect
did not occur until after the Second World War.

Various practical difficulties adversely affected the
growth of schooling for girls of which the most serious was
the acute shortage of women teachers. It was almost impossible
to recruit married women because they were preoccupied with
domestic duties while unmarried women were virtually non-
existent. In African tribal societies, for example, there
was no place for them. There were a few in the towns but
they were mostly of 'easy virtue'. (Harvey 1929).
Consequently, schools had to rely on the few European women
who were available. The often scattered population also
contributed to low enrolments because it was not considered
safe for young girls to travel any distance by themselves.

Criticism of the literary curriculum has already been
challenged by Foster. (Foster 1965). It is ironic that the
British should have been blamed for the bookish type of
schooling that developed when they were so opposed to it in
principle. One of the first tasks of the Advisory Committee
on Education was to formulate a set of principles to guide
the development of education in the colonies. These were
contained in a government white paper which embodied the
philosophy of indirect rule by insisting on the need to adapt
education to local needs and conditions. (HMSO 1925). This
view was endorsed a year later by the Secretary of State for
the Colonies at the Imperial Conference of 1926:

> Our whole endeavour now is to substitute for a
> purely literary education, not suited to the needs
> of the natives, a type of education more adapted
> to their mental aptitude - a type of education which,
> while conserving as far as possible all the sane and
> healthy elements in the fabric of their own social
> life, will also assist their growth and evolution on
> natural lines and enable them to absorb more
> progressive ideas; it aims above all, at the building

up of character on the part of the native, at
giving him an understanding of his own environment, at making him useful in his own environment rather than at giving him the kind of
education which is really only suitable in the
environment of a country like Great Britain.
(HMSO 1926 p.123).

The Advisory Committee's white paper received a mixed
reception. It was intended that it should provide a set of
broad principles as guides to action, but that local administrations should be left free to implement them as they saw
fit. Unfortunately lack of resources and a dearth of educators with appropriate anthropological training prevented the
white paper from having any significant effect. (Cox 1965
p.131). Failure to implement the ideal was also due to its
rejection by the indigenous people themselves. They quickly
appreciated the economic and social advantages of an English
academic schooling as J.S. Furnivall pointed out in his study
of South East Asia and Burma. Primary vernacular education
languished everywhere because it had no economic importance.
It was merely an instrument of welfare. (Furnivall 1956
p.392). Efforts to promote technical education likewise
suffered from lack of popular support. The thinking of the
Advisory Committee on Education was strongly influenced by
the Phelps-Stokes report on education in Africa which appeared
in 1922. (Jones 1922). The report visualised a static rural
society and a practical type of education based on the rural
environment which would hopefully minimise the conflict of
forces between the old world and the new. Unfortunately,
this does not work in practice. The forces of change cannot
be contained nor can schools survive unless they respond to
the perceived needs of society. Africans and Asians alike
viewed an English academic education as the means to social
and economic advantage and, for some, eventual political
power. Anything less was regarded as second rate. In retrospect, it seems rather pointless to condemn the British for
circumstances beyond their control.

Criticism of the motives which prompted state intervention
in education is equally suspect. Surely it is a little too
facile to claim that the British were concerned merely to
provide a source of cheap clerical labour. In the early 1920s
it was soon apparent that the missions would be unable to
meet the rising demand for schooling solely from their own
resources. It was also questionable whether they should
enjoy a virtual monopoly in the supply of schools. Considerations of this sort coupled with the moral responsibilities
of trusteeship largely explain increased government involvement in education after the First World War. As the administrative function of government expanded in the colonies so it
became necessary to recruit more local civil servants but

schools were not started exclusively for that purpose.

Finally, what of the argument that colonial education imparted a subservient mentality to its recipients. Unfortunately, leading writers in this field like Martin Carnoy adopt an ideological standpoint which largely inhibits debate. (Carnoy 1974). If one accepts that British colonial expansion was predominantly motivated by the desire of the strong to exploit and to dominate the weak, then it follows that schools colonised the intellect. But perhaps the motives behind imperial expansion were more complex as suggested in a recent study by D.K. Fieldhouse. (Fieldhouse 1973). The fall of Singapore in 1942 undoubtedly constituted an event of the utmost psychological importance to the colonial peoples of Asia but the extent to which they had been conditioned into accepting European hegemony by the schools remains an open question. Western education undoubtedly highlighted the scientific and technological leadership of the western world but it also generated political awareness and the eventual demise of colonial rule.

Academic arguments about the relative merits of colonial rule will continue for some time yet but there is surely no need to write as an apologist about British colonial education policy. The discrepancy between what was stated and what was achieved was not altogether the fault of colonial officials. The ambivalent nature of colonial objectives between the two world wars and the numerous practical difficulties associated with the implementation of any coherent policy were genuine enough. Modern critics might well ask what realistic alternatives were available. Experience in numerous developing countries since 1945 has demonstrated the unsettling effects of educating youth for non-existent jobs and inculcating them with socio-economic expectations which cannot be satisfied. In the final analysis the major characteristics of British colonial education policy owed more to the volition of the governed than to the persuasive powers of colonial officials. (Brown 1964).

The above paragraphs have stressed the need for a reassessment of British colonial education policy. If glib generalisations are to be exposed for what they are, greater emphasis must be placed on more detailed case studies of educational development in individual colonies. More research is also needed into the influence of the Advisory Committee on Education in the Colonies. No attempt has been made here to extend the argument beyond 1939 but there is an equally strong case for doing so. The work of Lord Hailey (Hailey 1938) who, like Lord Lugard before him, had a profound impact on colonial policy, and the Commonwealth Development and Welfare Acts of 1940 and 1945 respectively, ushered in a new era and philosophy of colonial development but by then time was fast running out. The full story of colonial education policy in the post-war years leading to the

dissolution of the colonial empire in the 1960s has still to
be written.

NOTES

     1. The author's research has centred on Fiji, Malaya
and Singapore. See also Felice V. Carter, 'Education in
Uganda 1894-1945', Ph.D thesis, University of London 1967;
S.P. Abbott, 'The African Education Policy of the Kenya
Government 1904-1939', M.Phil thesis, University of London
1970; A.R. Thompson, 'The Adaptation of Education to African
Society in Tanganyika Under British Rule', Ph.D thesis,
University of London 1968; J.C.E. Greig, 'Decision-Making in
Educational Administration: A Comparative Study of the Gambia
and Malawi during the period 1925-1945', Ph.D thesis,
University of London 1978.
     2. Figures are derived from The Colonial Office List
1924.

Chapter Three

EDUCATION AND UNDERDEVELOPMENT IN AFRICA: THE HISTORICAL
PERSPECTIVE

Brian Garvey

        Since those African territories which were formerly
controlled by Great Britain achieved political independence
in the fifties and sixties two types of criticism have been
levelled against the educational experiences of the colonial
period. The first, voiced before and in the years immediately
following independence, concerned the levels and structures of
educational provision which were inherited by new states from
colonial administrations. The second type of criticism which
gathered momentum during the seventies related to the purposes
and nature of educational experiences in the colonial era, and
the influences that such experiences still have on different
facets of national development. It will be the purpose of this
chapter to examine briefly the main structures contained within these critical approaches and then to attempt to put them
into an historical perspective, first by establishing a
rough periodisation of colonial educational development in
Africa and seconly be seeking the historical explanations of
certain selected criticisms.
        The first level of criticism is concerned with the
statistics of educational provision pertaining in each
territory at the time of the transfer of power. Four aspects
of educational provision have been frequently examined.
School populations as percentages of national age groups often
told a story of educational growth which, given the long years
of colonial and educational experience, had been extremely
slow. Thus, while Ghana with two hundred years of school
development had about 67% of the primary school age range
actually provided with school places, in Sierra Leone with a
similarly long history of educational effort school places
were available for only 21% of the age group. (Burns 1965).
On the other side of the continent, Zambia and Tanganyika with
much shorter but similar histories of educational growth had
primary enrolments of 54% and 24% of the age groups respectively.
At the secondary level, enrolments for these countries were
registered as 29% for Ghana, 3% for Sierra Leone, 2.6% for
Zambia and 2.1% for Tanganyika. Even the best provided was

faced therefore with an immense need for increased educational
opportunity if the level of modern sector employment which
existed at the time of independence was to be taken over by
autochtones.

Besides the levels of provision there were problems too
with the uneven distribution of schooling throughout populations
Nigeria provides a good example of these regional inequalities
which were partly geographical, partly religious, since at
the time of independence in the Western provinces there were
primary enrolments of 100% and secondary enrolments of 10% of
the respective age groups, while in the northern half of the
country fewer than 10% of primary age children were enrolled
in schools. The low enrolment in the north is partly accounted
for because missionaries were forbidden to proselytise in
this essentially Muslim area. Other territories had inequalities based on race. For example in Kenya, before independence
more capital had been invested in the education of the tiny
European and Asian minorities rather than on the African
majority which accounted for 97% of the population. (Kenya
1964). The reasons for this were as much economic as they
were political. The need to correct such inequities involved
tackling the fourth problem area inherited from the colonial
past, namely the uneven control by government over educational
provision which was an effect of the immense role played by
Christian missions in initiating, maintaining and developing
school systems over the entire period of British occupation.
(Scanlon 1966).

The second type of critical approach to colonial educational experience was expressed as new states began to formulate independent policies and began to attempt to enlarge
the political freedoms which had been sown by the acts of
political statehood. The concept of 'the development of
underdevelopment' as an indictment of colonial activity was
probably introduced by Andre Gundar Frank's examination of
Latin American experience, (Frank 1969), but was greatly
popularised in respect of Africa by the late Walter Rodney's
book How Europe Underdeveloped Africa. (Rodney 1972). This
has become the dominant theme in recent economic and social
histories of African states and has influenced writing on
mission history and education. (Carnoy 1974; Leys 1975;
Palmer and Parsons 1977; Linden 1974; Manu wuike 1978). The
general 'development of underdevelopment' thesis maintains
that the colonial experience subverted the social and economic
structures of colonised societies to such a degree as to
render impossible any self-developed movement to greater
economic prosperity or social coherence. In the context of
education three main criticisms are levelled against the
colonial experience. First it is said that both formal and
informal education of the colonial period was irrelevant not
only to societies as they had existed in pre-colonial times
but also to their chances of survival and properity in the

context of overseas involvement and change. Secondly it is
pointed out that formal education in particular had as its
main object the support of a new economic order based on
primary exports and only limited and dependent local industrialisation. Thirdly it is claimed that, because of its
foreign social base, the educational systems of colonial
states were thoroughly disruptive of local communities and
were incapable of adaptation to African needs or to the support
of genuine developments in African society.

The point might be made here that much polemical writing
such as that of Rodney can too easily be dismissed because of
its evident faults: the idealisation of the pre-colonial past,
and the universality of its condemnations, where for example
colonisers are blamed both for not having provided enough
schools and for having had the temerity to provide schools at
all!! It has to be admitted however that criticisms such as
those listed above do not appear intrinsically unreasonable,
though they certainly stand in direct opposition to much
historical writings on the growth of education in the colonial
areas of British Africa. (Sumner 1963; McWilliam 1959; Weiler
1964; Snelson 1970). What will interest the historian is the
evidence for the various claims of both the 'development of
underdevelopment' school and the more orthodox critics of
educational growth in Africa and any indication of change over
time which can point to the way in which various aspects of
educational provision actually influenced the social cohesion
or the economies of African communities. This approach would
require micro-studies of the sort illustrated for Central and
Southern African economic development by the collection edited
by Palmer and Parsons (1977). What follows is at most a
possible framework for the study of educational experiences
in Africa.

Despite the immense differences in language, culture,
length of exposure to colonial influence and the actual spread
of both literacy and schooling by the time of independence,
all African territories under British rule went through the
same sort of motions in the development and change of formal
education. Of the many possible ways of analysing such changes,
the most convenient seems to be that which examines the
relationships between the actual providers of education and
the territorial colonial administrations. Thus we can posit
a rough periodisation within any territory over four stages
of educational growth:

1. pioneering educational activities by church or other
   initiatives;
2. educational activity directed by missionary groups but
   under some control of the colonial administrations;
3. education directed by and financed by colonial administrations, but purveyed through missionary organisations;
4. education systems directed, financed and run by colonial

governments with the assistance (gradually diminishing
in importance) of existing missionary organisations.

   The pioneering phase in the educational history of any
territory was of a duration determined by the level of colonial
political control. Early educational activities were usually
fragmented and frequently interrupted. Thus during the
eighteenth century the West Coast saw many attempts by trading
companies to establish some form of schooling for castle
populations or client villages, attempts which depended not
only on the goodwill of individual Governors, but also on the
lifespans of individual missionaries, schoolteachers or
philanthropic societies. (Wise 1956). When a century or so
later missions were initiated in South, Central or Eastern
Africa by larger and better organised and financed missionary
societies, there was still a great dependence on the successes
of a handful of able individuals, while the organisations
themselves were often torn between the rival strategies of
consolidating a base or extending apparently successful work
into new unpenetrated zones. The spread of Protestant
activity from the South African base at Lovedale is a good
example, particularly since its pioneering element (Robert
Moffat and David Livingstone) is so well known and its overlap with other mission innovators, such as Francis Coillard
and Frederick Arnot, well attested. (Shepherd 1941). During
this crucial pioneering phase schooling was certainly restricted
to basic literacy, numeracy and religion, and strictly sub-
ordinated to a non-educational objective: the pacification of
a castle village and the diffusion of Christian doctrine.
   The link between education and social control explains
the often early attempts by colonial administrations to
control educational activity in and around colonised areas.
Given that such administrations were not in any position to
imitate their own school systems, the favourite instrument
of control became the 'education ordinance'. Ghana's earliest
ordinance, that of 1852, was prompted by the public order need
to occupy and suitably to train youth in the area of the
trading posts. As British interests in Africa grew, the
objectives of educational control became less positive.
Malawi and Zambia both received their first ordinances in
1919 after the disturbances around the mission church of
John Chilembwe persuaded the colonial administrations to
attempt to limit and control teaching by 'native' pastors.
(Snelson 1970 p.130). Within the limits set by such ordinances,
missions or other groups were usually free to pursue their
own educational objectives according to their own methods,
but it is clear from the frequent differences and misunder-
standings between colonial officials and mission teachers
that the objectives of both sides of the colonial penetration
were not always identical. (Ranger and Kimambo 1975). Only
when state finance became an important element in mission

educational development did the need to co-ordinate such
objectives became apparent to both interests.

While in West Africa there had been a tradition of limited
government expenditure on schools, even with some short-lived
attempts to establish administration-run institutions, the
whole of British Africa was affected by the establishment of
the Advisory Committee on African Education by the Colonial
Office in 1923. (Mason 1959). The formation of a colonial
policy on education was strongly influenced by missionary
experience, and was preceded by the two church-supported
Phelps-Stokes commissions which toured Africa and made
recommendations based both on the history of school development in British colonial territories and on the growth of
Negro education in the post-civil war United States of
America. (Lewis 1962). However, comparatively few of the
detailed suggestions of the commissions were put into effect.
In practice each territory worked out its own educational
objectives and strategies for growth.

The most important innovation of the period was undoubtedly
the considerable injection of financial aid into the mission
systems, and the parallel establishment of colonial education
departments though the latter did little more at first than
administer those finances. There is no doubt that the availability of funds persuaded missionary societies to extend
their school activities, and Roman Catholic orders for example
were pressed by the Apostolic Visitor of 1928, Bishop
Hinsley, to use the educational strategy much more in their
evangelical endeavours than had hitherto been the case.
(Garvey 1974). Not unnaturally the existence of rival
churches seeking funds from the colonial administration
occasionally led to unseemly squabbles and in some areas,
the more attractive ones especially, to an overconcentration
of educational institutions. (Ekechi 1972 p.280).

Unlike the earlier periods of educational development,
there was now some standardisation in provision and much
closer collaboration between administration and agencies on
the objectives of learning. However, church autonomy was
not completely relinquished largely because colonial administrations did not have enough money to develop government
financed schools. The result was that more of the direction
and much more of the financing than had been envisaged in
discussions in the 1920s was left in mission hands. The
latter point has not always been fully realised about the
development of school systems in Africa before the Second
World War: the educational pyramid stood on a vast network
of 'schools in the bush' wholly financed by the voluntary
agencies and staffed by teachers trained outside the administration-run normal school system. Until well after the war,
colonial administrations were paying the smaller proportion
of the educational expenses of their territories, while the
larger share was found by the mission agencies. (Garvey 1974

p.287). It can hardly be argued, therefore, that colonial
governments deliberately used schools as a means of social
control.

This state of affairs began to change in the decade before
independence from the early 1950s onwards when revenues
increased and a larger proportion of them was devoted to
educational development. During this period various organisational changes in all colonial territories brought schooling
more directly under government control. Teacher education
systems were enlarged and funded by government. Teacher cadres
were unified. There were positive moves both to continue the
extension of primary education and to build more secondary
technical and tertiary institutes. By the time of independence
nine territories had embryo university colleges. Mission
influence remained of course, and many independent states
were to make use of this missionary presence since missionary
expatriate teachers were likely to provide the backbone of
secondary and tertiary institutes for some years to come.
The secularisation of education was under way however, with
important possibilities for the early years of independent
nationhood though the speed at which it took place very much
depended on the political complexion and financial capabilities
of the newly independent governments.

The educational history of most British African territories has been written in terms similar to the above, with
emphasis on establishment and administration, on mission
foundation and gradual government involvement. That schools
were by and large a good thing is normally assumed by writers
who themselves have often been beneficiaries of and even paid
auxiliaries of the colonial educational system. The 'development of underdevelopment' thesis challenges such assumptions.
Given that mission penetration was part of colonial penetration,
that mission educational objectives were accepted by colonial
administrations as worthy of financial investment, the onus
is perhaps on the defenders of the educational past to justify
not only what did not happen (in respect of lack of development) but what did happen in localities infused by Western
schooling. Historians might be wary here of assuming 'guilt
by association', but the majority of mission educators did
not show themselves to be out of line with the thinking of
their political masters and the association did include
accepting the shillings offered by the colonial administrations.

According to Rodney, however, 'colonial schooling was
education for subordination, exploitation, the creation of
mental confusion and the development of underdevelopment'.
(Rodney 1972 p.264). Rodney's criticisms need to be taken
seriously if only because of their widespread influence on
present and future educational thinking in Africa as well as
because of their reflections on the past. If one takes the
first of the criticisms mentioned above which is directed at
the Christian Europeans and not at the Muslim Arabs, namely

that education was irrelevant to the true development of the communities who were supposed to benefit from it, it would be useful to examine the notion of 'relevance' against the periodisation of educational development that has been outlined. Schools established by pioneers before the full politicisation of large areas by colonial powers served one of two purposes: the spread of the Christian gospel by enthusiasts or the social control of embryonic communities by administrators. The relevance of the gospel message to African rural societies will be argued by believers and doubted by non-believers. But from this distance in time it is now possible to appreciate that such societies had over long periods developed their own systems of religious and rational belief which reflected the needs of their own social and economic structures. (Parrinder 1962; Mbiti 1969). But it would be wrong to consider that such beliefs, or indeed the structures which embodied them, were immutable. One can recall Horton's thesis that 'world' religions, such as Islam or Christianity, accord with the needs of societies with strong outside links and therefore become attractive to tribal societies as those societies form trade or other relationships with the wider world. (Horton 1971). However, in advance of dramatic social change, the teachings of European understandings of Christian belief, understandings with strong historical roots in eighteenth and nineteenth century European social history, might not have appeared relevant to African communities and might indicate why such teaching was comparatively ineffective before commercial and political interference began to change African society. Extending Horton's argument one can point to the gradual Islamisation of 'black' West Africa as a result of the spread of trans-Saharan trade, but the influence of European trade and politics was much more sudden and violent. Where schools were introduced in castle villages and their client communities one can see that the relevance of Christian indoctrination was to the advantage of the foreign traders. But in many other cases schools were part of a Christian pioneering activity not sympathetic to the parallel penetration of commerce.

After the pioneering phase, formal education accompanied and was increasingly part of the growth of colonial control. Despite increasing government support for school systems, the tension caused by the different objectives of mission teachers and colonial administrators continued. But it is clear that just as officials found mission schools a useful tool of political control, so educators found administrations useful both financially and politically as government pressure was put on African communities to accept and support schools. (Snelson 1970 p.221). That the leaders of these communities did not always find schools relevant to their needs is also evident. African society was being subjected to a large number of disturbing influences: foreign styles of government,

alienation of traditional land, labour migration etc. Schools
were either an additional burden which it would be wise to
avoid, or a means of learning how to make use of the new
economic and social order. In North Eastern Zambia mission
teachers of one Roman Catholic order found at one time that
young men were abandoning their schools to attend the Living-
stonia mission in Malawi, because the teaching there was in
the economic language, English, and at another peiod their
trainee schoolteachers were leaving the normal school as soon
as they had acquired enough skill to obtain paid employment
elsewhere. (Garvey 1974 p.265, 283). In this respect formal
education was relevant to the changing demands of the new
colonial society and in fitting Africans to contribute to it,
schools also fitted them for making use of it.

This becomes more apparent when we look at the last
period of educational development in the years immediately
preceding independence. African elites became more important
in school, church and commercial spheres at the time that
their peers were claiming political powers previously denied
to natives of colonial territories. Educational agencies,
those of the administration as well as those of the missions,
were responding to the newer needs of development which included
the need to nurture leadership as well as to develop the
practical skills in educational institutes. Here the missions
had a much better record. The preparation of Africans to take
over the direction of local churches had always been a part of
mission educational enterprise. Junior seminaries often
preceded secondary schools, and theological colleges certainly
preceded most other forms of higher education. The relevance
of such leadership to the needs of colonised populations can
again be debated but the churches became what their leaders
made of them. The assumption of the educators was that the
institution itself was worthwhile irrespective of economic or
social circumstances. Such institutions survive where they
contain the flexibility to render themselves relevant. Given
the disturbed situation of African local politics in the years
since independence it would be unwise to condemn the churches
as unhelpful to African national communities.

Another criticism levelled against the colonial school
system is that the main purpose 'was to train Africans to man
the local administration at the lowest rank and to staff the
private capitalist firms owned by Europeans'. (Rodney 1972
p.263). Formal education certainly played an important part
in the economic re-orientation of African communities away
from their evolved systems of production, distribution and
reward. The organisation of agricultural and mineral production
for world markets in support of overseas industry demanded
much greater social disturbance than the establishment of
schools. Resources were alienated by political acts, workers
were obliged to move to new areas and activities by taxation
systems and everywhere traditional agricultural economies were

changed. The results of such change differed from territory
to territory. In South-Central Africa subsistence farming
became 'sub-subsistence' farming carried on without men and
involving a growing dependence on imports of food from the
foreign commercial enterprises. In Kenya similar pressures
caused other results as the Kikuyu fought back with their
ability to out-produce the foreign growers and compete success
-fully against them in world markets. In West Africa post-
slave trade developments were less dramatic as foreign economic
interests made use of local produce and only gradually and to
a limited extent took over the activities of production.
(Tignor 1976; Dickson 1971).

It is not within the scope of this paper to trace the
economic history of each territory and to consider the relation
-ship between changes in economy and changes in formal
education. However, in the context of different parts of
Africa one can see a congruence for example between the
economic style of Central Africa and the spread of Malawian
clerks from the Scottish missions across the administrative
and commercial systems of Zambia and Zimbabwe, or between
the independent agriculture of the Kikuyu and their insistence
on alternative, locally controlled schooling, or between the
absorption of West African farmers into the 'capitalist mode'
and the strong influence of West African educators on the
growth of their European-oriented school systems. Was there
any resistance by educators to the tendency of formal education
to support foreign and disruptive economic movements? Teachers
were not usually political economists. African educational
history is scattered with enough experiments in rural or
technical training to indicate that teachers were trying to
prepare pupils for the economic challenges of the present.
(Clarke 1937; Bittinger 1940; Griffiths 1953). That alternative rather than imitative economies were not developed can
be blamed, just as the African predilection for 'academic'
rather than 'practical' education can be blamed, on the informal
side of education.

Another criticism is that 'in Africa both the formal
school system and the informal value system of colonialism
destroyed social solidarity and promoted the worst form of
alienated individualism without social responsibility'.
(Rodney 1972 p.280). One may of course doubt the absence of
unsocial individualism in pre-colonial communities but it
must also be admitted that post-colonial societies exhibit
problems of acculturation, alienation of social responsibilities
and untraditional competitive behaviour. Rodney rightly said
that much of this influence arose from the colonial society
which surrounded African communities, but it can be asked
how formal education and in particular formal Christian
education was itself disruptive of traditional social life.
Most eighteenth and nineteenth century evangelism was concerned
with developing the consciousness of individual guilt and

merit while developing a whole series of new attitudes in
social behaviour which were contradictory to customary African
practice. At the same time the educators were themselves part
of the informal education system, embodying as they did the
values and culture of the colonial society. To what extent at
different periods education caused changes in the ways of
living of African communities would require very careful
micro-studies. There can be a temptation to see change where
very little exists. Studies of rural education in independent
Africa show how little traditional life is affected by teaching which relates solely to modern sector living or employment.
It is perhaps an indication of the failure of schooling to
change rural communities that independent societies are
demonstrating the development of 'two nations' in the modern
and traditional economic cultures. (Zanelli 1971; Brownstein
1972).

It is not the function of the historian to make judge-
ments on the values of former teachers on the basis of criteria
which would have had little meaning in the past. One may however judge outcomes in relation to stated aims and ask whether
formal education of the colonial period achieved what it was
intended to achieve.

Quantitatively there can be no firm answer to such a
question because neither missions nor governments set themselves anything but the shortest term quantitative targets.
Given that for most of the period the heaviest financial
burdens were being supported by voluntary organisations, long
term goals would have been unreasonable. Qualitatively it is
probably true that colonial educators achieved over the years
their most important aims. School systems were established,
as churches were established, and they survived the transfer
of political power to African elites. If African economies
were developed as contributing subsidiaries to the economies
of industrialised nations the objective of school systems has
always been that of enabling educated individuals and educated
communities to make use of the economic tools available. The
level of local involvement in modern sector industry or commerce
will spell the success or failure of education in each
territory in that respect. The struggle for relevance in
teaching and learning continues. Colonial teachers emerged
from the social revolutions of industrial growth in Europe
and attempted to serve African societies according to their
own current images of social and individual development.
That they are condemned by hindsight as having contributed to
underdevelopment rather than a post-independence interpretation
of genuine development indicates that with the limited vision
that any teacher will have they were by and large successful.

Chapter Four

THE CONTRIBUTION OF MISSION SCHOOLS TO EDUCATIONAL DEVELOPMENT
IN SOUTH EAST ASIA*(1)

Keith Watson

THE EARLY PIONEERS

The influence of the Christian missions in the field of
education in South East Asia, especially in Thailand, Malaysia
and Singapore, has been enormous and it is generally acknowledged that the development of modern education in these
countries came about as a direct result of missionary
influence(2). Yet although the story of missionary involvement in education largely begins with the expansion of the
colonial powers and is therefore mainly a nineteenth and
twentieth century phenomenon, it is worth pointing out that
missionary activity in South East Asia began during the
sixteenth and seventeenth centuries.

The first Christian missionaries in the region were
Roman Catholics brought by the Portuguese to Malacca in 1511,
but the first known school, with 120 pupils, was not established
until 1548 by St. Francis Xavier, the pioneer of education in
Malaysia and the Philippines. However with the seizure of
Malacca by Dutch Protestants in 1641 there followed over one
hundred and fifty years of persecution and rivalry until the
British East India Company authorities, responsible for what
came to be known from 1825 until 1946 as the Straits Settlements (Penang, Malacca and Singapore), granted religious
toleration in 1824.

The first missionary contact with Siam, as Thailand was
known until 1939, and other parts of mainland South East Asia
was also in 1511, though serious Roman Catholic missionary
activity did not begin until 1555 (Downs 1968). Since then
Roman Catholic missions, in spite of periods of difficulty,
have been resident continuously.

The main educational thrust, however, began during the
seventeenth century, with the creation in Paris of the French
Societé de Missions Etrangères, generally known as the French
Mission, in 1659. The aim of the French Mission was the
conversion of Indo-China, and ultimately of China. Initially,
however, it was to convert and train native born clergy so

that they could run their own churches in 'Further India' and
the following instructions were issued by the papal curia in
Rome:

> The motive inspiring the Curia in its despatch of
> Bishops to the Far East was to foster every
> opportunity and every means for training the youth
> put there to acquire such aptitude for Holy Orders
> that ultimately they would assume full charge of
> the Christian community in those parts under your
> guidance. This therefore is the goal which you
> should ever keep before you - to bring in, teach,
> and in due course promote as many suitable
> candidates as possible for the Priesthood.
> (Hutchinson 1933).

The first missionaries were bound for Cochin-China and
Annam but because of shipwreck they were forced to land on
the coast of Siam and in 1662 settled in Ayuthia, the then
thriving capital of the country. Very quickly they opened a
seminary and attracted novices and trainees from the neigh-
bouring countries of Burma, Cochin-China and Cambodia as well
as the sons of Chinese settlers in Siam. The college was
divided into two sections, an elementary school and an upper
school for aspirants to Holy Orders. In 1665 the king, Narai,
even allowed ten royal princes to attend the school, but
numbers remained small even though the school survived until
1767 when the Burmese sacked Ayuthia. As far as we know this
was the first long lived mission school to be established in
Asia. Others quickly followed in Burma, Cambodia, Malaya
and Vietnam, since wherever the French Mission established a
centre it also opened a dispensary and a school. (Hall 1955;
Watson 1980b).
In spite of the disfavour into which the Mission fell
after the abortive attempt by the French to convert King
Narai to Christianity in 1688 (Collis 1965), the indignities
suffered by both missionary and indigenous Christians in Siam
during the eighteenth century, and the chaos into which Siam
was thrown as a result of wars against Burma and Cambodia (3)
the tradition of mission schools persisted until the early
nineteenth century when increased funds from the Paris based
Ouvres pour la Propagation de la Foi (founded in 1811) and a
papal decree of 1827 granting the Apostolic Vicar of Siam
jurisdiction over Singapore and other parts of South East
Asia gave the missionary enterprise a considerable boost.
By the middle of the nineteenth century in Siam therefore
there were ten schools for boys and girls and two convents
for girls, all of them small, but nevertheless the beginning
of influential schools. The Mission also continued to work,
with mixed results, in Cambodia and Vietnam until annexation
of these territories by the French in the latter part of the

nineteenth century provided a degree of official support on the ground.

THE GROWTH OF MISSIONS IN THE NINETEENTH CENTURY

There is little doubt that the real credit for arousing interest in and providing the basis for public and secular education, as opposed to education offered in Koranic schools and Buddhist temple schools, must go to the various Protestant and Roman Catholic missions that penetrated the region during the nineteenth century. Although it is easy to denigrate them for misguided zeal their motives were of the highest and their impact was to be profound. (Neill 1964).

In Siam Catholic penetration began as a result of the friendship of Bishop Pallegoix of the French Mission with King Mongkut (1851-68) while the latter was still a monk. The story of this remarkable king's influence on the development of Thai education and society has been told elsewhere (Bruce 1968; Watson 1980d; Waugh 1970) but his eagerness to learn Latin, French and theology from Bishop Pallegoix and English from American missionaries, his curiosity to learn things Western and in 1856 his recognition of the right of the Thais to choose their own religion had a long lasting impact on the development of missionary education. Even now the King of Thailand is regarded as the Patron and Protector of all Faiths, even though he himself is a Buddhist. During King Chulalongkorn's reign (1868-1910), Pallegoix's successor, Bishop Vey, opened in 1885 what was in time to become one of the leading and most influential schools in the country, Bangkok's Assumption College, and by the time of his death in 1909 there was a network of orphanages, schools and colleges throughout the country, enrolling several thousand pupils.

Other Catholic missions established themselves in Thailand during the late nineteenth and early twentieth centuries (e.g. the Brothers of St. Gabriel, the Sisters of the Sacred Heart, the Ursulines, the Jesuits and the De La Salle Brothers) and by the time of the Second World War there were well over one hundred Catholic Mission schools established up and down the country. Although a number of these have now closed, thirteen of Bangkok's leading secondary schools are run by Roman Catholic missions and there are over thirty religious orders working in the country. Thompson observed a number of years ago that missionaries realised that 'the extension of their influence throughout the school years has a much more lasting effect on character than gratitude for relief from pain which evaporates very swiftly'. (Thompson 1941 p.653). Hence there was a growing emphasis on involvement in education rather than in medicine, although the latter has never been forgotten as can be seen in some of the key hospitals and dispensaries.

Impressive though Roman Catholic missionary activity in Thailand might have been it was the Protestant missionaries

that aroused the greatest interest in modern education in that
country. The first Protestant missionaries arrived in 1828
from Singapore with the intention of proselytisation though
their activities were rapidly confined to the small Chinese
population only. Appeals for help were sent to Holland,
England and America and during the 1830s several US missionaries arrived. Initially their main concern was for medical
work and even to this day missionaries in Thailand are often
referred to as 'moh' (doctor). As one modern missionary has
observed,

> It is hard to recapture, in this day of massive
> government aid and loan programmes, the influence
> exerted by individual missionaries in those earlier
> days. Advisers, teachers and friends to kings,
> queens and royal children, they enlarged the thinking
> and liberalised the minds that opened Thailand to
> the West. That Thailand had to confront the West
> was a matter of historical inevitability. That it
> was prepared for the encounter by sympathetic and
> generous minded men was the earliest and one of the
> greatest contributions of the Christian Church.
> (Downs 1968 pp.33-34).

Of these early Protestant missionaries Dr. Dan Beach
Bradley (Lord 1969) stands out as a pioneer not only in
medical work but in the development of printing. The earliest
printed works in Thai were the Ten Commandments, an edict
banning the smoking of opium and a newspaper. King Mongkut
saw the possibilities and developed a government printing
press and as Jumsai (1951 p.17) has noted 'printing started
and promoted by royal patronage has since become one of the
most important tools of education in the country'.

During the 1840s and 1850s several Protestant mission
schools were opened, including one for girls, but so little
interest was shown that missionaries had to offer inducements
to get children to attend (Sukontarangsi 1966), a situation
repeated in many territories. However, following King
Chulalongkorn's decree of Religious Toleration in 1878,
obstacles to parents sending their children to school were
removed and mission schools began to flourish in the North
and North East as well as in the Central Plain of Thailand.

By the beginning of this century missionaries in Thailand
could claim to have introduced Siamese type, developed the
first printing press for printing textbooks and royal decrees,
written the first Thai dictionary, founded the first girls'
schools, pioneered a network of secular schools and provoked
the monarchy - in the form of King Chulalongkorn - to develop
a state education system. (Wyatt 1969). In fact one Thai
official has observed that 'it is owing to the King's
(Mongkut's) enthusiasm for Christian education that King

Chulalongkorn, his son, embarked upon educational reform in 1871'. (Sukontarangsi 1966).

The influence of Christian missionaries on educational development in Malaya and Singapore has likewise been enormous. Because, as in most colonial territories, the colonial government tended to ignore education in favour of the maintenance of law and order, defence and economic 'development', missionaries and voluntary bodies were allowed, and even encouraged, to develop Western-type schools largely unmolested. But although government policy was superficially one of 'laissez-faire' mission societies were never allowed an entirely free hand to do as they wished. The British authorities supported them when they believed it was in their interest to do so, but restricted them when necessary (e.g. from proselytising amongst the Malays) because they believed that that was also in the best interests of the government and the governed.

In fact colonial governors were always sensitive to local religious sensibilities and were not only content to leave indigenous methods of schooling amongst the Malays - e.g. Koranic schools - largely untouched, but they even included a 'conscience clause' in the mission schools of the Federated Malay States. The code of Regulations for Government and Grant Aided Schools (FMS 1902) stipulated that 'no child shall be compelled to be present when such religious instruction (i.e. Christian) is given, nor may any child be refused admission to a grant-in-aided school on grounds of religious belief'.

Although ostensibly Christian, the chief aim of the mission schools was 'to provide a general education and a better standard of moral life based on the tenets of Christianity'. (Wong Hoy Kee 1971 p.15) rather than proselytisation and on this basis they can only be judged as highly successful. Their early work lay in promoting English and vernacular education, but gradually, as the Chinese opened their own schools and the government took over responsibility for Malay vernacular education and insisted on the plantation companies providing some elementary education for the children of estate workers, missions came to provide predominantly English medium education. Moreover because, with the exception of a few Chinese middle schools in Penang and Singapore, vernacular education tended to be provided at primary level only, mission schools were the only ones to cover the whole range from primary to post secondary. Their most constructive role, however, was to bring together in the school all the races that went to make up Malaysian society, Malays, Chinese, Indians and Europeans, so that they could learn together and could share with and understand one another. As the Education Report of 1954 (HMSO 1954) was to comment 'The English schools everywhere co-operate to create the feeling of cohesion between the different races of the country which is the best hope for

75

the emergence of one nation'.

During the early nineteenth century mission schools flourished in Singapore, to a lesser extent in Penang but hardly at all in Malacca, the third element of the Straits Settlements, because it remained economically backward and the demand for education was limited. With British intervention in the Malay States from 1870 onwards and the subsequent rapid economic and population growth, demand for mission education, especially from amongst the Chinese, rapidly increased. In the Unfederated Malay States mission schools were neither encouraged nor given grants-in-aid and although the American Methodist Mission struggled to keep two schools going in the backward state of Kedah, it eventually had to surrender them to the government.

Because mission schools tended to open where there was the greatest demand, though not necessarily need, unless both are equated, it meant that the majority, though by no means all, were situated in the urban areas of the West Coast of peninsular Malaya and Singapore. Consequently those who benefitted from the education offered were the immigrant communities, especially the Chinese. From the middle of the nineteenth century the Chinese formed the majority of pupils since they, far more than their Malay counterparts, appreciated the value of English education as a passport to a career. Not until the late 1920s/1930s did Malays and Tamils begin to show any real interest in missionary education and the benefits that could be derived from continuing formal schooling beyond primary level. By then it had become widely recognised that mission schools provided socio-economic advantage, as well as educational advantage on those who attended them.

The earliest Roman Catholic activity was in the northern Malay States. It was undertaken by the French mission based in Siam and persisted during the eighteenth century before the British, in the form of Francis Light, arrived in Penang in 1786. Thereafter there was expansion of educational activity. A separate school for Catholics was created in 1826 and in 1852 it was taken over by the Christian Brothers and renamed the St. Xavier Institution. In time it became the oldest Roman Catholic and senior mission school in Malaya, with its nearest rival, St. Joseph's, in Singapore.

It was the arrival of the De La Salle - or Christian - Brothers and the Sisters of the Holy Infant Jesus, invited by Father Beurel of the French Mission, that provided the impetus for Christian educational work in the Malay archipelago. (Wong Hoy Kee 1966). It can hardly be said that the Christian Brothers were the spearhead of the British colonial effort, however, since many of them were not even English speaking. There were Dutch, Belgian, and Irish brothers, though gradually all used the English language. Wherever they took over existing schools (as for example with the boys school (1875) and the girls school (1902) in Malacca or St. Paul's Institute,

Seramban (1899)) standards rapidly improved and wherever they opened new schools, as for example in Taiping and Kuala Lumpur, they pioneered a curriculum that was both academic and practical in its bias. Thus while French, English, Malay, Chinese, mathematics and literature were taught as basic, commercial subjects such as book-keeping, accounting, typing, shorthand, needlework and carpentry were also included. In this way pupils were guaranteed employment. The Christian Brothers also pioneered boarding education, which conveniently brought together different races. By the mid 1970s there were eighty-two Infant Jesus Convent Schools and fifty-one De La Salle schools. (Casey 1976).

Protestant activity has also been extensive. Protestantism was first brought to Malaya via the Anglican chaplains appointed by the East India Company to Penang (1805) and Singapore (1826). They were supposed to look after the servants of the company and were forbidden from proselytisation but several chaplains found ways around these regulations and men like Rev. E.S. Hutchings founded Penang Free School (1816) and advised Sir Stamford Raffles on his plans for opening the Singapore Institute; and Rev. Courtenay founded Malacca High School. Other schools also opened with Anglican connections. During the early part of the nineteenth century, however, it was missionaries from the London Missionary Society (now the Congregational Council for World Missions) who pioneered vernacular education amongst the Malays and Chinese and who opened several girls schools, most notably St. Margaret's Chinese girls school in Singapore (1842), before the Chinese edict banning missionary activity was lifted in 1843 and the LMS missionaries departed for mainland China. Although Cooke (1966) questions the interest of the LMS in Malaya their pioneering work was to have lasting results.

Of the other Protestant missionary groups that arrived in the country during the nineteenth century it was undoubtedly the American Methodist Mission that had the greatest influence on educational developments. The AMM's main concern was for educational provision regardless of racial groups and it was fortunate that it began its work at the beginning of the Malayan economic expansion in the 1880s when the demand for English medium education was increasing rapidly, since it was able to go some way towards meeting this demand. Thus it opened a number of Anglo-Chinese schools as well as a number of girls' schools. By 1900 thirteen of their twenty-three schools were for girls. The problem confronting the AMM, however, was whether its staff should be proselytising or simply providing English education, especially since the education codes of the FMS and Straits Settlements made little provision for Religious Education in schools. In the eyes of many, proselytisation and conversion were after all the main raisons d'etre for providing mission schools. This uncertainty was clearly expressed at the 1894 annual conference of the mission:

> With the increasing attendance at our schools and the
> spirit of competition engendered by government inspec-
> tion and the grant-in-aid system, we must steadfastly
> withstand the secularising influence of the conditions
> under which we labour, and bear in mind with studious
> and jealous vigilance our solemn duty to impart as far
> as possible, along with secular instruction, a know-
> ledge of the saving truth. (AMM 1894).

A compromise solution was reached whereby it was recognised
that education was as important as evangelism, but fears that
educational work had grown disproportionately during the next
few decades led to a special committee from the USA being sent
out in 1930 to review the situation. Although critical of
government financial policy, which it was argued stifled
initiative because of its insistence on minimum standards and
examination results in order to receive grants-in-aid, the
committee could find nothing but praise for 'a Christian
educational project of the first magnitude'. One result of
this endorsement of policy was that during the economic
Depression Malaya was one of the few mission fields that
continued to expand simply because of its large educational
programme.

By the time of independence in 1957 there were one
hundred and twenty two aided schools with enrolments of over
130,000. Not only did the missions provide schools in smaller
towns as well as in the large towns but they developed
vocational and some technical education and catered for
certain groups. Tamils and other Indian groups have a special
need to be grateful to the missionary enterprise for, in
spite of government use of Indians in Public Works, Post and
Railways Departments the government provided no schools for
Tamil children in the Settlements before World War II and
only thirteen schools in the FMS. (FMS 1937). As a result
Indian vernacular education was left to missionaries and
Indian philanthropists, but even this was insufficient for
the needs of the majority of Indians. (Arasarathnam 1970).

The development of girls' education in Malaya and
Singapore also owes much to the dedication of missionaries.
The pioneers were the Society for Promoting Female Education
in the East (SPFEE) and the LMS who sent out several woman
missionaries in the early nineteenth century to open girls
schools in Malacca, Penang and Singapore, a number of which
are still in existence. In the latter part of the nineteenth
century the Catholic Sisters of the Holy Infant Jesus, whose
work in this field can only be viewed with admiration, began
to open girls schools and to recruit local staff. Where they
could not persuade girls to attend school the sisters taught
them at home. The Methodist Mission also used similar tactics

and even provided carriages, rickshaws and bullock carts to
take girls to school. (Cheeseman 1948). In the early years
the government was far less persevering. If girls did not
wish to avail themselves of education, the government was
unwilling to provide schools. Although the position was
modified as demand increased - it was almost impossible to
meet demand by the mid 1930s - by 1940 80% of all girls'
education was conducted in mission schools and over 50% of
those learning through English medium were also in mission
schools. It was not until 1935 that a teacher training
college was opened for women - in Malacca. Hitherto the only
trained teachers had been missionaries and those trained on
the job by missionaries. As a result many thousands of
Malaysians and Singaporeans had educational opportunities that
would otherwise have not been made available by the colonial
government and they have every reason to be grateful to the
many dedicated staff who served in the mission schools. Some
indication of the impact of these schools can be seen from
the fact that before World War I 74% of boys and nearly all
girls in English medium schools were being educated in mission
schools.

Elsewhere in Asia missionaries also pioneered educational
provision as part of their evangelistic work. The result of
the famous 1854 Education Despatch of the East India Company
which argued in favour of education as 'a blessing to the
native peoples' and as 'a sacred duty on the part of the
British Government' to see to its provision, which encouraged
mission societies and voluntary agencies to establish schools
and which promised aid to those in need of financial assistance,
and which was to become the cornerstone of British Indian and
British colonial policy was to open the floodgates for missions
to open schools at all levels throughout India, Ceylon, Burma
as well as Malaya and Singapore. In China missionary education
'was one of the outstanding features of the period between
1875 and 1914' (Neill 1964 p.337) and by the time of the
First World War Christian schools, colleges and universities
were an essential part of the educational scene in China,
having graduated over 80,000 believing Christians as well as
thousands who had accepted mission education but not the
Christian faith. It is little wonder that many Chinese
respected and feared mission institutions as the spearhead
of Western penetration into China. In Japan three mission
schools founded shortly after the Meiji revolution - Kumomoto
School, Sapporo School at Hokkaido and Doshisha School at
Kyoto - were also to have a profound impact on future developments in Japan since many of the pupils from these schools
were to play a leading role in the modernisation of Japan.

RECOGNITION OF THE ACHIEVEMENT OF MISSION SCHOOLS

The achievements and contribution of mission schools to

educational development of specific South East Asian countries
were recognised by a wide variety of people over a long period
of time. Towards the end of the last century an ex-regent of
Siam said that 'Siam has not been disciplined by English and
French guns like China, but the country has been opened by
missionaries to whom Siam owes the introduction of printing,
European literature, vaccination, modern medicine and surgery,
modern education and many useful mechanical appliances'.
(Backus 1884). Anna Leonowens, governess to Prince Chulalongkorn and other children of King Mongkut, was even more
eulogistic when she wrote 'in their united influence Siam
unquestionably owes much, if not all, of her present advancement and prosperity'. (Leonowens 1870). In 1928 the last of
the absolute monarchs of Siam, Prejadhipok(4), praised the
work of the Protestant Missions in Siam for their benevolence
and stimulus to the nation, while in the late 1930s the
pioneering work of foreign mission schools in 'modern education,
both primary and secondary, and more especially of education
for girls', (Chaplin 1937) was clearly recognised. Even
during the 1960s it was suggested that 'Christian private
schools continue to make a contribution to Thai education out
of all proportion to the numerical strength of that faith
among the country's population'. (Cobb 1966).

Similar recognition comes from Singapore and Malaya. The
1924 Annual Report on Education for the Straits Settlements
stressed that '...the missionary aided schools provide a useful element of competition and rivalry in our educational
system and furnishes valuable religious and ethical teaching
to various sections of the community'. (SS 1924). While the
Annual Report for 1926 went so far as to say that 'while
missionary bodies have done so much for boys' schools they
have done almost everything for female education. A few years
ago there was no demand for the education of girls: that the
attitude of parents has changed is due among other causes to
the work of the convents and other missionary societies'.
(SS 1926).

The Report of the Central Advisory Committee on Education
in Malaya of 1950 'recognised gratefully' the efforts of
missionaries in furthering education in Malaya while the Razak
Report stipulates that 'we desire to record a thankful tribute
to the work which they have done'. (Federation of Malaya
1956). A more recent recognition comes from a headteacher of
one of the mission schools:

> The Church school in many countries is dependent on
> the wealthy and the middle class for maintenance
> and support, so it caters in large part for them.
> In Malaysia it is quite different. From the very
> beginning there was no distinction either of race,
> religion or social class. Malays, Indians,
> Eurasians, Chinese were accepted. It did not

matter whether they were Muslims, Hindus,
Christians, Buddhists or Taoists, all were
welcome, and people of all these races and
religions were equally generous in helping to
build schools ... Today, as in the past,
children of Royalty sit side by side with
children of labourers. (Casey 1976).

CRITICISMS

Not all has been praise however. Far from it; and it is
worth recording some of the main criticisms levelled at
mission schools and European education overseas generally.
J.S. Furnivall (1943) castigated mission schools because they
replaced the existing schools, 'instruments of civilisation'
with 'instruments of economics'. They trained children how
to earn a living rather than how to live. Although the
mission schools of India, Burma and Malaya produced the best
type of public servants and were successful in providing
government employees of a high standard, as instruments
designed to improve the social environment through the
Christian ethic they were not particularly successful.
'Western statesmen had looked to transform oriental society
by education. They brought into existence a new society not
however by education but by economic forces; and this new
society transformed the character of education'. (Furnivall
1943 p.47). Because mission schools tended to be located in
towns rather than rural areas only a relative few benefitted
from them. If, as in the case of Malaya, these few were
largely of immigrant stock, Chinese and Indians, then the
benefits were even more unfairly allocated.
Other criticisms have been that the curriculum offered
was too academic and too Western in approach and hence helped
to undermine the traditional values of society, as for example
the view that 'missionary education, like the Western
education on which it was originally based, has been concerned
with teaching pupils ... what could be learned from books
about a number of different things. It has too often failed
to develop in the pupil a consistent philosophy of life'.
(Brown 1933 p.242). Because of this youngsters were divorced
from their home community, developed a dislike for manual
work and in spite of the high moral standards taught in school,
many youngsters turned to petty crimes when away from their
home community and environment. How easy it is to prove this
latter accusation is difficult to say. Certainly a common
criticism voiced about mission schools is that their products
were often scholarly but restless and out of touch with their
own people.
The main criticisms however must be that many saw
evangelism as a top priority; that education and evangelism
were perceived from a European or American standpoint and as

such were not rapidly or even adequately adapted to the local South East Asian environment; that they failed to keep abreast of educational thinking in Europe and America particularly; that denominational rivalry led to confusion in the minds of the recipients; and that they were slow to prepare indigenous peoples to assume leadership and roles of responsibility.

While it is easy to criticise what was obviously an imperfect system, the measure of success of the mission schools lies in how easily they adapted to and were absorbed into the growing state systems of education and in whether they made any longstanding contribution to educational developments in the countries where they operated.

DEVELOPMENTS AND ADAPTATION IN THE TWENTIETH CENTURY

Because the Thais were never colonised in the conventional understanding of the term and because the church had gradually become 'Thai-ified', there has generally been a spirit of tolerance and goodwill shown towards missions in the country. There have been periodic lapses, but private mission schools are still seen as having an important role to play in the nation's education, if for no other reason than that they have high academic standards and moral teaching and because they ease the burden on the education budget. This does not mean, however, that mission schools have been free to do as they pleased.

Moves to regulate mission schools began as early as 1892 when they had to register with the new Ministry of Public Instruction, but it is since 1919, when the first of a series of Private Education Acts designed to control all private schools, that they have been brought into closer contact with the state system. In 1936 they had to re-licence, Thai was to be used as the language of instruction and principals and teachers had to qualify in Thai language examinations. Since 1954 private schools have had to be prepared to accept children of all religious faiths and have had to conform to Ministry regulations and curricula though mission schools have been allowed to supplement the Ministry of Education prescribed curriculum on morality with Christian religious instruction. Most Buddhists and Taoists amongst pupils attend lessons on Christianity and acts of Christian worship without any conflict of conscience and it is not uncommon to find Buddhists who would also profess to be Christian.

Missions were able to comply to regulations without too much anguish because since the 1910 Edinburgh Conference on Missions there has been a gradual recognition that churches should come under national leadership, though it was not until 1934 that an independent Thai church, made up of an amalgamation of a large number of Protestant missionary churches, was created; and not until 1957 that the Church of Christ in Thailand finally took over the running of mission

schools, of which there are over forty. Although the Roman
Catholic church has remained as a separate organisation it co-
operates very closely with the Church of Christ in educational
matters(5). Some of the country's most famous schools -
Assumption College, Bangkok Christian College, Wattana Wittaya
Girls School (all in Bangkok) and Prince Royal's College,
Chiengmai - are mission schools whose standards have influenced
the State sector.

In Malaya mission schools did not have to accommodate to
developments in the State sector quite so early since independence was not granted until 1957, but since then they have
become fully integrated into the state educational system in
a way that is unusual in Asia, possibly in the world. It was
possible after independence that there would have been conflict
between mission schools and the newly indpendent Malayan
government becasue of the latter's desire to use education as
a means of fostering nationalism through a common type of
school, common syllabus, common examinations and above all
through the national language, Bahasa Malaysia, and because
of the recognition of Islam as the State religion. The 1957
Education Ordinance, moreover, could have exacerbated conflict
because it created a unified and transferable teaching
profession thereby limiting control of mission schools over
the appointment and dismissal of staff. The gradual replacement of English by Bahasa Malaysia as the medium of instruction
in all schools, the gradual replacement of expatriate staff
by indigenous staff, and the ten year limit imposed on the
time a foreign missionary can serve in the country have all
had an effect on the role of 'mission' schools. Schools in
Singapore have been under far less pressure because governmental policy in this secular, multi-racial, multi-faith
society, has been to recognise equal rights for all citizens
regardless of race or religion. As such mission schools have
been encouraged to become part of the state education system
but their Christian message has not been diminished and many
former 'mission schools' have continued to hold pride of place
in the educational hierarchy.

One reason why, in both cases, mission schools have
adapted to changed situations is that from the beginning they
showed no discrimination on grounds of class, race or religion.
Thus when the Malayan Parliamentary Paper of 1954 observed
that 'We affirm unanimously our belief that multi-racial
schools are essential for the education of the future citizens
of a united Malayan nation' mission schools could justly point
to the fact that they were already multi-racial, though the
number of Malays in schools was small compared to the Chinese
largely because, as has been shown, missionaries were not
allowed to operate in the Islamic regions of the country.
However as the policy of Malayanisation intensified it meant
that many of the teaching posts held by Europeans, especially
those of headships, had to be filled by Malays, the majority

of whom were (and are) not Christians. The then Minister of Education, Encit Abdul Rahman Talib, made this abundantly clear to the Guild of Assisted Catholic Schools in 1964 when he said:

> As you know it is the policy of the government to encourage the country's own sons to lead the people not only in the field of economics and administration but in education as well. All schools in the country, especially those which are fully aided, are required to implement this policy. I hope that those schools which have not Malayanised their posts of principals will do so as soon as possible regardless of race and religion. (Straits Times 1964).

After independence in 1957 mission schools were given the option of going fully private or of becoming assisted government schools. The unanimous decision was for the latter, regardless of cost, in the belief that standards and racial harmony were less likely to be adversely affected. By an act of parliament of 1961 mission schools were classified as fully assisted schools under the control of the Ministry of Education and as such became part of the federal education system. Although they were guaranteed 'maximum consultation' regarding the appointment of principals, they lost their independence over the appointment of staff and the admission of students or of restricting numbers. They have thus been forced to take on more puils than they might have wished with the resultant large classes: they have had no say over the official syllabus nor over the excessive concentration on examinations. Because many of the European staff took out Malayan citizenship and because missionaries did not take full government salaries they have earned the respect of the authorities. They are allowed to teach Christianity outside the offical school hours provided similar provision is made available for the teaching of Islam by qualified staff. Mission schools still continue to pioneer the way in curriculum development in subjects such as mathematics, home economics and commercial subjects, in 'setting' for specific subjects; and in forging close links between schools and parents in the community. (Casey). Thus while they have lost their distinctive 'missionary' touch they nevertheless have a key role to play.

THE MISSIONARY CONTRIBUTION

What then can be said of the contribution of mission schools to educational development in selected South East Asian countries?

In the early years especially in their work in Thailand missionaries were often arrogant and intolerant. They were

more concerned with conversion than with getting alongside the
Thai people and understanding them socially and psychologically
and they owed their right to stay in the country as much to
the farsightedness of the Chakri kings as to their own abilities
and sense of purpose. The early education offered was too
intensive and far less related to daily life than that
offered in the monastic schools. As a result it led to
failures. (Thompson 1941). That the picture gradually changed
was mutually beneficial and mission schools stimulated
successive Thai governments to provide state education,
education for girls, technical and agricultural education.
They also set standards for state schools to emulate. As a
result they helped in the process of modernisation and by
encouraging indigenous involvement in state education they
helped prevent this modernisation from becoming Westernisation.
Unfortunately other forces, most notably US economic investment and the presence of large numbers of US 'advisers'
during the Vietnam war undermined this gradual process of
modernisation and led to some distorted aping of the West(6).
  Perhaps the most lasting influence has been a subtle
one since some Christian ideals have infiltrated aspects of
Thai society. There has been a greater concern for individual
rights and freedoms, a concern for social welfare and medical
help, an element of competition and individualism, a belief
that promotion should come from merit and educational achievement and not simply from patronage as happened in the past
and 'if Mrs. Leonowens or any other nineteenth century critic
of Siamese society were to return today they would find it
hard to recognise that present attitudes towards social welfare,
economic development and medical care came from the same race
of people whose indifference they so roundly condemned'.
(Watson 1980a).
  The same comments could to some extent be applied to
Malaya and Singapore except that there, apart from challenging
ancient religious beliefs, missionary education also helped
bring together under one roof, through the medium of a
common language (English) diverse groups of people, racial
and religious. It was not the fault of the missions that
Malays were largely excluded from the economic and social
advancement brought about as a result of English medium
education. It was colonial government policy that missionaries
should be excluded from the rural areas and the Malay
Kampongs, that Malay vernacular education should be government
controlled and for the primary level only with the result
that 'Malay education in the Kampong was so restricted in
content that the rural Malay was isolated and even divided
from the minority who were English educated ...' (Ryan 1967
p.168). Had mission schools been allowed to open in these
regions as well the situation of having to weld together
different races into a sense of nationhood after World War II
might not have been so problematic.

Above all, however, the mission schools helped to produce an educated elite capable of formulating ideas based on Western humanism and liberalism, of which the most potent has undoubtedly been that of nationalism, which in Asia is largely a twentieth century phenomenon. 'It developed as a struggle to establish equality for Asian peoples and nations with the rest of the world and was, with different levels of intensity, a form of protest against colonial domination and Western attitudes of indifference and arrogance of which many missionaries were accused of being guilty'. (Pannikar 1969). As another Asian writer has pointed out, 'The idea of nationhood in every Asian country is therefore a product of imperial law and order, Western education which developed an elite committed to liberal values and the English, French or Dutch languages which made possible communications among leaders from different regions, religions, racial and ethnic groups ...' (Thomas 1966).

Nationalism and the belief in nationhood in the multiracial societies of South East Asia especially are seen as vital forces in the process of social and economic development. If the contribution of mission schools was none other than the spread of nationalism it would be a contribution worth being proud of. The fact that they continue to operate and pioneer new developments in the curriculum, classroom organisation, non-formal education and rural development programmes is indicative of the value with which they are still regarded.

REFERENCES

1. Although reference is made to other parts of South East Asia this paper concentrates on development in Malaya, Singapore and Thailand.

2. Even though Wyatt's book on developments in Thailand (Wyatt, D.K. (1969): The Politics of Reform in Thailand: Education in the Reign of King Chulalongkorn. New Haven: Yale University Press) argues in favour of royal intervention, it is nevertheless hard to avoid the influence played by missionaries in sowing the seeds for educational expansion.

3. Not until this century did the population of Thailand reach what it had been before the wars with Burma in the early eighteenth century.

4. Siam became a constitutional monarchy in 1932.

5. When Chiengmai University was opened there was close co-operation between the Jesuits and the Protestants over establishing a joint student project in the north.

6. One notable exception has been the establishment of Ramkamhaeng University, an 'open university' with over 500,000 students enrolled, a novel and very Thai solution to social demand for higher education. See Danskin, E. (1981): The Open University as the Route to Higher Education Expansion

86

The Contribution of Mission Schools to Educational Development

in Developing Countries: the case of Ramkamhaeng University
in Thailand, unpublished Ph.D thesis at the University of
London; and Watson, J.K.P. (1981): The higher education
dilemma in developing countries: Thailand's two decades of
reform. Higher Education. 10, 3, 297-314.

Chapter Five

EDUCATION AND COLONIALISM IN PENINSULAR MALAYSIA

Keith Watson

INTRODUCTION

Historians and educationists have argued for a long time
about facets of colonial involvement which have shaped education systems in the Third World. From the hindsight of the
1980s, it is easy to denounce colonial education policies as
leading to underdevelopment of human and economic resources
or at the least, to misshapen development (e.g. Carnoy 1974).
What is often overlooked, however, is that many colonial
administrators with or without a specific brief for education,
acted from the highest motives, according to the conventional
wisdom of that time such as introducing an academic, neo-
classical curriculum, or paying grants-in-aid. Many others
developed an ad hoc policy on the spot. Such a situation was
undoubtedly the case in Malaya in both the Straits Settlements
and the Federated Malay States. As for the argument put forward by Eisenstadt (1978) that colonial involvement in Asia
was little more than a passing phenomenon which in a long
historical time scale has had remarkably little impact on the
course of events and on the relationships between different
peoples of the region, this is patently untrue in the context
of Malaysia, as it is hoped that this chapter will show.
For the purposes of our discussion, colonial influence
on education is divided into traditional classical colonialism, internal colonialism and neo-colonialism, as discussed,
amongst others, by Altbach and Kelly (178). Classical colonial
ism is interpreted as the domination of one group or country
by another, in this case British control of Malaya. Internal
colonialism is interpreted as the dominance of one ethnic/
political/religious group over others within the nation
state, in this case Malay political dominance over the Indians
and Chinese within Malaysia. Neo-colonialism is interpreted
as the continuing influence or control, often invidiously or
indirectly of the former colonial power over educational
developments within its former colony.

Education and Colonialism in Peninsular Malaysia

    Not only are all three types of colonialism applicable
to Peninsular Malaysia, but Malaysia also provides an excellent
example of the way traditional education policies led to the
development of a political urban, ethnic elite, which in turn
has sought to use the education system to perpetuate its own
position after independence. (Watson 1979, 1980b; Salvaratnam
1974). While it is hard not to accept some of Carnoy's
analysis of education and colonialism - that colonial schools
were designed to maintain the status quo and rewarded those
who were already privileged; that they created a class of
highly educated non-Europeans who accepted European standards;
that they attempted 'to make children fit a certain mould,
and to shape them to perform pre-determined rules and tasks
based on their social class'; and that they aimed 'to build
a cultural dependency amongst the educated and ruling classes
so that revolutionary overthrow would never be a likely
alternative' (Carnoy 1974) - it is questionable whether this
was deliberate policy or was an incidental result of policy.
However this chapter is not intended to be polemical. It is
intended, as far as possible within the constraints of space,
to provide as balanced and objective a view as possible, of
educational policies in Peninsular Malaysia both before and
after independence.

THE MALAYSIAN BACKGROUND

    Although Malaysia as a political unit is of relatively
recent nomenclature the term has frequently been used by
historians to refer to the Malay archipelago since the early
nineteenth century. Modern Malaysia is a parliamentary democracy based on a federal system of eleven equal states each with
its own hereditary sultan. It has an elective constitutional
monarchy and the king is chosen for a five year term of office
from and by the sultans. It was created in 1963 as a means
of balancing the power and influence of the Chinese in Singapore with the Malay speaking world around and now consists
of the former Federation of Malaya (Peninsular Malaysia),
Sarawak and North Borneo (now Sabah). Singapore was a member
briefly until its 'expulsion' in 1965. Covering an area of
52,000 square miles (approximately the size of England) and
stretching south from Thailand, Peninsular Malaysia is
largely made up of tropical rain-forests and alluvial plains
with settlements predominantly along the river banks and
coastal regions. The population of 10.5 million consists of
Malays (53.1%), Chinese (35.5%), Tamil Indians (10.6%) and
hill tribes and Europeans (0.8%). The majority of Malays
live in the relatively economically backward part of the
north east and east coast regions, while the bulk of the
Chinese and Indians live in the more economically advanced
west coast regions, the Johore plain and the south.
    Malaysia is one of the richest nations of South East

Asia (GNP per capita = $1370 US) with an annual growth rate
between 1960-79 of 4% (World Bank 1981) though this distorts
the considerable regional and ethnic variations in unemployment and income. (Wong 1979). The economy is mainly based
on rubber, tin, date palm oil and timber. The economic
infrastructure and the population complexity are directly
attributable to British intervention.
        Little is known of Malaya's early history. There is
evidence of ancient settlements and contacts with South China
and like other South East Asian nations with long influence
from China and India, (Hall 1955; Fisher 1964) evidence shows
that there was some Indian influence on the patterns of court
households, even though these were often little more than
superficial. For centuries Malaya was divided into a number
of sultanates with society divided into a hereditary sultanate,
a feudal aristocracy and a peasantry made up of the ra'ayat,
the subject class of farmers and fishermen. Islam was brought
by Arab traders during the thirteenth and fourteenth centuries.
In spite of the fall of Malacca to the Portuguese in 1511,
Portuguese involvement in the sixteenth century, and Dutch
involvement in the seventeenth, the European impact on the
Malay people and their way of life was slight. What was
ultimately to change the course of the country's development
was the arrival of the British in Penang and Malacca at the
end of the eighteenth century and their gradual involvement
in Malay affairs, during the nineteenth. What resulted was
greater political stability, an end to the internicine
fighting between rival Chinese gangs, the exploitation of the
country's wealth and an increase in population. Malaya's
role in world trade became increasingly important as it became
a leading producer of tin, rubber and date palm oil. It was
the importation of non-Malays to help the country's economic
development that led to dramatic social changes and to the
creation of a multi-racial society with the Malays actually
forming a minority during the 1930s.

A. CLASSICAL COLONIALISM

BRITISH INTERVENTION

        It has often been argued that Britain acquired her
empire by accident rather than by design. (Cross 1970). This
was certainly not true of British involvement in Malay affairs.
The purchase of Penang in 1786 by Francis Light on behalf of
the East India Company was a deliberate attempt to find an
alternative dockyard to Madras. It was also an attempt to
curb Dutch influence in the region. The acquisition of
Singapore by Sir Stamford Raffles in 1819 was likewise a
deliberate attempt to establish an outpost in what had
previously been a predominantly Dutch trading area. Only
Malacca, initially ceded to Britain in the Napoleonic Wars,
and returned to the Dutch after the war 'voluntarily' became

British in 1824 as a result of the Treaty of London(1). These three settlements, Penang (including a strip of mainland known as Province Wellesley which was purchased in 1800), Singapore and Malacca became known as the Straits Settlements (1826) because of their strategic position overlooking the Straits of Malacca. Until 1858 they were loosely administered by the East India Company, initially from Penang, later from Calcutta and eventually from Singapore(2). After the loss of the China trade in 1833 the Company lost interest in the Settlements which suffered from benign neglect as a result.

There the situation might have remained but for the growing violence amongst different Chinese groups working in the tin industry in a number of Malay sultanates, (Purcell 1966) which led to British commercial interests demanding protection for their legitimate trading rights and threatening to seek German protection if British help was not forthcoming. In 1874 the Pangkor Engagement was signed(3). This was the first of a number of agreements signed with Malay sultans allowing British Residents 'to advise' local Malay chiefs on all matters except religion and custom and to 'protect' the States from disorder and political anarchy.

Gradually and inevitably the involvement of Residents led to greater administrative control and the creation of the Federated Malay States. (FMS). On 1 July 1896 the FMS of Perak, Salangor, Negri Sembilan and Pahang were formed under British protection. Schools, hospitals, postal services, roads, railways and an administrative framework were all gradually developed. Unfortunately little responsibility was assigned to Malay rulers who resented the fact that the earlier promises of indirect rule had in reality become more like direct rule. Although a Federal Council involving the Sultans was created in 1909 in practice this did little to alter Malay grievances and weakened the importance of the Sultans. One of the first effects of British intervention, therefore, was the gradual transformation of administration and government, though as we shall see the class system of rulers and ruled remained not only untouched but was reinforced by British educational policies.

In 1909 British control extended northwards to the states of Kedah, Perlis, Kelantan and Trengganu. In that year, in return for a loan for railway and bridge building, the Thai monarchy yielded its claims of suzereinty. However while a British Resident was accepted as an adviser in each of the States, all four firmly refused to join the FMS and became known as the Unfederated Malay States (UMS). In 1914 Johore made a similar agreement. The result was that these States retained a degree of independence, remained largely untouched by many of the developments taking place elsewhere and, with the exception of Johore, remained both economically and educationally backward(4).

Although the division between the SS, FMS and UMS prevailed

until the end of World War II, there were conflicting views
amongst officials over the need to develop a federal system
and over the need to integrate the different ethnic groups
whose presence was becoming increasingly obvious and whose
latent nationalism was growing. It was not until after the
war that views were reconciled in the Federation of Malaya
Agreement of 1948(5), though ironically the Agreement coincided
with the beginning of the communist Emergency (1948-60) and
the period of increasing Chinese - Malay bitterness. The
Malays accused the Chinese of supporting the Communists, just
as the Chinese accused the Malays of collaborating with the
Japanese during the period of occupation. It says much for
the leaders of all parties that the British were able to hand
over power to the new Federation of Malaya in 1957, even though
underlying racial tensions remained.

The second major effect of British involvement was undoubtedly the changed population structure. In 1850 the
population was 0.5 million. By 1911 this was 2.3 millions,
by 1947 4.9 millions, and by 1979 10.5 millions, a more than
twenty fold increase since the 1850s. The impetus for such
rapid population growth came about largely as a result of
immigration in the latter part of the nineteenth century of
Chinese and Indians, encouraged by the stability of British
rule and by the prospects for economic advancement. The peak
period for immigration was 1890-1920 when the basic ethnic,
economic and political patterns were laid down. (McGee 1964:
71). The Chinese, forced to leave southern China because of
economic depression were attracted by the economic possibilities
of Malaya, though they brought with them their clannishness,
languages and regional groupings. (Purcell 1966). They were
certainly not discouraged by the British because of their
contribution to the economic development of the country
through the tin industry and import/export houses. The
Indians were brought from Madras and southern India to work
as indentured labour on British-owned rubber plantations many
of which were rather isolated. No attempt was made to curb
the flow of immigrants until 1929-30 by which time the Chinese
made up 41.5% of the population, the Malays 34.7% and the
Indians 22.2%. Although the balance was partly redressed in
the 1930s, Chinese still outnumbered Malays by 43%:41% at
the outbreak of war.

The problems posed by the growth of a multi-racial society
were not simply ethnic, however. They were closely linked
with urbanisation, employment patterns and above all education.
Because numerous treaties and agreements reached between the
British authorities and the Malay rulers granted special status
to the Malays, the rural Malays were left largely undisturbed
by the population and economic changes taking place. Part of
those agreements preserved Malay custom (adat) and religion
(Islam) from outside interferences and Christian missionaries,
who were largely responsible for establishing modern secondary

education, were debarred from proselytising and from establishing schools amongst the rural Malays. The result was that the
English medium schools that opened were mainly in urban areas,
largely attended by non-Malays. A recent survey of urban
settlements shows that by 1921, two-thirds of urban settlements were dominated by Chinese and even in 1970, 68.36% of
urban centres were still dominated by Chinese. (Sidhu 1976).
Thus it was the Chinese and to a lesser extent Indians and a
few urban Malays who benefitted from these schools.

A further result of these patterns of urbanisation and
policies regarding immigration and employment was that the
economic structures of the country were also largely divided
along ethnic lines. Thus, while urban Malays and Malays of
aristocractic lineage were encouraged to join government
service after 1910, with the result that 62% of government
employees are Malays, the majority were left as subsistence
farmers and fishermen. It is estimated that 80% of all small-
holders are Malays and 60% of Malays are associated with
agriculture. On the other hand the Chinese control the major
businesses, import/export houses, banking, insurance, transport, rice milling and above all the tin industry. In spite
of government economic policies of the 1970s enshrined in the
New Economic Policy of the Second and Third Malaysia Plans
(1972-76 and 1976-80) in 1978 61% of all manufacturing industry
was still in the hands of Chinese Malays and 75% of all
executive and managerial posts were held by Chinese. Twice
as many Chinese are in commerce and industry as Malays and
Indians combined. 51% of Indians are in the plantation industry.
The Indians and Chinese dominate the professions as lawyers,
doctors, accountants, scientists. Many others are in railways,
menial government employment or are humble clerks. However,
divisive such a situation may be the seeds of economic and
cultural separatism between the different ethnic groups arose
largely as a result of colonial educational policies.

BRITISH EDUCATIONAL POLICIES

Prior to the arrival of the British there were two
existing school 'systems'. There were Koranic schools for
Malay boys, where the rudiments of Arabic were taught so that
boys could learn and recite large chunks of the Koran and
where religious observances were instilled, (Wilkinson 1957),
and Chinese writing schools, where Chinese boys were taught
the classics and the rudiments of reading, writing and
recitation. (Purcell 1936). Neither 'system' was widespread
and neither was anything like universal.

Until 1867 when the Colonial Office assumed responsibility
for administering the Straits Settlements, there was no
official education policy with the result that the early part
of the nineteenth century is often regarded as a period of
'laissez-faire' in educational matters. However administrators
in the S.S. such as Governors Blundell and Cavenagh (Chelliah

1940) were influenced by developments in India and in due course
administrators in the FMS were influenced by both - what was
happening in India and in the Straits Settlements.

The two main strands of thought debated in both India and
Malaya were what have been described as 'conservationist' and
'diffusionist'. (Loh Fook Seng 1975). The former view was held
by orientalists who sought to preserve what was good in tradition
society by developing vernacular education, especially at primary
level. The second view, held by liberals from the 1830s onwards
was that the superiority of English medium education should be
acknowledged as the best vehicle for modernisation and for diff-
using Western knowledge and values to the masses. Macaulay's
famous Minute on Education of 1835, in which he championed the
diffusionist cause, may have won the day in India (Edwards 1968)
- though it has been argued that the diffusionists, in favour of
English education, would have won in spite of Macaulay (Mayhew
1926) - it did not have the same influence on developments in
Malaya. Whereas the diffusionist view led to the development of
elite English medium schools in the SS and a few English schools
especially the Malay College, 'The Star of the East', in the
FMS, the conservationist view prevailed amongst many of the FMS
administrators especially men like Sweettenham who feared the
spread of English education as seditious. (Perak 1890).

Several policy options were available to colonial administrators. They could refrain from any kind of educational intervention. They could support the rulers and offer them one kind
of education or they could develop an education system common
for both rulers and ruled. They could have imposed a British
type of education regardless of the consequences. They could
have provided a common education for Malays and other ethnic
groups which would have cut across ethnic lines or they could
have concentrated on Malay education only. As it turned out
several of these options were developed: vernacular education
for Malays, support for limited English medium education, especially at secondary level and comparative indifference towards
the education of the non-indigenous groups. It must be stressed
however, that the policies that evolved were gradual, largely
from men on the spot and not from the Colonial Office which took
little or no active part in defining educational policy except
to endorse (or criticise) views that were expressed by officials
in their reports. (Carnoy 139; Stevenson 1975: 69-70; Parliamentary Papers; Sadka 1968). It must also be stressed that
British officials in Malaya were influenced by their own conservative, traditional upbringing, by current developments in the
UK and by what they saw happening in India. The result was the
development of a four-language system of education - maintained
Malay vernacular primary schools, assisted or maintained English
medium primary and secondary schools, private Tamil medium primary schools and private Chinese medium primary and secondary
schools, though in time these also came to be supported or
assisted by the government. Although by the

the 1920s/30s when it was apparent that the ethnic composition
of Malaya had been transformed, the government could have
worked towards developing a harmonious multi-racial society
by developing a monolingual (Malay) or bilingual (English and
Malay) education system, it chose not to do so, arguing that
its responsibility was towards the Malays and not towards the
other racial groups. The effect of these decisions on future
ethnic and economic developments was profound.

Until 1867 educational initiative had come mostly from
missionaries and individuals but from the 1870s onwards,
especially following the Woolley Report of 1870 (Woolley 1870)
which recommended the appointment of a Director of Schools,
and the growing British responsibility towards the FMS,
initiatives increasingly came from government officials. The
evolution of educational policies between individuals of
strong character with differing viewpoints makes a fascinating
study. (Stevenson 1975; Allen 1970). Suffice it to say here
that the British colonial authorities developed a dual policy
towards the Malays, one of conciliation and training for
leadership for the Malay ruling classes and one of minimum
or non-interference towards Malay villagers. One observer
has described it as 'a protective and paternalistic attitude
towards the Malays'. (Cooke 1966). There were several
reasons for this. The economic situation developing at the
time, with a thriving tin industry largely in the hands of the
Chinese, provided the British authorities with a lucrative
source of revenue without their being forced to depend on the
Malays. In any case the subsistence economy and widely
scattered communities of the majority of Malays would have
made revenue collection difficult. Many administrators
regarded Malay society as idyllic (e.g. Clifford 1898/9) and
Malays as 'gentlemen' (Weld 1883/4) and they did not wish to
upset the social stability and class system. (Perak 1890;
FMS 1898). They therefore sought to protect the Malays from
the immigrant Chinese and Indians (SS 1883; Parliamentary
Papers 1932) and to prevent a similar situation from arising
that had arisen in India, namely the appearance of the semi-
literate Babu. (Perak 1890; Parliamentary Papers 1892;
Mayhew 1929). Others feared that too much education,
especially English education, would lead to subversion.
(Maxwell 1932).

From the 1890s the British made a 'conscious attempt to
freeze the status quo and prevent any social or economic
change in the Malay village community'. (Stevenson 1975:55).
They did so 'as an act of political and administrative
expediency', though 'it represented for many of the administrators the attainment of a social ideal'. If one looks at
the views expressed by British officials of the time it is
easy to realise why so much of Malay education led to a dead
end. (FMS 1920; SS 1921; Watson 1973). Ironically it was
this policy which was to lead to the development of Malay

nationalism because teachers trained in the Sultan Idris
Training College in Malacca were made aware of the changes
taking place in their country and began to take the message
into the Malay kampongs.

Malay response to vernacular secular education was one
of indifference, suspicion or resentment because of fears of
proselytisation, expense, inconvenience and loss of earnings
of their sons, all good reasons why many rural people are
still uncertain about formal secular education. The authorities
used fines, compulsory attendance legislation and eventually
the co-operation of the rulers to extend Malay vernacular
education, but no amount of propaganda could conceal the fact
that Malay education was conservative, designed to maintain
the social cohesion of rural society and tended to isolate the
majority of the Malay community from the mainstream of social
and economic developments taking place elsewhere in the
country especially as it consisted of only four years of
primary level. There was no Malay vernacular secondary education (except teacher training and vocational training) until
after independence.

The exception to this state of affairs were the Malay
rulers, although for the first fifteen years of British
involvement no serious attempt was made to equip them for
government service. During the 1890s attempts were made to
develop an English medium school for the sons of rajas but it
was not until the 1903 Rulers' Conference had stressed anxiety
at how few Malays there were in the administrative civil
service that plans were developed to open the special
prestigious English-medium Malay College. (Stevenson, Ryan
1964). The Malay College that opened in Kuala Kangsar in
1905 was geared to a political objective - 'to give to future
Sultans, Malay chiefs and the traditional Malay elite an
approximate English public school education which could prepare them for participatory roles within the British administration. (Loh Fook Seng; 23-4).

By the 1920s preferential treatment for Malays in government service was not only recognised but was claimed as a
right by Malay leaders. This policy of support for the Malay
leadership and the suppression of rural Malays was to have
long term implications for the country's development.

The immigrant groups fared even less favourably for
whereas government policy was to encourage Malay vernacular
schools it was to avoid as far as possible involvement in
other vernacular schools. (FMS 1898; SS 1901). The British
approach to Chinese education therefore was one of 'laissez-
faire', leaving the Chinese to develop their own school
system which they did quite effectively, especially after the
reforms in China began to filter through to overseas Chinese
settlers. (Watson 1973a, 1976). There were strong links
between the overseas Chinese and China, both financially and
politically. It was the latter aspect that was to lead to a

change in British policy and attempts to contain the growth of Chinese schooling. Two events led to this policy change. The first was the beginning of the National Language Movement in 1917 and the decision to adopt Mandarin as the medium of instruction in schools in China and overseas with a common curriculum in all. British administrators began to fear subversion, especially after the second event, serious rioting following the Treaty of Versailles (1919) and the cession of former German possessions in Shantung province to the Japanese. (Watson 1973a). The result was the beginning of government intervention in Chinese schools to ensure that 'teaching shall not be of such a kind that it is against the interests of the government of the colony' and the passing of the 1920 Regulation of Schools Ordinance, demanding the registration of all schools, managers and staff. Although the ordinance affected all schools its chief target was Chinese schools. Thereafter began a series of measures designed to curb the political aspect of Chinese schools and to bring them under government supervision. Even so although by 1938 82.4% of Chinese pupils were enrolled in Chinese schools they received only 5.19% of government educational expenditure.

Tamil schools received some government support at a much earlier period. By 1905 the government felt it ought to establish Tamil schools as and when the need arose, though it preferred to leave provision to estate managers or to private individuals. The result was that schools varied enormously in quality, and opened and closed with alarming regularity. Although the 1923 Labour Code passed the onus on to plantation managers for establishing schools for children of plantation workers, many resented this because they believed that it should be a state responsibility. Standards in Tamil schools were low. Those who attended them were dependent on how good a particular teacher might be. The government provided grants from the 1930s onwards but this did little to alleviate a poor system. Tamil schools have been described as a monkery and the Cinderella of the system. (Arasaratnam 1970).

Separate vernacular schools simply helped reinforce ethnic and cultural differences. The only schools that in any way led to the development of ethnic harmony were the English medium ones, but they led to social and economic divisions because they led to the most prestigious positions in government and the economy; and because they were situated predominantly in urban areas they were mainly used by and favoured by the non-indigenous groups, the Malay aristocracy and a few urban Malays.

English medium schools had developed under the auspices of missionaries or private individuals and were open to all regardless of race, creed or colour provided they could pay the fees. Because of government policies English schools were beyond the reach of most rural Malays even if they could pay or wanted to attend. Gradually most schools became

government maintained or assisted. Although there were those
like Sir Frank Swettenham, who feared the indiscriminate
growth of English education, (Perak 1890) it met the needs of
government and commercial organisations for English-speaking
employees with the result that English medium schools had high
economic, social and educational value. Praise for their
role in Malaysia's development has been considerable (SS 1921;
Ministry of Education 1950; Razak 1956) but unless they were
of benefit to all groups in Malaya they were bound to be
divisive.

At the time of the Japanese occupation, therefore,
primary education was available in four language media - Malay,
English, Tamil and Chinese, the first two being government
provided or supported, the latter receiving small govenment
grants. Secondary education was available in two language
media, English (government supported) and Chinese (mainly
private) and some tertiary level education was available in
English. For the majority of Malays and Tamils therefore,
primary education led to a dead end. There was little realisation on the part of the British authorities that having been
largely instrumental in creating Malaya's pluralism they had
a responsibility to draw the different races together. As the
Aziz Commission of 1968 observed there was no national educational policy nor was there any attempt to create a national
outlook through common schooling. (Aziz 1968). Instead
policy was so often a piecemeal response to events and pressures
as they arose, not unlike most educational policy in Britain
itself. If there was a coherent policy it was to preserve
the status quo as far as possible.

Just as World War II changed attitudes in the UK, so did
it in Malaya. In the decade following the end of the war and
preceding independence British administrators finally recognised the need to create a harmonious multi-racial society on
a federal basis, especially since the Emergency showed how
few Chinese settlers had come to identify themselves with
their country of adoption. British post-war policy outlined
in 1946 aimed at the fullest educational development for every
section of the community and stressed the need to create 'a
sense of common citizenship' and above all to raise the
educational standards of Malays. (Council Paper 1946). In
this approach they were to point the way forward for post -
independence governments.

It has been suggested that the British showed the Malays
how to manipulate the civil service to their advantage.
(Allen 1970). They certainly pointed the way to showing how
the education system could be used as a political weapon. In
1951 the Barnes Report proposed the introduction of bilingual
schools, the gradual abolition of all non-Malay schools and
the introduction of a common type of school that would be
inter-racial and that would 'be purposely used to build up a
common Malay nationality'. (Barnes 1951). Although the

scheme was dropped because of mainly Chinese opposition (Fenn
-Wu 1951), based on the argument that their language and
culture was threatened, the seeds of future policy had been
sown, as was shown by the Razak Report (Razak 1956) published
on the eve of independence.

THE BRITISH LEGACY
What then can be said of the British colonial legacy?
British involvement in Malaya's affairs changed the political,
economic and ethnic shape of the country. By developing a
four language education policy, linked as it was with economic
opportunities, and by not pursuing a common policy for all
races ethnic divisions and pluralism were reinforced. The
Indians and Chinese were not encouraged to develop loyalties
to Malaya. Instead their primary loyalties lay elsewhere.
By pursuing a policy of leaving rural Malays as undisturbed
as possible yet providing a modicum of education without
prospects of more, the British authorities were guilty of
short sightedness. Not only did the new money economy largely
pass by the rural Malays but divisions were created in Malay
society, since, while the few Malays of aristocratic or
urban upbringing had a chance of entering administrative posts
in the country, the majority were debarred from so doing
because of their lack of English. By guaranteeing the
political power of the Malay aristocracy in treaty rights
and the Federal constitution, they paved the way for a new
form of colonialism based on ethnic dominance, and by
proposals in the Barnes Report they paved the way for an
ethnic elite to use education for political purposes.

B. INTERNAL COLONIALISM

At the time of independence the Alliance Party(6.), made
up of the leading political parties of the three racial groups
but dominated by Malays, was in power. After its election
victory in 1956 one of its first concerns was educational
reform and the establishment of the Razak Commission, the
result of whose report was to lead to the development of
an education system 'linguistically plural in form, national
in content, Malay in symbolism and developmental in purpose'.
(Rudner 1977). Since independence the Malays have system-
atically sought to strengthen their position using the education system for this purpose. (Watson 1979). They have
done so through reorganisation of the school system, pursuance
of a national language policy and restructuring tertiary level
education.

STRUCTURAL REORGANISATION
The first step towards the nationalisation of the education system was the development of a common syllabus for
use throughout all primary schools, regardless of language

media, in order to ensure a common outlook, a common loyalty and a basis for a common examination system. Since 1963 the Ministry of Education has exerted a strong oversight of the curriculum and the textbooks used, though there is some flexibility in the latter. Restructuring took the form of creating national schools (Malay) and national-type schools (other languages). The latter were eligible for government grants provided that they were subject to inspection and followed a common syllabus. In 1957 Malay secondary schools were introduced. This was generally recognised as an essential development, but the Chinese found it harder to accept when financial assistance was withdrawn from their own secondary schools in 1962. They were given the choice of making their schools English medium or of going private. The authorities of all except five schools opted to join the state system believing that English medium schools would remain thus ensuring the Chinese educational and economic advantage. One further step in restructuring was the decision taken in 1963 to abolish selection at the end of primary level, which favoured those attending English primary schools (the Chinese especially) and to introduce automatic promotion to a comprehensive lower secondary school, thereby helping the rural Malays. It could be argued that it was a discriminatory step in favour of rural Malays, although it was a logical development in a country whose economy was steadily growing.

LANGUAGE POLICY
     Language policy however, has always been and continues to be a crucial weapon in ensuring Malay dominance. As the Razak Report stated, one of the fundamental requirements of an educational policy was to orientate all schools to a Malayan outlook through the teaching of Malay.
     The position of Malay as the National Language is enshrined in Article 153 of the Constitution of 1957, though the use of English was allowed for a further ten years or more if it seemed desirable. Bitterness amongst many Malays over this concession nearly split the Alliance Party in 1959. The more extremist Malays have argued that Malay should be the national language not only because of Malay numerical predominance and because it is the lingua franca of the archipelego, but above all because of the political predominance of the Malays, and because of their special status, guaranteed by the British and enshrined in the constitution, which legitimises their political power. (Silcock 1964; Chai Hon-Chan 1922).
     Acceptance of the position of Malays by other ethnic groups occurred because they believed that English would remain widely used and English education, the passport to university and good jobs, would likewise remain. Unfortunately, to many Malays not belonging to the English educated ruling elite, 'English came to be regarded not only as the language of colonial education but also, after independence, as an

obstacle to the educational, social and economic advance of
the majority of Malays'. (Chai Hon-Chan 1977:27). As such
it had to go. The spearhead of this movement was the
Federation of Malaya Teachers' Association, mostly UMNO
supporters from rural areas. They were later joined by the
Malay National Action Front, a group formed in the mid 1960s.

For the first decade after independence the policy of
introducing Malay was a gradual one. The creation of the
Language and Literature Agency in 1959 did much to develop
the national language, translating thousands of scientific
and technical terms, developing textbooks, standardising
pronunciation, etc. In 1967 the National Language Act re-
affirmed Article 153 of the Constitution. Even this was
insufficient for extremists who felt frustrated at the slowness of Malayanisation and the small numbers of Malays
entering the tertiary level of education. As a concession
the government introduced the teaching of four minor subjects
in Malay in the first three primary grades. 1969 saw the
worst race riots in the nation's history and provided the
ruling Malay elite with the opportunity to exert its authority
over non-Malay groups. Bahasia Malaysia was declared the
national language. In 1970 the Rukunegara or National
Ideology was proclaimed laying down guidelines for the ideal
Malaysian but in effect listing the ideals of the Malay
elite. (Milne 1970; Alatas 1971). The Constitutional
Amendment Act of 1971 forbade any discussion of sensitive
issues such as the national language, the special position
of Malays, the sovereignty of the Malay rulers and the whole
question of citizenship rights which are partially based on
language ability.

In educational terms the 1970s have seen the gradual
replacement of English medium education by Malay medium
education. Beginning with the decision that from 1970 onwards Bahasa Malaysia was to replace English as the medium
of instruction at primary level, a change over that was
completed by 1976, other levels of the education system have
also been changed. By 1978, all National secondary schools
had changed over, and by 1982, all upper secondary schools
and by 1983, all tertiary level education will also have
followed suit. Exceptions are private schools which have to
have official recognition, and Chinese and Tamil medium
primary schools, which are allowed, provided they are requested
by fifteen or more parents. Also, since 1970, all applicants
for teacher training have had to have a pass in Bahasa
Malaysia in the Lower Certificate of Education - (a credit
pass for non-Malays) - and there have been massive retraining
programmes for non-Malay speaking teachers.

Further efforts to re-inforce the Malayanisation of the
education system have resulted in reform of the examination
system so that papers have gradually changed from English
medium to Malay medium. A credit pass in Bahasa Malaysia is

Education and Colonialism in Peninsular Malaysia

now necessary for Chinese and Indian Malaysians to be awarded
the certificate as a prerequisite for university entrance or
for government service, and more important for the non-Malays,
for permission to study overseas whether or not on a scholarship. These policies of the Malaysian government have been
viewed with growing misgivings by the non-Malay groups,
especially the Chinese. Having accepted slightly resentfully,
the unfair advantage accorded to the Malays through the quota
system in the matter of applications for public sector employment, they now feel themselves discriminated against in terms
of language, especially at tertiary level. The question of
restructuring higher education is one of the most sensitive
issues in modern Malaysia. Until the early 1970s, most
university faculties were dominated by the Chinese, but it
was precisely this point that angered the Malay extremists
who argued that they remained economically poor because they
were educationally under-represented at university level. As
a result of pressures from its supporters, therefore, the
government has sought to redress this imbalance.

RESTRUCTURING OF TERTIARY LEVEL EDUCATION
      The most striking aspect of positive discrimination in
favour of Malays by the ruling Malay elite therefore, has
taken place at tertiary level. Until 1969 the University of
Malaya was the only degree giving institution in the country.
Until the early 1970s, it was dominated by Chinese students
especially in the faculties of science, engineering, medicine
and economics. Since 1969 therefore, the government has
sought to redress the Malays' grievances by increasing the
number of universities (by three), by opening other tertiary
level institutions and by widening opportunities for Malays
to enter higher education. Perhaps the most interesting
document of recent years has been the Majid Report (1971),
which recommended that the racial composition of the university
as a whole, as well as each faculty separately, should represent the racial composition of the country 'as far as possible',
and that criteria other than academic criteria should be used
to select rural Malays; that scholarships should be used to
favour Malays and so alter the racial imbalances in science
and engineering faculties; and the process of using the
National language as the medium of instruction should be
speeded up. The result of these measures has been a
striking increase in the number of Malays enrolled in higher
education, with the result that by the late 1970s, they had
achieved a highly favourable position vis a vis the other
ethnic groups(7). As one observer has commented:

      The re-definition of the National education system
      to give prominence to the Malay medium of instruction
      and the recent efforts at engineering student enrol-
      ments represents the most comprehensive, and direct

attempts by the Malay governing elites to raise
the social and economic status of the Malays
through education. (Chee 1978:38).

Inevitably, the non-Malays have resented the steady
whittling away of their educational position. The Chinese
particularly resent the positive discrimination in favour of
Malays in government employment, examination results and
overseas scholarships. Although no Malay would say that their
educational policy is a form of colonialism, there is little
doubt that it is seen as such by other groups. In fact, 'it
is ironic that the two interlocking instruments of nation-
building, language and education, have divided rather than
united Malays and non-Malays'. (Chai Hon-Chan 1977:59).
While the more extreme ethnic policies were minimised during
Hussain Onn's period as Prime Minister (1976-81) and are
once again being advocated, it can be seen in hindsight that
during the twenty years since independence, the Malay elite,
feeling threatened economically and politically, used educational and language policies to reinforce its political
dominance over other ethnic groups.

C. NEOCOLONIAL INFLUENCE ON EDUCATION

Altbach (1971:237) defines educational neo-colonialism
as 'the continued post-colonial impact of advanced countries
on the education systems and policies as well as on the
intellectual life of developing areas'. Although it is less
easy to identify neo-colonial control in Malaysia than in
many former colonies, because of the rapid moves toward
Malayanisation of the bureaucracy, the educational system
and the curriculum, it nevertheless can be identified.
It can be seen in the structure and shape of the education system, which although changed since the days of
British rule, nevertheless still has the stamp of British
influence. This is particularly true of the upper secondary
and sixth form levels with their emphasis on preparation for
university entrance, and in the universities with their
faculty structure and examination system, which was originally
linked to that of London University. It is also evident in
the ethos of a number of schools and in the comprehensive
secondary school re-organisation that took place in 1964, a
hurried and unprepared operation that resembled the comprehensive secondary school re-organisation that took place in
England and Wales during the 1960s. Similar reasons to those
advocated in England were put forward by the Malay leaders for
developing comprehensive education, except that whereas in
England advocates of comprehensive education referred to the
need to redress selection based on class lines, the Malays
urged the need to redress selection favouring certain ethnic
groups. Pressures brought to bear on the Chinese schools

during the 1960s and 1970s, are also remarkably similar to
the tactics used by successive governments in England to
conform to government wishes. This is perhaps not surprising
since the bureaucratic structures are a direct legacy of
British rule and the ruling elite has been strongly influenced
by British attitudes and values. To some extent these attitudes
have been reinforced by the large number of Malaysian students
who have attended courses at institutions in Britain,
Australia and to a lesser extent, Canada and the U.S.A., under
technical assistance training schemes. The influence of such
training is impossible to quantify, but it nevertheless must
be considerable, especially as the largest single group of
overseas students studying in Britain come from Malaysia(8).
Likewise, the presence of a large number of expatriate staff
in the universities and special science schools must to some
extent, reinforce Western attitudes.

Altbach (1975, 1977) has argued quite forcefully that
European - and American - control of publishing houses is
also a form of neo-colonial control, since Western business
methods, management and policy makers influence textbooks and
other books used in schools. Some of the leading British
publishing houses which set up offices in Kuala Lumpur during
the period of British rule now have a very large financial
stake in publishing educational books, and have a sizeable
slice of the publishing market.

Perhaps the most striking neo-colonial influence however,
has been on the curriculum and examination structure, both of
which have been closely inter-linked. Originally, the School
Certificate and Higher School Certificate examinations were
set by the Cambridge Overseas Examination Syndicate. During
the 1970s, they were gradually replaced by Malaysian set
papers. Their names and their language medium are currently
being changed so that by 1982 all will be Bahasa Malaysia
medium. Thus, the Lower Certificate of Education at the end
of Form Six was replaced by the Sijil Rendah Pelajaran in
1978, the Malaysian Certificate of Education taken to the
end of Form Five was replaced by the Sijil Pelajaran Malaysia
in 1980 and the Higher School Certificate, taken at the end
of Form Six will be replaced by the Sijil Tinggi Persekolahan
in 1982. However, their selective purpose remains much the
same as in British colonial times, the format is still
remarkably British and the value and kudos attached to them
is still exceedingly high. (Lewin 1975).

It is however in the field of curriculum development,
especially science curriculum development, that British
influence can still be seen. (Watson 1980c). In many LDCs
science is seen as a major item on the school curriculum,
because it is believed it will lead to new attitudes of mind,
it will develop new approaches to learning and teaching, to
the understanding of the environment and to solving problems
such as water pollution, soil erosion and control of diseases.

Education and Colonialism in Peninsular Malaysia

In Malaysia it has been argued that by pursuing science and
mathematics reforms, the government was hoping to keep pace
with the advanced nations of the world. Since the late 1960s
and early 1970s, therefore, modified versions of the Scottish
Integrated Science Programme and the Nuffield Science Projects
have been introduced into Malaysian schools. British teachers,
familiar with both programmes, were sent by the British
Ministry of Overseas Development to help run Summer schools
and train Malaysian teachers in the techniques of Scottish
Integrated Science and Nuffield Science and to advise on the
modification of the curriculum to suit the Malaysian situation.
Several problems have arisen, though not necessarily of the
British advisers' making (Sim 1977). The schemes were introduced quickly. The Scottish Integrated Science programme, a
two year non-examinable course in Scotland, was stretched to
a three year examinable course in Malaysian schools. There
was a lack of teacher preparation and conceptual understanding.
Laboratory facilities were inadequate, and away from the urban
centres there was a shortage of trained laboratory assistants
and equipment; To overcome the latter, external provision of
expensive equipment from Britain has been considerable.
Perhaps the saddest aspect however, is that what is taught,
especially in the rural areas, is fragmented and not integrated,
and is more in tune with what is taught in Western industrial
situations rather than being closely linked with the technological, agricultural, health and hygiene needs of those
living in the rural areas. (Alam 1978; Watson 1980c).
Unfortunately, because of external influences and constraints
on these curricula developments, there has been too little
real attempt to re-orientate science teaching along lines
more suitable to the needs of rural peoples.

CONCLUSIONS

What lessons can be learnt from this study of education
and colonialism and is there any difference other than in
kind between the different forms of colonial control? There
would appear to be four lessons:

1. There was no long-term Machiavellian colonial education
    policy on the part of the British. The educational
    policy that developed was largely defined by individuals
    on the spot rather than by the British Government in
    Whitehall and the personalities and upbringing of
    individual administrators had a profound impact on develop-
    ments. While policy was often ambivalent and changeable
    according to the circumstances, there were a few constants
    - support for the Malay rulers, maintenance of the status
    quo for the Malay peasantry and until just before the
    outbreak of World War II, relative indifference to the
    education of immigrant groups. The result was that there

105

was no attempt to create a harmonious multi-racial society, there were different education systems conferring economic and social advantage on different ethnic groups and the independent Malaysian Government was left with the difficult task of trying to pull the different groups in society together.

2. British influence can still be seen in the administrative and educational structure, in the attitudes of many of the present elite, and above all, in curriculum development and guidance over examination reform.

3. The Malay elite since independence, has sought to use education to ensure its own political position. Whereas for the first decade after independence, moves towards developing a multi-racial society were gradual, it was the 1969 riots and the threat to their political as well as economic position by both non-Malays and radical Malays that led the more moderate Malay leaders to accelerate the process of ensuring their own political, linguistic and educational superiority.

4. Perhaps the most striking and disturbing conclusion however, is that the economic development of the country which took place under British rule, did so regardless of the lack of educational provision, except for a small English and Malay speaking elite, and that attempts to create a New Malaysian society via the school system, have sometimes led to resentments and have thus been counterproductive. Both these points must, therefore, still beg the question of how far is schooling important for economic and social development?

NOTES

1. In 1785 the Dutch Government issued the famous 'Kew letters' authorising the British to occupy Dutch colonies in an attempt to thwart the French: Malacca was returned at the end of the Napoleonic wars, but was finally ceded to Britain in 1824.

2. Until 1830 control was from the Presidency of Penang. This was downgraded to a Residency in that year when control passed to the Governor-General in Calcutta. In 1832 local Residential responsibility was passed to the Resident in Singapore.

3. This was so called because of a meeting held on board a ship anchored off Pangkor Island.

4. One interesting effect of this, is that in the former Federated Malay States, the Christian Sunday is observed, whereas in the latter, the Muslim Friday is.

5. In 1946 the British authorities had separated Singapore as a Crown Colony and proposed a Malayan Union. It was abortive because of Chinese opposition and because the Malay sultans feared a loss of power in their states.

6. The Alliance Party, in power since independence, is made up of the United Malay National Organisation (UMNO) the main partner, the Malaysian Chinese Association (MCA), and the Malaysian Indian Congress (MIC).

7. In 1970, Chinese students made up 49.2% of all degree courses, Malays 39.7% and Indians 7.3%. In faculty terms at the University of Malay, Chinese accounted for 93.1% of engineering places, 82.0% of science places, 66.1% of medical places and 64.2% of agricultural places - by 1975 Malays made up 57.2% of all degree students, Chinese 36.6% and Indians 5.2%. By 1977 the Chinese enrolment had dropped in the following faculties to 81.3% (engineering), 67.9% (science), 56.1% (medicine) and 13.3% (agriculture).

8. This was true until the academic year 1981-82, but as a result of the increase of fees for overseas students attending courses in Britain, the Malaysian government has taken the decision not to send any more students to Britain. Instead they will go to Korea, Japan and the U.S.A.

Chapter Six

COLONIALISM AND EDUCATION - VIETNAM

Dudley Hick

        If one regards colonialism as a political act with social
and economic consequences, the experience of Vietnam over two
millenia provides an interesting example of its effect on the
growth and development of a culture. The first colonists, and
those who remained longest, were the Chinese. They established
the kingdom of Nam-Viet in the second century B.C. and converted
it to a province of the Chinese Empire in 111 B.C., so to
remain for a thousand years. (De Jaegher in Lindholm 1959,
107). As to be expected the country was highly influenced by
Chinese culture, and in particular by the education system,
which was ultimately accepted and codified in 622 A.D.
(Hildreth in Lindholm 1959, 144). Yet the Vietnamese retained
much of their indigenous culture during this period, and indeed
themselves moved steadily southwards from their birthplace in
the north, reaching in the seventeenth century the tip of the
peninsula, which was to become known as Indo-China. This
nomenclature is in itself revealing, since the conjunction of
the two names neatly summarises the two vital influences on
the nation, Buddhism from India and Confucianism from China.
        In 939 A.D. Vietnam won its independence, which it was to
retain for almost another thousand years. It quickly developed
a strong centralised system and an administration that was
efficient and equal to that of many European nations. (Scigliano 1963, 7). At the same time a large degree of local
autonomy remained with the villages. Here the traditional
culture survived and thrived. A significant feature was the
worship of the ancestors, resulting from a strong attachment
to the land owned by each peasant, and his father before him.
In this way was forged a bond between the living and the
dead that provided a concept of immortality. Each individual
knew that his life's commitment would continue, as he himself
had carried on what his father had done before him. This in
turn encouraged filial respect, which, associated with the
collective nature of Vietnamese civilisation, led to a natural
obedience to authority, to which the western concept of intellectual freedom and diversity was completely foreign.

(Masson 1960, 54 et seq.).

The major impact on this culture stemmed directly from
the many centuries of Chinese colonial occupation. Confucian
philosophy pervaded the educational system and through it the
attitude and thinking of the mandarinate, itself a legacy of
the Chinese influence. It may be argued that the ordinary
people were hardly affected, (Marr 1971, 11) but certainly
those charged with the conduct of the nation's affairs were
subject to it. Confucianism was not a religion as such, and
was thus able to accommodate a variety of beliefs, including
the traditional animism and ancestor worship. It stressed
above all one's social obligations, including fidelity to the
sovereign, respect for the family, and a willingness to serve
the community. (Nguyen Khac Vien 1969, 91). This was a
strong contrast to Buddhism, which stressed the vanity and
unreality of things of this world, preached renunciation, and
directed thoughts towards the supernatural. The struggle
between these conflicting ideologies was not resolved until
the fifteenth century with the recognition of the ascendance
of Confucianism. (Nguyen Khac Vien 1975, 29).

The effect of this on Vietnamese culture is revealed
through the education system. The first state school was
established at Thang Long, Hanoi, in 1070 and in the course
of time there were schools serving the population throughout
the breadth of the country. (Nguyen Khac Vien 1971, 141).
From this base there evolved a comprehensive system of examinations designed to provide officials at various levels in
the public service. The detailed organisation differed in
some important respects from the Chinese mode, (Woodside 1971,
169 et seq.) but the influence is obvious, and certainly the
primacy of Confucian tenets was most apparent. At all levels
Confucianism dominated the curriculum, there was a great
emphasis on the study of literature and philosophy, leading
to what the French would call culture generale, but with the
important distinction that it did not allow the critical
analysis of philosophical ideas in the western tradition, but
assumed an acceptance of the basic principles of Confucianism.
As successful scholars generally entered the service of the
state, the result of this was to perpetuate a static society,
where any original interpretation of organisational policy was
unlikely to occur.

It is of course unjust to judge the system by extrinsic
standards, and it is evident that Vietnamese society was
complex and well-developed. Within it scholars were held in
high esteem, and this rose in accordance with the level of
scholarship acquired. At the apex were those who obtained
the doctorate. In the millenium after the opening of the
Temple of Literature in the late eleventh century, only some
two thousand were successful in obtaining this. (Nguyen Khac
Vien 1975, 18). Unsuccessful candidates presented themselves
for re-examination at three-year intervals, and many did so

until the twilight of their years. In the meantime they
engaged in further study and were often employed in village
schools, preparing a future generation to follow the same
path.

UNESCO computations indicate that some 80 to 85 percent
of the population were literate at the time the French colonists
arrived in the middle of the nineteenth century, and that the
literacy rate had fallen to between 15 and 20 percent when
they finally left in 1954. (Naughton 1979, 101). It is
likely that this occurred by default rather than intention.
The southern part of the country fell under direct French rule
as the colony of Cochinchina, the remainder was governed
indirectly as the protectorates of Tonkin and Annam (Hoang van
chi 1964, 27). The total administrative purpose was to further
the economic exploitation of the country for the benefit of
the French, instead of sustaining the traditional society
based on irrigated agriculture. (Scigliano 1963, 9).
Initially no attempt was made to interfere with the prevailing
education system, and it was allowed to continue. But as the
indigenous administration was impotent, there seemed less and
less point in undergoing a rigorous preparation to serve it.
In consequence the system declined and decayed, and, with
nothing to replace it, there developed an educational vacuum.
(Marr 1971, 79).

The general acceptance of Confucian principles, with
their insistence on unquestioning obedience to legitimate
authority, had ensured a stable and just society, with a
profound sense of popular sovereignty, albeit expressed in
ways unknown to the western world. The delicate balance of
authority and consent was destroyed as people realised the
helplessness of their own rulers, and resented the servitude
to their foreign masters. By using the forms of the traditional
regime whilst stripping them of their substance, the French
allowed moral principles to be eroded and condoned widespread
corruption in the mandarinate. (Hammer in Lindholm 1959, 40).

Christian missionaries had worked in Vietnam since the
middle of the seventeenth century, although their impact on
the society had been minimal. After the French had established the colonial regime, the Catholic church was encouraged
to expand its operations. It was hoped to train some young
Vietnamese in western ways and so to begin the process of re-
orienting the country from its Chinese cultural allegiance,
and in particular from Confucianism. (Ennis 1936, 167). Not
surprisingly this aroused resentment, and the schools did not
prove popular. Acknowledging this, a policy was introduced
in 1865 of sending children away to be educated at catholic
schools in France. This too proved of limited value and the
scheme was eventually abandoned. (Osborne 1969, 90). In the
long run the Church did itself a grave disservice by co-
operating in this manner, since its converts in later years
were identified with reactionary forces and regarded as

unpatriotic. (Nguyen Khac Vien (ed) 1975, 32).
    After the turn of the century the need for suitably
educated Vietnamese in the colonial administration became
imperative, and the Escole de Thai Ha Hap was founded in 1906.
In the following year the University of Indo-China was established, and in 1915 Sarrault introduced a replica of the
French educational system with its three divisions of primary,
secondary and tertiary. (Masson 1960, 101). The curriculum
was that of metropolitan France and instruction was mainly in
French. The effect of this system was to train Vietnamese
children to acquire an alien tongue, to follow a French
curriculum and so in fact to gallicise them, estranging them
from their own culture. A few of the most able continued their
tertiary education in France, and as a result there evolved
an intellectual elite who, like the mandarins of the past,
lived apart from the people, and who in many instances were
unable to speak and write their own language correctly.
(Nguyen Khac Vien 1975, 45).
    Between the two world wars educational provision increased
substantially. In 1936 there were nearly half a million children at school, the vast majority in the primary schools, and
only a few hundred at the senior secondary level. (FLPH 1975,
112). This is not a large number when one considers that the
population of the entire country was over 18 million, but it
was more than enough for the jobs available, and it created
disaffection. Many young people had learnt about liberty,
equality, fraternity only to find that they were not for them.
(Fitzgerald 1973, 82). Thus the increase in educational
opportunity was paralleled by the development of a powerful
nationalist resistance movement. The assassination attempt
on the Governor-General in 1924 was followed by the formation
of a varity of underground revolutionary groups, and these
were unified in 1930 with the formation of the Communist
Party. (Chesneaux 1966, 135). The leaders were mainly 'petty
intellectuals', the clerks and teachers, trained by the
French, who were close to the peasants and whose fortunes they
shared. Unwittingly the French had created conditions to
suit their immediate needs that were to have great import for
the future, in that the inevitable nationalist movement was
to be led by a small but well-organised and educated communist
party.
    The second world war provided the opportunity for the
resistance movement to gather momentum. After a short period
of Japanese occupation an independent state was proclaimed in
August 1945. The previous colonial regime was rejected completely, and with it the French educational structure. It
was replaced by a system of general education lasting nine
years on the Soviet polytechnic pattern. The language of
instruction was Vietnamese, and the comprehensive nature of
the scheme ensured that children from all strata of society
attended school and received an adequate education. (FLPH

1968, 33). At the same time all the previous youth organisations run by Catholics, Buddhists and others were incorporated in the one movement, the Lao-Dong, so that the aims of
the developing socialist society could be most efficiently
achieved. (Fall 1960, 317). This also required a literate
population, and consequently a mass literacy campaign was
inaugurated through the introduction of complementary education.
This programme, which involved people in their workplace, and
husbands teaching wives and other members of the family, was
so successful that illiteracy was almost eradicated within a
decade. (FLPH 1975, 104).
    A remarkable feature of this extension of educational
opportunity to practically the whole population was that it
occurred at the same time as the French were attempting to
re-impose their earlier colonial administration. Schools and
adult classes were established in the guerrilla zones where
they thrived openly. In much of the occupied zones they
operated clandestinely and successfully. (Nguyen Khac Vien
1971, 26). It was in fact the foreign challenge as much as
anything else that gave an impetus to educational effort.
Popular education was seen as an expression of patriotic
nationalism, and each class became in its way a cell of
resistance to the French colonial aspirations, and every
teacher a propagandist for the cause.
    The campaign against French colonialism was led by the
National Liberation Front. This organisation attracted
people of many political persuasions, but the one thing that
they had in common was a determination to set their country
free from any form of foreign domination. The best organised
group within the NLF was the Communist party, and this for all
practical purposes provided the leadership, and with it the
ideology which influenced the organisation and curriculum of
the school system. Ironically the United States had supported
the Viet Minh in the last stages of the second world war as
the most effective resistance group against the Japanese.
Roosevelt had proposed granting independence to the country
instead of a resumption of French colonialism, but the
ardour for this course of action cooled as the Marxist nature
of the movement became apparent. (Scigliano 1963, 190-1).
    Ho Chi Minh had warned of the danger of separating manual
from intellectual labour, and it became a prime requisite
that instruction should be polytechnic and follow the Marxist
doctrine of combining study with productive labour. It was
believed that political goals could be achieved through the
education system, which should have a truly national,
scientific, and popular character. (FLPH 1968, 52). Every
village had schools for children and illiterates, and they
became centres for the distribution of news and propaganda.
The work and study approach meant a better understanding between the peasant and the scholar, and a sense of community
with each other. By the time that the French were compelled

to abandon their reconquest of the country in 1954, a great
number of people were literate, politically aware, and ready
to participate with their leaders in the next stage in the
establishment of a socialist state, and to continue, through
the school system, the endeavour to create the socialist man.
(Nguyen Khac Vien 1977, 22).

Following the French withdrawal, the country was divided
along the seventeenth parallel, and an independent republic,
the DRVN, was proclaimed in the north. Its destiny was to be
the progenitor of the eventual creation of a national government of the whole country, and its leaders were confidently
aware of this. Immediate steps were taken to extend the
system of general education to all children in the north. The
educational reform of 1956 formalised this with the introduction of three levels lasting ten years. It was also
ordained that instruction should be in Vietnamese and textbooks
were produced accordingly. (FLPH 1968, 53). There were about
one million children in pre-school and first level education,
lasting five years - pre-school one year, and then four years.
There were about 63,000 in the three years of second level
education, and some 3,400 in the following three years of third
level education. By 1974 these enrolments had risen to five
million, 1,3000,000 and 120,000 respectively, a remarkable
achievement in the light of the political and military events
of the period. (FLPH 1975, 113).

Complementary education was continued and extended for
those in the former occupied zones. Its aim was to complete
the eradication of illiteracy and to reach for political
purposes those who had not passed through the formal system.
The number involved reached a peak of some two million and
declined by 1970 to just under one million. (Nguyen Khac
Vien 1971, 174). This is indicative of the success of the
schools in reaching the great majority of the population, and
by 1975, when the country was eventually unified, complementary
education was concentrated almost wholly at the second and
third levels.

There was an equally dramatic increase in the provision
of tertiary education. Where there had been only one
university for the whole of Indo-China at independence in
1945, there were thirty-seven further education colleges and
universities in 1974, and one hundred and eighty six
vocational schools operating at the tertiary level. (Nguyen
Khac Vien 1977, 92). Under the French, courses of advanced
study served the needs of the colonial power. The significance
of this increase lay in the fact that the courses were designed
to serve the new society, and to supply the trained technical
cadres needed in the transition from a mainly agricultural
economy to an industrialised socialist state.

The aim of this enormous commitment to the education of
the people was the training of the populace in socialist
ideology, from which arose naturally the necessity for a

literate, informed, and technically competent population.
There was a clear need to build the material and technical
bases of socialism, and so to train a new generation and to
form cadres who would be responsible for future economic and
cultural development. The French system had been designed to
provide clerical workers, junior managers and basic technical
support for their colonial regime. This was replaced by a
curriculum which laid more stress on the manual and technical
skills needed, and which provided a content more suited to
the inculcation of national pride and which reflected the
need for scientific advancement.

By 1961 the education system had been unified, illiteracy
had been practically eradicated in the delta, and great progress had been made in the countryside. Each rural commune
had at least one first level school and often a second level
one. Each district had a third level school. (FLPH 1975,
105). More attention was now given to the ethnic minorities
who composed 15 percent of the population and occupied two
thirds of the territory. (Kahin 1972, 580). Their rights
were guaranteed in the constitution and instruction was
given in the mother tongue. Experimental schools were
established, such as the one at Hoa Binh, where the children
spent half their time studying and half in productive agriculture work. By 1970 the school covered all three levels
of general education, had successfully demonstrated the
possibility of linking study with the activities of the
locality, and was in fact economically self-supporting. (Thai
Quang-Nam 1979, 95). In all this enterprise, teachers had
an important role to play. They were expected not merely to
impart knowledge, but to communicate a communist outlook on
the world and life. This required a stress on the work and
study policy, which was often interpreted as study to avoid
productive work, a social problem of some magnitude. (Nguyen
Khac Vien 1977, 84). Their work was reinforced informally by
the home and family, parent organisations, and other social
groups. All had a part to play in preparing working people
to be the 'collective masters of society'. (Thai Quang-Nam
1979, 92). This often involved khiem thao, group discussions,
the admission of errors, and the resolve to seek a true
understanding of the nature of the incipient developing
society. (Fitzgerald 1973, 272).

The great expansion of educational effort was scarcely
affected by the interference of U.S. armed forces, an event
that was commonly regarded as an endeavour to reimpose a
colonial regime in another guise. Following the threat and
the actuality of aerial bombardment and military action in
the border zones, schools and institutions of higher learning
were evacuated to the countryside, where they continued to
function. (FLPH 1975, 106-7). All over the country, schools,
carefully camouflaged and concealed from aerial observation,
went on with their allotted tasks. Indeed it was said that

the added stimulus of national defence and patriotic determination rendered the schooling even more effective.
(Nguyen Khac Vien 1971, 12).

With the division of the country in 1954 the southern
half also became ostensibly an independent country. Yet the
French colonial influence persisted. The general structure
of the administrative system was modelled on the French
pattern, and French principles were evenly more strongly
engrained in the judicial system. (Scigliano 1963, 34-5).
The education system too retained its strongly French character,
particularly at the secondary level. Much of this was
financed by the French Cultural Mission to Vietnam and the
classes were taught in French, by French teachers, or by
Vietnamese who had been trained in France, and using textbooks
which had been printed in France. (Hildreth in Lindholm 1959,
148). Superimposed on this however was an additional force
which was to increase in weight and compass.

The Americans did not come to Vietnam as colonists, yet
it is difficult to distinguish in what important respect they
were not. Their avowed aim was to support a legitimate
independent government, but the process of increasing economic
subvention led to total foreign dependence, thereby negating
and invalidating the altruistic goals. Between 1954 and 1960
there was a shift in trade away from France in favour of
America, as the aid programme developed. In 1960 most major
industrial countries were excluded as suppliers and Vietnam
became heavily reliant on American goods and services.
(Scigliano 1963, 109-110). There was a plethora of American
commissions and with them a stream, and then a flood, of
civilian and military personnel. The inevitable result of all
this was a steady and progressive deculturisation of Vietnamese
urban society, and the manifestation of the outward and more
materialistic trappings of American culture.

This economic and social colonialism was accompanied too
by other aspects of American life. In 1968 a new constitution
was introduced that was similar to the American presidential
system. (Devereaux 1968, 628). Changes were made to the
education system following recommendations by various visiting
delegations. The purpose may have been to get rid of the
unsuitable French legacy, but the result was the substitution
of another equally unsuitable heritage. Advanced students
were sent to America for further training, where previously
they had gone to France. In 1972 more than 80 percent of
tertiary students were enrolled in the social sciences, which
did not correspond with the need in a developing country for
engineers, technicians, doctors and pharmacists. (Nguyen
Khac Vien (ed) 1975, 132-9).

It must of course be understood that the government in
Saigon was only nominally that of the whole of Vietnam. It
would be more accurate to consider it as a confederation of
city-states, such as Saigon, Hue, Da Nang. For all practical

purposes the NLF controlled most of the countryside outside
the principal towns, and here it established a complete school
system organised in three levels and providing much the same
ideological preparation as in the north. In every village
cadres formed schools, classes for illiterates, and centres
for the dissemination of news and propaganda. (Fitzgerald
1973, 247). American influence was absent, except for the
direct and deadly military presence, and the system flourished
despite the hardships and setbacks suffered. Over the years
there was a steady increase in the number of pupils benefitting
from the teaching, austere and primitive as were the conditions
under which they studied.

After the liberation of the southern half of the country
in April 1975, steps were taken to begin the process of re-
unification of the country, and with it the education system.
The Socialist Republic of Vietnam, SRV, was proclaimed in
July 1976 and in the same year the Fourth Party Congress was
held to prepare the next five-year plan, 1976-80. The reform
envisaged the abolition of existing structures and their
replacement with the New Improving Education, in which all
pupils would follow a common course of general education.
Pre-school education and first and second level education
would be combined as a Basic Primary School of eight years
duration, with the intention to extend this eventually to
nine years. The third level would become a secondary course
lasting three years and require different types of schools
according to the branches of study.

The purpose of this re-organisation into an integrated
structure was to build a regime of socialist collective
mastery, and to develop the new socialist man. (Vo Thuan Nho
1977, 1). Such a society needed a firm educational base and,
at the higher education level, specific provision for the
development of skills in specialist areas. This was achieved
by a vast expansion of tertiary education and a rejection of
the western concept of universality. Specialist institutes
such as the College of Medicine, College of Agriculture,
College of Railway and Road Transport were established. In
these there was a judicious mixture of theoretical study and
productive labour and experimentation, in accordance with
marxist principles. (Vietnam Courier, 63,4). There are now
over fifty universities in Vietnam, of which only a few,
where studies are theoretical, are controlled by the Minister
for Education. The majority come under the various ministries,
such as Agriculture. The Ministry for Transportation, for
example, has three universities to train its high level cadres
and the budget comes through this ministry. There is thus a
strong impetus for the study and learning to be directed at
specific vocational goals. This greatly facilitates the
requirement that study should be combined with productive
labour, since all students work during their studies at
projects directly connected with the ministry. There are also

some three hundred vocational schools, mostly situated in the north. These schools provide the middle-level technicians required by the emerging socialist society, and they play an important role in the future economic development of the country.

In the south the problems are considerable, and it is not expected that the reformed system will be operating properly for some time. In the first place there was at the time of liberation a very high level of illiteracy. Secondly there were far too few schools at the second level for any serious attempt to introduce the Basic Primary School of eight years in the near future. Thirdly, there was the great problem of re-educating a large number of people to understand the new political philosophy, and moreover to accept it and work towards its goals. As an interim measure many teachers and graduates from the northern institutions were relocated in the south, where they set an example of combining study and productive labour by assisting in such practical activities as water conservation measures, teaching and working in the New Economic Zones, and helping to eradicate French and American attitudes and traditions in the southern schools and universities.

An early start was made with the programme of re-education. In December 1975, 1,200 intellectuals underwent a political course in Ho Chi Minh City for four months. They studied the history of the Vietnamese nation, the history of the revolution, and the character of socialist education. These were key people in the education system, and it was claimed that the course was very successful. (Nguyen Khac Vien 1977, 125-6). At the same time numerous political education centres were founded. All ex-army personnel had to register, and short political courses were held for the ordinary citizen in the evenings. (Donnell 1976, 6).

Whether or not these programmes succeed, there can be no doubt that educational opportunity has been vastly extended. By the end of 1978 there were some 15 million in the system. 1,300,000 in pre-school education, 12,000,000 in general education, 1,600,000 in complementary education, and over 200,000 in vocational and higher education. (Vietnam Courier, 77,6). The increase in educational provision, the campaign to eradicate illiteracy, the attempt to train great numbers of fairly unsophisticated people to undertake skilled tasks in the economy, all these are impressive, and a challenge to the leadership and the people. Vietnam is a country ravaged by war for thirty years. Throughout this period there was a consistent attitude that it was a revolutionary war of liberation, a people's war against French and American imperialism. (Fifield 1977, 877). With victory achieved the immediate goal was naturally the removal of every trace of French and American culture. To this end a conference sponsored by the Ministry of Culture and Information was held in Ho Chi Minh City in January 1978. (Vietnam Courier, 70,21). The slogan was the 'Struggle to eradicate all traces of neo-colonialist culture', and it was agreed that the Americans had deliberately introduced their way of life to destroy national consciousness and undermine the class struggle, and to dehumanise people by encouraging them to live a luxurious and parasitic life satisfying vile, animal passions.

Couched in these extravagant terms, the sentiments expressed reveal the deep concern to rebuild a disintegrated society. In the south particularly, under the blatant veneer of American culture, persisted a blend of Chinese and French traditions, a reverence for the Confucian scholar combined with the ideal of classical elegance. (Winston 1970, 4). For more than a thousand years Vietnamese education had been presented in a foreign language, Chinese and then French. This was ended with the requirement that teaching at all levels should be in the vernacular. The fact that half of the teachers involved were women was said to be a certain guarantee of the demise of the ancient Confucian patriatchy. (Woodside 1977, 661).

The provision of general education for all, in conjunction with a curriculum that stressed national pride, the common purpose, the dignity of labour, and the acquisition of practical and technical skills, was designed to dissipate the remote intellectualism of the French and the vulgar sophistry of the Americans. But by replacing these with a political philosophy based on Marxist-Leninism, an outdated nineteenth century credo, there is the obvious danger that a colonial domination based at various times on imperialist ambitions, economic motivation, political and military hegemony, will be replaced by another kind, ideological congruity. Vietnam is ideologically close to the Soviet Union, was indebted to it during the years of war, and became somewhat dependent economically. This has lessened recently, and the refusal to join Comecon, the Soviet economic organisation, (Horn 1979, 604) suggests a reluctance to surrender a hard-won national independent identity for another kind of colonialism.

NOTES

The figures given in this chapter come partly from official sources and partly from conversations with officials in the Ministry of Education in Hanoi. They cannot be regarded as absolutely reliable, but the general picture is. Many of the references listed at the end of this volume are published by official sources or by sympathisers with the regime. There is a dearth of objective writing on the topic, but care has been taken to assess the evidence accordingly and in the light of the writer's experience in his observations during an extended visit to the country.

Chapter Seven

THE LEGACY OF COLONIALISM IN WEST INDIAN EDUCATION

Colin Brock

INTRODUCTION

It is necessary at the outset to define the terms of
reference within which this chapter has been constructed. A
number of authoritative studies already exist on various
aspects of the educational history of the West Indies, and it
would be presumptuous to attempt to parallel these within the
scope of a single essay. It would also be inappropriate to
attempt a synthesis or epitome. Rather one would wish to
concentrate on a particular aspect or concept within the
broad field of education and colonialism as evidenced in part
of the Caribbean in the late twentieth century. Hence the
selection of the legacy of colonialism in educational terms.

It could well be that the educational legacy of colonialism has been the most invidious of all, with its debilitating
inertia enveloping and constraining local cultural initiative.
For as has been remarked by a leading student of Caribbean
societies, the greatest affliction of dependent societies is
the 'colonised condition of the minds of the people', (Beckford 1972, 235). This is no mere whimsical irritant to do
with parrots and pieces-of-eight, but a latter-day bondage
more subtle and enduring than physical slavery. Almost the
entire educational scene in the West Indies is a legacy of
colonialism, but looked at in more detail it is seen to
comprise a bundle of residual legacies each deriving from
particular aspects of the colonial experience. Even then,
successive and overlapping elements of colonialism serve to
qualify the degree of discretion likely to be evident in
relationships apparent between particular formative influences
and particular educational provisions and practices.

Continuing now with terms of reference, it is necessary
to indicate how 'education' will be defined and viewed below.
The essay will not be confined to a consideration of formal
institutionalised provision, though this strand has acted,
and continues to act most strongly as a purveyor of metropolitan values. For West Indian societies, perhaps more than

most, attitudes, assumptions and aspirations, and above all
the question of identity, have been fundamentally moulded by
contextual factors which include non-formal educational
influences. Foremost among these factors has been the continued dependency of the West Indies, cultural and economic, with
the latter having prime significance in terms of sustaining
colonial attitudes. Slavery was abolished but plantations
were not, and we shall need to examine at least some aspects
of the relationships between education and human ecology.

A third definition is required in terms of the geographical scope of the essay. The term 'West Indian'(1) is
preferred to 'Caribbean' since we shall be concerned primarily
with the island nations of that area. However, because
emphasis will also be placed on the 'British West Indies' -
a colonialist term if ever there was one(2) - then Belize and
Guyana, both mainland territories, must be included. In order
to facilitate geographical recognition, two maps are included.
This is done at the risk of offending some readers, but an
evident and remarkable ignorance of the basic geography of
the West Indies is itself a legacy of colonial education.
One may take this point further and suggest that even an
elementary geographical appreciation of the area on the part
of those responsible would have rendered any idea of a
federal state comprising the 'British West Indies' a definite
non-starter. This is to say nothing of the very real and
national identities of the component units of the Federation
of the West Indies, most of them multi-cultural, and so it is
not surprising that the scheme aborted in 1962, after only
four years in being.

Figures 1 and 2 also show former metropolitan affiliation
and help to illustrate the variety of colonial connections in
the area. Although most of the 'British West Indies' is now
politically independent, there are some that are still
colonies, and others that have the status of 'Associated
States'.(3) Several small island nations have expressed a
desire to remain colonies, and one (Anguilla) removed itself
from federation with two others (Saint Kitts and Nevis) in
order to return to that status. This was on the grounds of
concern about the domination of the troika by the largest
partner, Saint Kitts, and Nevis has subsequently attempted
to emulate Anguilla but so far without success. Indeed one
of the clear political legacies of colonialism here is the
desire of even small states to have their own colonies:

'Smallness has condemned the islands to a history of
tutelage and, in some cases, to microscopic versions of
political dependence. A decade and a half ago only the
three largest units - all in the Greater Antilles - were
independent, and some of the smallest islands were dependencies of dependencies. Carriacou, subordinate to Grenada,
boasts its own fief, Petite Martinique'.
(Clarke 1976: 8).

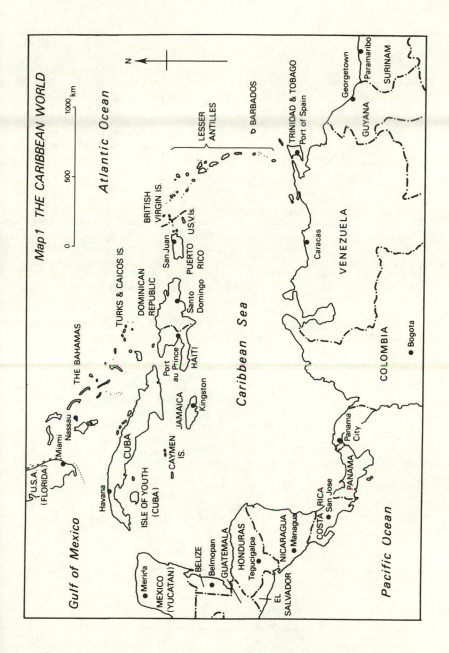

Map 1   THE CARIBBEAN WORLD

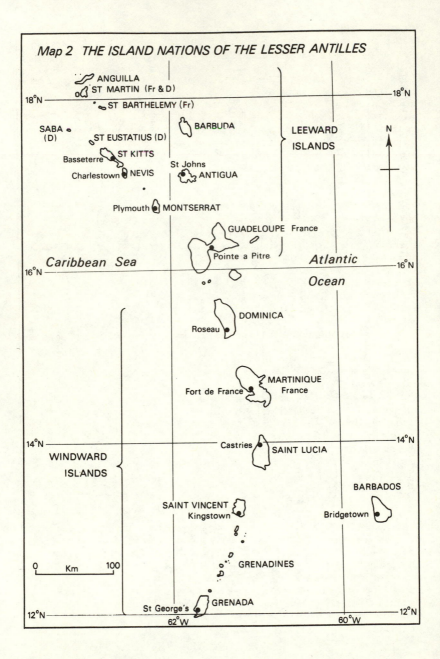

Map 2 THE ISLAND NATIONS OF THE LESSER ANTILLES

ANGUILLA
ST MARTIN (Fr & D)
18°N — ———————————————————————— 18°N
ST BARTHELEMY (Fr)

SABA
(D)   BARBUDA   LEEWARD
ST EUSTATIUS (D)   ISLANDS   N
Basseterre   ST KITTS
Charlestown NEVIS   St Johns
                      ANTIGUA

Plymouth MONTSERRAT

                GUADELOUPE France

Caribbean Sea   Pointe a Pitre   Atlantic
16°N — ———————————————————————— 16°N
                                Ocean

                    DOMINICA
         Roseau

                        MARTINIQUE
Fort de France   France

14°N — ——————————— Castries SAINT LUCIA —— 14°N
WINDWARD
ISLANDS
                                        BARBADOS

        SAINT VINCENT
        Kingstown   Bridgetown

                GRENADINES

0   Km   100

                GRENADA
St George's
12°N — ——————————————————————— 12°N
        62°W   60°W

The Legacy of Colonialism in West Indian Education

Given some understanding of the cultural and ecological facts of life on even very small West Indian islands, it is not at all self evident that political federations within the area are either necessary or desirable, as Clarke and Lowenthal (1981) convincingly illustrate in their spirited protaganism of Barbudan secession from a state of political dependency on Antigua which has obtained since 1860.(4) Smallness and insularity may not necessarilly be beautiful, but given political independence it may well have distinct advantages: An island that rules itself can prime its own pump. Like any local industry, a unit government creates business and employment. Autonomous islands can take advantage of money-raising schemes, like special coinage and postal issues for collectors, seldom available to dependencies. And their strategic location may gain them valuable bargains with great powers. The cost of self-government is more than compensated for by help from international agencies, little of which filters down to mere dependencies. Moreover, a self-governing island can set its own welfare priorities, allocating funds for services that a larger country would find unnecessary or uneconomic, while foregoing other expenditures that a larger state might require.' (Clarke 1976, 468).

Whether the colonial forces at work such as the possessive tendencies of larger islands, the desire of Britain to divest itself of former colonies and the neo-colonialism of the eudcational system will combine to thwart an independent option on the part of smaller islands remains to be seen. But it is already clear that the initiatives of CARIFTA and subsequently CARICOM(5) have indicated a capacity within the 'British West Indies' to accommodate both local and regional interests within an overall drive to reduce dependency in economic terms. Regional organisations in the educational field seem not to have been as successful, and this may have something to do with the capacity of colonialism to effect an infiltration of culture to the point where it becomes endemic.

With the exception of Haiti, the Francophone West Indies is politically part of France, and so the very direct form of colonialism characteristic of the former French Empire persists - the pros are also the cons. Surinam is now independent and so the Netherlands Antilles comprises only five-and-a-half small islands made up of the Leewards in the south and the Windwards in the north(6). Their political relationship with the metropole is that of junior partner in the Joint Kingdom of the Netherlands and the Netherlands Antilles, and therefore midway between that of the French Antilles and the majority of the 'British West Indies'. The remaining countries are either part of Latin America (Cuba and the Dominican Republic) or, to all intents and purposes, of the United States of America (Puerto Rico and the U.S. Virgin Islands), leaving Haiti, the first independent West Indian nation(7), to bring up a characteristically anomalous rear.

Having defined the use of the terms, legacy, education and West Indian in respect of this essay one must now take the fourth key word, _colonialism_, explain its variants and their place in the formulation of the analysis. As a starting point it is useful to consider the three forms of colonialism as defined by Altbach and Kelly (1978): classical colonialism, internal colonialism, and neocolonialism, and then add a fourth category: post-colonialism.

For the purposes of this analysis one would wish to divide classical colonialism into two phases: (i) pre-emancipation colonialism and (ii) post-emancipation colonialism. The watershed comes in the mid-nineteenth century as the effects of emancipation began to be felt in accordance with other manifestations of the political and economic development of post-Napoleonic Europe. Of particular significance for the West Indies was the shift from a simple pre-capitalist plantation economy to a corporate plantation economy with some capacity for diversification within the dependent territory. (Cross 1979). Concerning internal colonialism within the context of the West Indies one sees this as operating mainly through the development of formal instutionalised systems of education in the various dependencies, but also in some measure evident in post-independence regional structures. Neocolonialism is not merely a tendency for metropolitan influences to exhibit various forms of inertia after the granting of political independence. Indeed it constitutes the deliberate policies of the industrialised nations to maintain their domination. It may function through foreign-aid programs, technical advisers, publishing firms, or other means.' (Altbach and Kelly:30).

Here again, educational systems provide an obvious example of continued and contrived dependence. In view of the indirect rule operated by Britain in respect of its West Indian colonies, it is not suitable to view the onset of neocolonialism as being contemporaneous with the granting of political independence to the 'British West Indies' in the form of the aforementioned and ill-fated Federation in 1958. In any case, upon its demise in 1962 some components reverted to colonial status before, in most cases, moving on to full political independence as individual nation states.

So the three forms of colonialism as identified by Altbach and Kelly cannot be viewed as chronologically distinct, but so long as the problem of overlap is born in mind it is not unreasonable to take them in the same order as above, when examining each in terms of educational legacy. Before proceeding to this, however, one must consider the question of post-colonialism, by which is meant trends and movements

relating to colonialism as a phenomenon, operating in the
West Indies since the formal cessation of British colonialism
but not necessarilly related to it. It is obvious that neocolonialism comes into this, but we should also recognise (i)
new colonialism, (ii) regional metropolitanism and (iii)
decolonisation.

New colonialism is exhibited in the West Indies by
political powers other than those historically involved in
colonialism here (Britain, France, Netherlands, Spain, U.S.A.(8),
seeking to influence the island nations whether politically,
economically or culturally. The most obvious example of this
is the influence of the U.S.S.R. in Cuba, (Crozier 1973) which
although in detail is beyond the scope of this essay, nonethe
less has implications for the whole area. There are also the
colonial aspirations of nearby Latin American states such as
the consistent and organised interest of Venezuela in the
Windward islands, and Guatemalan claims on Belize. Indeed
the Caribbean region as a whole is regaining some of the
strategic significance on which many of the myths and stereo-
types of the West Indies so characteristic of imperial adven-
ture stories for British children were based. The stability
of the Caribbean is now a matter of considerable international
significance and concern. (Moss 1973).

The term regional metropolitanism refers to the tendency
in an area comprising a number of newly independent nations
for one of them to become dominant. This is very evident with
respect to groups of tropical island nations (Brock 1980),
and in terms of the 'British West Indies' is not just a case
of 'Jamaica versus the rest', it is rather a division between
the MDC's and the LDC's(9) with the virtual hold over higher
education enjoyed by the former group acting in a very metropolitan manner in respect of the latter. The regional university is an institutionalised example to which we shall
return in some detail, but the phenomenon of regional metropolitanism can also operate through such media as ideological
propaganda and various forms of aid to smaller nations, which
is not meant to indicate here that either is more or less
desirable. That would obviously be a matter for the target
nation(s) to decide, but it would likely bring some response
from other interested parties. Here again the influence of
Cuba, first in Jamaica and latterly in the Windward islands,
especially Grenada, has had significant effects on some
aspects of post-colonial educational philosophy and policy.

Finally in this introductory section we come to decolonisation, which has much to do with the development of indigenous culture and identity (Demas 1975). In the 'British
West Indies' with its historic subjection to the various forms
of colonialism already mentioned, such an objective is at
once both crucial, and very difficult to attain. It is
crucial because in the context of insularity and political
independence there will be little margin for error in the

125

future in respect of achieving a harmonious relationship
between the various elements comprising the island ecosystem.
As Spate (1963) rightly indicates, some sort of attitudinal
change is required that will accept the parameters of the
island ecosystem, while at the same time being sufficiently
flexible to absorb the effects of change in external forces
and relationships. Education systems inherited from the
colonial past and sustained by the neocolonial present do not
have the appropriate outlook. Their only demonstrable success
is to effect the escape of those selected and 'successful'.
They are so intrinsically colonial as to be a major constraint
on radical thinking. To achieve decolonisation is one thing,
but to learn to live with the consequences is another. Where
is such a radical change to come from but through the non-
formal strand of education, including the creative and
expressive arts?

HUMAN ECOLOGY, SOCIAL STRUCTURE AND CULTURE

It is now necessary to look in more detail at the
educational legacy of colonialism, bearing in mind that the
impact is sometimes direct and sometimes by proxy. Non-
education factors induced by colonialism may well have profound effects in educational terms, for education is in many
respects subordinate to context.

Despite, or perhaps because of, the fact that almost no
educational facilites were established during the first and
longest phase of colonialism in the West Indies, the legacy
of this period is probably more profound than any other in
educational terms. The period of pre-capitalist plantation
colonialism lasted from the early sixteenth century to the
mid-nineteenth century, and was based upon the supply of
slave labour from Africa. The story of the slave trade is
well known, and need not be repeated here, but the effect of
the system on the nature of West Indian societies as they
evolved is of prime significance to our consideration of the
colonial legacy in respect of education.

In the larger and more prosperous Spanish colonies of
the early days (Cuba, Hispaniola, Trinidad and to a lesser
extent Jamaica), where slavery, at least in terms of African
labour, was minimal, some seminaries were established.
Jamaica became a British colony in the mid-seventeenth century
and soon became the major importer of negro slaves in the
West Indies. It also ceased to be Catholic dominated and
acquired an Anglican base subsequently joined by the various
nonconformist churches. However, while slavery persisted
very few churches or missions in Jamaica or elsewhere in the
'British West Indies', with the possible exception of Barbados,
succeeded in establishing schools. There was no economic need
for the potential products of schooling in the economy then
obtaining, and the moral arguments of a minority of clergy

were easily contained by the power of the plantocracies.
Nonetheless, the formation of certain patterns of economic
and social structure during this period did provide a distinctive context for the post-emancipation development of educational provision. Three contextual elements will be
discussed here, all of which have retained their significance
right up to the present day. They are: human ecology, social
structure and culture.

Human ecology is concerned with the dynamic relationship
between man and his environment, in terms especially of
economy and domicile. This has to do therefore with patterns
of land utilisation and human settlement. The plantation
system imposed a situation whereby the bulk of the productive
and flat land was redered unavailable for family farming or
for settlement. This still obtains in many islands. In the
pre-corporate period the economic system acted against the
development of significant urban centres, with all that that
implies for education. Escaped, and later freed slaves had
to establish a new peasantry, not only without the skills
normally imparted in such societies through traditional non-
formal education, but also in locations most unsuitable for
rural settlement. The degree of marginality ranged from
extreme in the mountainous Windwards, to variable in Jamaica
and minimal in Trinidad and Barbados. It was not merely a
matter of physical geography, and certain social factors
assisted the moderation of disadvantage in some locations.
(Brock 1978).

Plantations survived emancipation, and still occupy land
that in Europe for example would have supported a more stable
rural economy and society. In the West Indies, when social
conditions eventually allowed the missions to establish
schooling, the more inaccessible the rural settlement clusters
the more difficult it was to provide it. Although a rural/
urban dichotomy in respect of educational provision and
performance exists in most countries of the world, the extra
geographical dimension applied here, conspires to maintain a
degree of rural disadvantage out of all proportion to the
small scale of the nations involved.

There are many variants of social structure in the West
Indies, but in most the relationships between race, colour
and class are a result of the combination of the rigid
divisions of a racist plantation system and a certain concept
of social class derived from the colonial society. Consequently
even before emancipation and the emergence of educational
provision, most societies of the 'British West Indies' exhibited
a tripartite structure compising a small white upper class,
the plantocracy, who sent their children to school in England;
a small creole class(10) - of mixed race and resulting from
liaison between planter and slave - who were favoured by the
plantocracy in terms of status and some educational support;
a large lower class, mostly black and with no access to

education. Although the relationships between race, colour
and class are less rigid and formalised today, there is still
a clear correspondance in terms of education and of status.
Status may be seen as the invidious ranking of others in terms
of deference, and 'what sets the colonial connection in the
Caribbean apart is that this pattern of deference is firmly
based on 'race' and the degree of approximation to white
ethnicity. It is a system which has endured and justified
descriminatory action from Carriacou to Cuba and which has
had the unanticipated consequence of encouraging urban
residence and deepening the mythology that places a rural way
of life at the lowest point on a hierarchy of personal aspir-
ation.' (Cross 1979: 118).

As we shall see below these social divisions tend to be
maintained by an educational system which in most West Indian
nations has developed on the principles of elitism and selection.

The third legacy of the first phase of colonialism that
has had important implications for education is that of culture, and one would wish to identify three elements of this in
particular: language, identity and religion. When slaves
were brought across from Africa they were deliberately dis-
persed within the West Indies so as to minimise communication
between them. In this way the cultural links with their
African origins were reduced almost to the point of extinction,
and this was especially significant with respect to the
linguistic structures developed by plantation slaves, and
also groups of escaped and later, freed slaves. In so far as
slaves were required or allowed to have language this normally
involved only a rudimentary acquisition of whatever elements
of English were deemed necessary. Since there was no formal
education at this time a wide variety of differing vernaculars
emerged even within individual islands, and these contained
both English and African elements. During this stage of
colonialism there was considerable competition for territorial
possession as between the various European powers, and it was
not uncommon for islands to change hands. This further
complicated the linguistic problem, especially if the colony
ended up under a colonial power which had not been dominant
there before. For example, Dominica and Saint Lucia were for
most of this formative period French colonies, but became
British in the post-Napoleonic rationalisation. Consequently
their people have a patois vernacular, but are required to
undertake their schooling in standard English. Even where
the vernacular is English based, there is still often a
conflict between the language of home and school, especially
as the local languages are often unwritten.

Problems of language deriving directly from the formative
period of colonialism, constitute a legacy with profound
educational implications for West Indians in Britain as well
as in the Caribbean. (Edwards 1979). A policy of mother

tongue teaching in the early years of schooling has proved
widely successful in terms of facilitating general linguistic
development in many parts of the 'developing world', but has
limitations in the West Indies due to the nature of patois
and creole vernaculars. It has also not been helped by the
sometimes ill-disguised contempt displayed by some members
of the educated, and therefore more colonised, elite who have
held responsibilities for educational policy and administration.

Religion, like language, in West Indian societies is
largely European derived but with an African input that varies
in discretion from place to place. As has been remarked
above, the churches and missions made little impact pre-
emancipation in providing schooling. But the formal sector
is not the only education, and the general religious activities
of the churches may be defined as being educational as well
as spiritual. At any rate they certainly strongly influenced
the social context into which formal education was eventually
introduced, and they were also the media of introduction.

As Barrett describes with respect to Jamaica, the
Catholic and Anglican churches confined their activities to
the white elite so that 'The urge to consider the state of
religion maong the slaves was brought about by the entrance
of the Moravians in 1734, the Methodists in 1736, the Baptists
in 1783, and the Presbyterians in 1823. These nonconformist
denominations were a real threat to the establishment, finding
ready ears among the slaves and winning over large numbers to
their cause. The loose rituals of these churches - especially
the early Methodists and Baptists with their spirit-filled
enthusiasm - fit beautifully the exuberant religion of the
slaves and brought about an early syncretism between
Christianity and various African religions.' (Barrett 1977:20).

Although the practice of African religions among the slaves
was forbidden, it was carried on clandestinely in modified
form. This is generally known as 'obeah' and is associated
with sorcery and witchcraft. In that this was to some extent
a ritual aggression against slavery and white domination, it
provided in pre-emancipation societies in the West Indies a
basis on which later Afro-Christian movements were to develop.
Some of these are very significant today, and in general act
against the operation of formal schooling, which when added
to the normally reactionary stance taken by the Christian
churches in respect of educational reform in current West
Indian societies places religion clearly in the vanguard of
influences constraining the radical rethinking demanded by
Demas as an essential component of decolonisation.

This brings us to identity, obviously closely related
to language and religion, but also to insularity. In the
West Indies, despite a considerable development of independence, confidence and status when viewed from outside in the
brief post-colonial period to date, there is still an endemic
even paranoic concern with the question of identity. This is

a problem for colonised peoples throughout the world, but it
has been rendered chronic in Caribbean communities by the
virtual destruction of true links with the African cultures
from which the slaves derived, and the incomplete and fragmented acquisition of European cultural elements during the
formative colonial period. The result has been a tendency to
denigrate local products be they agricultural, manufactured
or even cultural. One of the strongest legacies of slavery,
and deepened by insularity has been a yearning for the culture
and identity of the metropole. The creation of artifical
communities on tiny areas of land with in most cases no
conceivable future in terms of widespread modernisation is
deeply resented. The legacy of colonialism is that they are
tnere at all, stuck between past and future with imperfect
connections both ways. One modern Caribbean writer, albeit
more pessimistic than most has categorised the West Indies
as 'manufactured societies', 'labour camps' and 'creations of
empire'. Building on the issue of bondage he has written:
'It has been said that in concentration camps the inmates began
after a time to believe that they were genuinely guilty.
Pursuing the Christian-Hellenic tradition, the West Indian
accepted his blackness as his guilt, and divided people into
the white, fusty, musty, dusty, tea, coffee, cocoa, light
black, dark black. He never seriously doubted the validity
of the prejudices of the culture to which he aspired. In
the French territories he aimed at Frenchness; in the Dutch
territories at Dutchness; in·the English territories he
aimed at simple whiteness and modernity, Englishness being
impossible.' (Naipaul 1969: 73).
     One of the implications of all this for the development
of education when it was eventually allowed to exist in the
post-emancipation period was an uncritical acceptance of its
structures and contents, and a profound belief in the
efficacy of educational attainment in terms of upward social
mobility, and an attendant identity. That such a faith has
been for most unfounded and misguided is only becoming
apparent in the post-independence context of constraint,
whether it be within the narrow confines of a sub-tropical
mini-state or the beleaguered Caribbean enclaves of British
cities. So despite the virtual absence of educational
initiative and provision in the first phase of classical
colonialism its legacy has been a profound and decisively
negative one in terms of the ecological, sociological and
cultural context bequeathed to its successors.

THE GROWTH OF INTERNAL COLONIALISM

     The second stage of classical colonialism in the West
Indies, that of the diversifying economy of the corporatist
plantation system occupied approximately a hundred years,
from the mid-nineteenth century to mid-twentieth. During

this period of more concentrated and politically systematised colonialism, occurred the establishment of systems of formal schooling in the various territories. We may therefore associate the phenomenon of internal colonialism with this process since not only did the structures of the education systems institutionalise the social divisions already evident, but in addition the colonial culture was instilled through the curriculum. There are aristocratic and conservative modes of control in a former slave society. There must also be notions of subordination and superordination and forms of social differentiation which create an educated leisurely class. This class is saved from manual work of any kind. While it is subordinate to the class of English rulers, it is superordinate to the vast majority of the population. Colonial education supported such a system. (Jervier 1977: 20-21).

Formal schooling was established on the momentum of emancipation. The 'negro problem' largely ignored for centuries, began to claim the attention of benefactors and humanitarians, to say nothing of the churches. It might not be an exaggeration to suggest that for a brief period in the mid-nineteenth century schooling and teacher training, especially in Jamaica, claimed more attention among the English liberal establishment than did the indigenous poor whom the churches were seeking to exclude from educational opportunity. Nonetheless this fleeting altruism soon became appropriated by the contextual forces already obtaining and discussed in the previous section: human ecology, social structure and culture.

Corporatism assisted urbanisation but maintained the plantations, and thereby the continued exclusion of the peasantry from the best land. But this was now a peasantry swollen by emancipation, and so while for a few urban opportunity appeared, for the majority rural disadvantage deepened. The churches set about the task of providing primary education on the assumption of it being terminal, especially in rural areas. There was little or no articulation with secondary education, which emerged as a highly selective sector access to which was already appropriated by the whites and creoles who were in any case associated disproportionately with the expanding urban economies. Education was synonymous with selective secondary schooling, and yet the vested interests behind such schools, often denominational, rendered them something apart from the system. Whereas primary school teachers were rarely educated beyond that level, secondary teachers were often graduates of British universities.

Despite a considerable amount of individual effort, the erection of innumerable systems of educational administration, and the formulation of a number of major reports (Gordon 1963, 1968) after a century of educational development, clear characteristics of divisiveness, elitism, disparity,

irrelevance and above all inertia prevailed. Another major
scholar of West Indian education observed of the secondary
sector in the mid-twentieth century, that 'the curriculum is
divorced from the real needs of the community and the activity
and experience of the pupils, with the qualification that it
might be said that the secondary school virtually makes a
fetish of this unreality.' (Williams 1951: 31).

Such characteristics were assisted in their persistence
by the   lack of any policy on education in the West Indies on
the part of Britain unitl 1923 when The Advisory Committee on
Education was set up. Even then, since this body was concerned
with British colonies throughout the world only minimal
attention was paid to the West Indies. In fact for most of
the period in question the organisation and financing of
education in each territory was a local responsibility.
Consequently, not only was each system unique in detail, some
were much better resourced than others. Each island also had
a particular combination of religious influences responsible
for schools, though most tended to be very traditional and
conservative. Furthermore colonial administrators under the
Crown Colony system had the power to indulge their individual
whims with respect to education inter-alia, and sometimes did.
In view of the social origins of such individuals they rarely
took the form of a critical appraisal of educational provision
and performance in terms of the needs of the local economy
and the mass of the population.

Crucial to the maintenance of an elitist system is of
course the question of selection, where again, differentials
of race, colour, and class are significant. Scholarships to
secondary school tend to be won by urban primary pupils who
are more likely to be well prepared, at home as well as in
school, for selection examinations. Where there is less of a
divide between urban and rural society, as in Trinidad and
Barbados, the free scholarship record of rural children is
correspondingly better than in say Jamaica where a combination
of physical geography and a more severe legacy from slavery
in sociological terms, still engender rural disadvantage.
Despite the odds, however, the elitism enshrined in that
greatest of glittering colonial prizes, the island scholarship,
concentrated the efforts of urban and rural pupils alike in
intense competition. They 'plagued' the curricular system,
selecting a field more susceptible to cramming, which on the
whole meant the furthering of the status of classics and
literature. Foner (1973) was able to illustrate very clearly
the aspirations of certain rural Jamaican communities in
respect of their children, and how these hopes are enhanced
in successive generations. There can be a blind, almost
desperate faith in education as a panacea, so that:
'Educational statistics and reports do not record the pathetic
efforts made by parents to afford the high fees and so provide
the secondary education that is the avenue to white-collar

jobs. Rather one would have to consult the records of people's co-operative banks and local money lenders.' (Williams E.:39).

During this period the development of higher education in the West Indies was almost entirely confined to the establishment of teacher training colleges as part of the drive to support negro education in the nineteenth century. But these were few, concentrated in the larger islands and operated a curriculum of secondary rather than tertiary level. The real higher education dominating the curriculum and aspirations of West Indian secondary education was the university sector in the metropole to which the various island scholars migrated. Many such scholars remained in Britain - an intellectual exploitation every bit as colonialist as its economic counterpart. A number of abortive attempts were in fact made to establish some sort of university in the area during the period of classical colonialism, notably in Bermuda, Barbados and Jamaica, but the white and creole classes were unsupportive, preferring to enjoy the established facilities and status of Oxford, Cambridge or London.

Eventually, in the early years of this century a true institution of higher education was established in Trinidad of the 'West India College of Agriculture', but this soon became the 'Imperial College of Tropical Agriculture' catering for the entire British Empire, and supported by vested colonial agricultural interests. In the event it was not until almost mid-century that a university was created in the West Indies, and then it was profoundly colonial, for: 'although vaguely conceived of as serving West Indian interests in a West Indian context, the University was primarily thought of as a projection of the best of British abroad. The University was not to be autonomous, but would develop as a college of the University of London. ....The fact that the British government was prepared to make a capital grant meant that local legislatures and politicians never came to grips with the serious problems of financing a university in the area. The affiliation to London guaranteed the middle classes that the 'standards' to which they were accustomed would not be violated.' (Braithwaite 1965: 79).

By the end of the period of classical colonialism then the 'British West Indies' had acquired an education system of an extremely elitist and selective nature because its prime objective was to serve the needs and interests of the West Indian intelligensia as perceived by themselves and their colonial masters. Institutionalised education of this type merely confirmed the profoundly pluralist nature of West Indian society according to the qualifications put forward by Farrell (1967), and based on Smith (1965). Given the widespread provision of primary schooling by 1960, the picture of educational attainment portrayed in the Commonwealth Caribbean Census of that year and abstracted by Roberts and Abdulah (1965) is a clear condemnation of the disparate and divisive legacy of colonialism as operated under 'indirect-rule'.

Table 7.1 Educational Attainment 1960: Population 15 Years and Over

Island	Percentage of Total Adult Population				
	No Education	Primary Education	Secondary, No School Certificate	Secondary, with School Certificate	University
Antigua	3.3	83.1	9.4	1.9	0.4
Barbados	1.8	80.2	11.4	4.5	0.6
Dominica	13.4	79.0	4.8	1.6	0.5
Grenada	6.7	84.7	5.4	2.3	0.5
Jamaica	16.8	74.4	3.9	2.8	0.3
Montserrat	11.1	81.1	2.3	2.0	0.4
St. Kitts Nevis	3.8	89.1	4.1	1.8	0.4
St. Lucia	26.2	69.7	2.2	1.1	0.3
St. Vincent	7.9	85.4	4.2	1.6	0.3
Trinidad and Tobago	11.3	72.9	9.9	3.7	0.7
Virgin Islands	3.2	88.0	4.0	2.2	0.5
All Islands	13.4	75.3	6.2	3.0	0.5

Note: Percentages for 'not stated' are excluded.

(Source: Braithwaite 1965: 145)

The Legacy of Colonialism in West Indian Education

It is very clear from Table 7.1 that the disruption and
disadvantage faced by the majority of West Indians in the
form of slavery had not been significantly recompensed by the
provision of a form of secondary education particularly as
the latter was difficult of access. The contextual factors
of plantation economy, human ecology, social structure and
culture, especially language find their further limiting
expression through an education system acting even more
effectively than most as an agent of internal colonialism.
Such was the legacy with which so many hopeful West
Indian migrants set off for England in the 1950s and 1960s.
Presumably they saw their journey as one of decolonisation,
but little did they know that the colonial experience
peculiar to the slave societies of the Caribbean had already
condemned them to a greater educational disadvantage in the
metropolitan system than that encountered by their fellow
immigrants from Asia. Such was, and is, the degree of
correspondance between the structurally and linguistically
divisive educational systems of Britain and the 'British West
Indies' that they simply moved from the bottom of one heap to
the bottom of another.

THE POST INDEPENDENT COLONIAL LEGACY

Returning to the Caribbean we have finally to consider
the legacy of colonialism in the 'Post-Independence West
Indies'. To what extent have the forces of neocolonialism,
new colonialism and regional metropolitanism affected
educational provision during the last twenty years, and what
are the educational implications of a definite commitment to
decolonisation?
Political independence as enjoyed by most of the 'British
West Indies' for well over a decade, albeit by some of the
Windwards and Leewards in the form of Associated Statehood
for all or most of that time, has provided an opportunity to
rectify or at least moderate some of the significant constraints
of the colonial legacy in education. As Jervier (1977:8)
rightly states, in the Caribbean milieu, 'Jamaica often serves
as a role model', and it is here that the earliest and most
extensive attempts to widen access to schooling were carried
out. Junior Secondary schools were introduced in both urban
and rural areas to offer a higher general education to those,
the majority not proceeding to selective secondary education,
i.e. grammar schools.
They were conceived as a radical alternative, but subsequently became appropriated by the elitism of the ongoing
system, and were upgraded and redesigned as New Secondary
schools. In his analysis of education and society in contem-
porary Jamaica, Miller (1976) shows clearly how both schooling
and further/higher education are still very closely related
to social strata differentiated on the basis of both colour

The Legacy of Colonialism in West Indian Education

and class. He also indicates that while all areas of post-
school education are more open in this respect to people from
the lower social classes, in fact they still tend to be under-
represented at this level due to the greater degree of discrimination active at school level. It is through the selective
secondary sector, and also a strong private sector that
Jamaica remains elitist in terms of education despite genuine
large scale efforts to widen educational opportunity. He
concludes that because of its relationship with the social
order, education 'cannot be expected to operate in such a way
that it would create radical, revolutionary or even substantial
changes in the social order. The best that can be expected
is that dysfunctionality will occur, because of tensions between social strata, and that this will result in certain
evolutionary changes both in the educational system and the
social order.' (Jervier: 65).

However it is also clear in Jamaica and in other nations
of the 'British West Indies' that powerful groups with vested
interests will seek to appropriate, divert or at the very
least, minimise reforms with egalitarian objectives. Thus in
many islands the middle or professional classes and the
churches have argued for the status quo inherited from
colonialism. In so doing the churches are fighting for their
distinctive and historic role as the provider of education
and in particular the status of the selective secondary school.
Thus it would seem that structurally at any rate a neo-
colonialist inertia is still effective in the compulsory
sector.

What about curriculum reform and development with respect
to reducing colonialist influences? In order to break the
colonial connection and influence the nations of the 'British
West Indies' have collectively instituted the Caribbean
Examinations Council, with headquarters both in Jamaica and
Barbados. This is to replace the Cambridge and London GCE
examinations currently still being offered at 'O' and 'A'
level. Progress has been slow and co-operation between member
states difficult to obtain in some areas, due to the genuinely
individual nationality and culture of different West Indian
states. The outcome has on the whole been to produce
syllabuses and examinations not radically different in style
from their predecessors. In other words the colonial model
has persisted. Such an outcome has been inevitable, given
the anxieties of parents in particular in respect of the
status and equivalence of the certificates gained, for
proceeding either to employment or higher education. In the
context of certain subjects there has been a marked shift
towards the West Indies, and even individual home environments.
Social Studies has been especially flexible in this way, but
unfortunately is often available only to less able classes
in some secondary sectors.

The delicate position of the CXC, balanced as it is

between radical decolonising pressures on the one hand and
reactionary neocolonialist forces on the other can be sensed
in the guarded phraseology of a fact sheet it produced in
1978 partly to attempt to allay public apprehension at the
time of the first papers: 'It (CXC) looks forward to authorising syllabuses, conducting examinations and issuing certificates
which will reflect and satisfy the needs and aspirations of
the vast majority of the English-speaking Caribbean public.'
(Caribbean Examinations Council, 1978). CXC has clearly had
some success in decolonising parts of the curriculum, and has
potential for more, but it is not yet a radical reply to the
problem.

Curriculum change has also been in the hands of individual
governments, especially in respect of primary and lower
secondary schooling, and some have established curriculum
development centres. However the style and organisation of
such innovations is, like CXC, for the most part based on
British and North American models. The School of Education
of the University of the West Indies has also been involved
in a number of regional schemes of curriculum development,
notably in mathematics and science. Such projects normally
involve 'experts' provided under the auspices of various aid
agencies such as UNDP, USAID and ODA, and this has both neo-
colonialist and new colonialist implications.

Indeed the University of the West Indies itself,
'conceived of as a "parting gift" of the United Kingdom
Government', (Braithwaite: 79) represents the major motor of
neocolonialist inertia in West Indian Education. Like CXC,
but to a much greater extent, it also operates as a force for
regional metropolitanism. In a comparative examination of
this phenomenon pertaining to the Caribbean and the South
Pacific island groups one may conclude that problems 'are
especially evident in the areas of higher education, external
examinations, teacher education and curriculum development.
All are associated with intra-regional political friction and
rivalry and the role of the university. Clearly nations of
this size cannot support a university each, and so in both
regions all member states contribute proportionally to the
costs of, respectively the University of the West Indies and
the University of the South Pacific. Inevitably the main
campus of each is located in the largest and most powerful
nation i.e. Jamaica and Fiji. UWI also has substantial
campuses in Trinidad and Barbados, both classified as 'more
developed countries' within the Caribbean Community. It is
clear that both UWI and USP tend to benefit the core rather
than the periphery of their respective regions. Quite apart
from academic considerations, they represent a growth industry
in the form of a multiplier effect, stimulating a large number
of jobs. More seriously perhaps, a fair amount of intellectual
talent has been drained from the smaller to the larger islands.'
(Brock 1980: 76-77).

Although the University of the West Indies has carried
out research programmes beneficial to the local economy, in
general it is too near the academic model of a British university to be a constructive force for post-colonial reconstruction
One cannot apportion blame to current staff who are bound to
operate through the normal channels of a university system of
world wide inter-connections concerned mainly with teaching
and research. In the context of the West Indies, Braithwaite
would like to see three other functions foremost in the role
of the university, namely: the maintenance of cultural
traditions on the higher level; the development of national
cultural patterns; and an advisory and leadership role in
modern society. It is difficult for a university representing
a group of nations so unified in some respects, yet so diversified in others to meet such a variety of radical needs in
the post-independence context of increasing insularity and
economic stress.

CONCLUSIONS

One would conclude that in its various forms, colonialism
has been a dominant force in West Indian education, and
continues to be so. It provided the context, ecological,
social and cultural, within which education had to develop.
Unlike Asia, Africa - excepting the south of South Africa -
and to some extent Latin America, West Indian societies began
with colonialism(11), and consequently do not have what
Naipaul describes as 'their own internal reverencies' to be
returned to them after political independence. They are, in
their very being, one of the most enduring legacies of
European colonialism to be found anywhere in the world.
Looking briefly to the future, the nations of the
'British West Indies' face the challenge of a life and
economy more insular and restricted than before. For
education this means adaptation to more localised objectives.
Given that the whole emphasis of colonialism on and within
education in the area has been in the opposite direction,
this is going to be a monumentally difficult task, and a
truly revolutionary one. For the smaller island nations this
will be particularly difficult, unless, as in the case of
Barbuda already referred to, there exists an evolved ecological
relationship that appears to be well adjusted, and which can
be preserved from the perils of any new, more regional
colonialism. Such examples are rare in the Caribbean.
It is then in a context of endemic and all pervading
colonialism that any call for decolonisation must be evaluated,
and given that educational systems in the West Indies have
been in the vanguard of cultural bondage, it is somewhat
ironical that some of the most strident calls for decolonisation made by Demas have been made in the form of addresses
at graduation ceremonies in the Universities of the West

Indies and Guyana respectively. 'One is·struck by the slowness
with which new ideologies of development and social change
relevant to the West Indian experience and West Indian needs
are developing. For the most part we remain prisoners of
either explicit or implicit ideologies (whether of Liberal
Capitalism, Communism or West European Social Democracy)
developed abroad to suit other peoples experience and needs
decades and sometimes even centuries ago. Undoubtedly we
are still to a large extent intellectually colonised.'
(Demas: 55).

This being so, one would suggest that the necessary
shift in educational philosophy to achieve such a fundamental
reversal of attitudes, cannot be operated within the existing
structures of schooling. As with all forms of dependency, the
connivance of the local elite is a necessary element, and it
is particularly difficult to convince such a group of the
inappropriateness of the very quality that set them apart.
In any case, bearing in mind the faith of the mass of West
Indians in 'education for salvation' any espousal of radical
change in this field would be tantamount to political
suicide. There would seem to be not only a dilemma but an
impasse.

NOTES

1. The term 'Caribbean' comprises not only the West
Indian islands, but also the Caribbean Basin and the surrounding
land and sea areas, the Circum-Caribbean.
2. The less obviously colonial term 'Anglophone Caribbean'
is inappropriate here becasue attention is not given to the
American Virgin Islands or The Dutch Windwards in this paper.
3. An internally self-governing state with foreign
affairs and defence in the hands of the United Kingdom.
4. This was a British, not an Antiguan decision, and
the link has never been integral.
5. Following the failure of the political federation
(1958-62) members of the British West Indies have attempted
economic links instead, first CARIFTA, the Caribbean Free
Trade Area, and the CARICOM, the Caribbean Community.
6. This is comprisingly the reverse of the 'British
West Indies' islands of the Lesser Antilles where the Windwards are in the South and the Leewards are in the North.
7. Haiti became independent as a result of the slave
revolt led by Toussant L'Ouverture in 1880.
8. On a smaller scale and for limited periods of time,
Denmark, Seden and some of the German states had Colonies in
the 'West Indies'. Also Portugal was also active in the area.
9. Within the 'Caricom' group, Jamaica, Guyana, Barbados
and Trinidad and Tobago are recognised as 'More Developed
Countries' (MDCs) while the remainder are 'Less Developed
Countries' (LDCs).

10. Also known as 'free people of Colour'.
11. The indigenous Caribs and Arawaks having been virtually exterminated by the early colonisation of the West Indies.

Chapter Eight

NEOCOLONIALISM AND EDUCATION IN LATIN AMERICA

Beatrice Avalos

BACKGROUND

In Latin America neocolonialism is the state by which the
region remains to a large extent economically dependent on the
industrialised world after almost two centuries of political
independence. Whether this is the consequence of structural
requirements of the advanced countries to maintain their
status quo is a matter of judgement.

After the depression of the 1930s it was thought that by
emphasising national development, industrial modernisation,
and social reforms aimed at greater popular participation the
Latin American countries would progress toward economic development and would assert themselves as independent nations both
economically and culturally(1). The decade of the fifties
manifested however a growing process of concentration of
capitalist production under the hegemony of the United States.
The emergence of multinational corportations and their
increasing control over the resources of the nations the
world, especially the poor world, slowly led to the realisation
that a contradictory force was at work: it would be difficult
for the poor nations to accumulate sufficient capital and
increase their production in order to compete with the power
of anonymous trans-national corporations. In practice this
process seemed to indicate that dependent economies are not
simply confined to being exporters of raw materials but that
they are also internally characterised by an increasing de-
nationalisation of capital, the acceptance of outside technology, and the submission to control by outside markets
(Labarca et al.1977). Thus, nearing the end of the sixties
Latin Americanists were denouncing the former beliefs that
'Latin American development is the work and creation of a
nationalist, progressive, enterprising, and dynamic middle
class, and the social and economic policy objectives of the
Latin American governments should be to stimulate "social
mobility" and the development of that class' (Stavenhagen 1969).
No matter how rapid the growth of the middle class in Latin

America the growth of the lower income groups in the countryside and the city was even greater. On the other hand, the
middle classes did not appear to want independence in any true
sense of the word. Instead they are:
economically and socially dependent on the upper strata; they
are tied politically to the ruling class; they are conservative
in their tasts and opinions, defenders of the status quo; and
they search for individual privileges. Far from being nationalists, they like everything foreign - from imported clothing
to the Reader's Digest. They constitute a true reflection of
the ruling class, deriving sizable benefits from the internal
colonial situation. This group constitutes the most important
support for military dictatorships in Latin America.'
(Stavenhagen 1969).

These words become all the more clear when one considers
for example the situation of Chile after the 1973 military coup
The coup was possible due to an encounter of external power
and interests supported by the United States(2) with efforts
from former power groups and the middle classes in Chile.
Thus, six years after the events the effect of redistributive
policies of former governments (in the sixties and early
seventies) had been practically annulled, allowing a few
economic groups to control the country's economy (Dahse 1979)
and minimise nationalised industry(3). What has been however
most interesting in this process is the total acceptance of
economic dependency as an inevitable fact thus reversing the
belief of the earlier populist-nationalist movements in Latin
America. Santiago, the capital city of Chile, like other
South American capitals is filled with imported products to meet
the tastes of the upper middle-income groups while unemployment continues to near 14%.

There are a number of ways of interpreting the dependent
relationship between the poor countries and the developed
world which fall under the general umbrella of dependency
theory(4). Fairly widespread is Theotonio dos Santos' (1970)
characterisation of a new dependency opposed to and distinct
from the older colonial financial and industrial dependecy
prevalent at the end of the nineteenth century. The new
dependency is linked to the emergence of the multinational
corporations at the end of the second World War and is of an
industrial-technological kind. It is the situation by which
the economy of the dependent country is conditioned by the
expansion of another economy to which it is subjected. The
economy of such a country (the dominant one) 'can expand and
can be self-sustaining, while the other countries (the dependent
ones) can do this only as a reflection of that expansion which
can have either a positive or a negative effect on their
immediate development' (Santos 1968: 6). From another theoretic
perspective Lagos and Godoy (1977) consider the notion of
'international stratification'. They define the world as a
'vast social system composed of many nation-states occupying

142

varying positions within the system, each nation interacting
with the others. The position of a country within a strati-
fied international system can be expressed in terms of
economic status, power and prestige; these three factors
determine its real status (pp. 12-13). Economic status is
indicated by the level of economic and technological development; power by the use of technology for development of
resources, the ratio of its defense budget in relation to its
GNP and the financing necessary for participation in the
technological component of the arms race; prestige is the
synthesis of a country's economic and military status, and the
degree of harmony between its international conduct and those
said principles and values considered to be essential to the
international system. To give a simple indication of the
position of the Latin American countries in this respect,
Lagos and Godoy refer to the fact that total annual sales
registered by the three largest United States corporations
surpass the GNP of Brazil and that the total annual sales of
the ITT surpass the combined GNP of the five Central American
countries.

HISTORICAL NOTES

   To understand in what way economic neocolonialism may be
linked to cultural and educational dependency it may be of
use to refer to some aspects of Latin America's educational
development.
   From the start of their independent history the Latin
American nations looked to Europe for inspiration to model
their new educational institutions. The early ideas of
independence were born through contact with the French
Enlightenment and nurtured by British liberalism. Education
was seen as a means of preparing the political leaders and
the widening of its coverage would stimulate the needed
process of national integration. Thus faced with emergency
requirements the Lancasterian system of schooling was introduced in the newly independent countries of Chile, Argentina,
Peru and by Simon Bolivar in the north of South America.
The system also reached Mexico.
   The conflict between conservatives and liberals in the
nineteenth century reflected the European struggles regarding
the role of the State and the participation of the middle
classes in power politics. In this struggle, the expansion
and control of education became an essential issue. Latin
American liberalism supported the notion of the State as
responsible for education thus opposing the conservative
notion that education is a private concern and it should
come under the control of the Church. Liberals considered
education as a powerful means of building up the new nations
and civilising its population by bringing it into the mainstream of European culture. An early link between culture

and economics can be observed through the thought of some educationists such as the Chilean Manuel Montt and the Argentine Domingo Faustino Sarmiento who hold that education is not only a spiritual process; but that it leads to practical concerns that have to do with economic development. Hence, their admiration for French culture and for British economy is noticeable. At the root of the establishment of the University of Buenos Aires, for example, there is the French model of education which was also to be adopted throughout South America. As Weinberg (1977) puts it, the new university represented a clear break with former patterns, inasmuch as one perceives through it a sense of nationality and secularism on the one hand, while on the other its criteria respond to the new ideas coming from Europe but above all to something quite significant: the Agricultural and Industrial revolution which not only endeavours to express the new relations of production and commerce, but also to inspire a new attitude to life, society and culture. (1977: 32-3).

The second part of the nineteenth century evidenced the emergence of the notion of 'popular education'. As expressed by the Mexican statesman Benito Juarez primary free education is a basic human right but its exercise is limited because of poverty: 'The will to know and to learn is innate in all men. If you remove the barriers caused by poverty and oppression man will learn naturally, even without direct protection. The causes of such poverty are well known amongst us'. (1871: 561-62). In the Southern Cone, Domingo Faustino Sarmiento is the most powerful exponent of 'popular education'. His source of inspiration was largely the American Horace Mann and fascinated by the possibilities of the European industrial and agricultural revolution and by the frontier expansion in the United States, he advocated the transformation of the rudimentary livestock-economy of Argentina into an advanced agricultural and cattle-raising economy(5); the development of primary education was an essential condition for such a purpose. By preparing needed human resources education could become a decisive variable in the social and economic transformation of the Latin American countries (Weinberg 1977). Given this sort of emphasis, secondary education was seen as directed only to the elite that would later attend the university and constitute the political leadership of the Latin American countries, a picture not too different from that prevailing in Spain and Portugal.

The influence of positivism permeates the latter part of the nineteenth century and the early part of the present one. In its Spencerian and Comtean variations and as expressed in local terms positivism pushed for order as a means to progress even when such order might mean curtailment of freedom. Its social philosophy justified the expansion of the economy to benefit the landowners by the building of roads, railways, bridges to improve communications and exports. The requirement of political stability for such a programme of material improvements led the liberals to adopt more conservative positions which went to support the position of the bourgeoie and landowners but had nothing to say for the neglected indigenous population (Weinberg 1977). It was not to their Indians that the Latin Americans would turn for help in the development of their countries but to European immigrants such as the Germans in Chile and Brazil.

With the emergence in the mid-thirties of more nationalist and populist types of governments in Mexico, Brazil, Peru, Bolivia, Chile, there is renewed concern to look at educational provisions, especially at the coverage and quality of the system. However, not much was altered of the French structure already dominating secondary and higher education, nor of the encylopaedic contents of such education, which borrowed from German ideas. But the new American pragmatism had also begun to pave its way into the systems, at least through its rhetoric of 'education for democracy'. As in the late nineteenth century primary education continues to be a central policy for populist governments; but they advocate such expansion in the hope of securing support from the industrial urban proletariat who demand greater opportunities in the educational system to secure their chances for social mobility.

Looking back on the nineteenth and early twentieth century developments in education there are two facts that stand out: the emergence of educational ideas that draw on European culture but that also consider the particular context of Latin America, and the elitist character of educational provisions that only slowly expanded to incorporate segments of the working class. There was, therefore, a certain degree of cultural dependency but also a great deal of internal colonialism that in fact ruled out the indigeneous groups from participation in the educational process.

The discussion of neocolonialism in current day education in Latin America is complex. On the one hand, the type of cultural dependency that has been observed through the above historical notes does not seem to have been substantially altered, while on the other hand, the new economic conditions of the world and the ideologies that support these conditions present new forms of influence less linked to the needs of the Latin American nations. Thus, although it was possible to speak in the nineteenth century of a Europeanisation of culture and of French and German influences, these were mediated by thinkers such as Andres Bello or Sarmiento who maintained a sense of national concern. Today, even though such thinkers exist, the power of the media, the international system of diffusion of culture and the rise of what one might call the 'technocracy of education' make it extremely difficult for Latin America to pursue its own thinking about education in a way such that it might deal with the region's social, cultural, and economic transformation.

Neocolonialism in education and culture can be seen as
the power exerted by industrialised nations to attract Third
World elites to their centres of intellectual life (Altbach
and Kelly 1978) and the interest that these elites have of
maintaining educational systems in their countries which
secure their position. In the particular case of Latin
America cultural neocolonialism seems to be rooted in the
region's economic dependence, particularly on the United
States. As Celso Furtado (1969) indicates the question of
Latin American development is 'what type of "development" the
United States envisages for Latin America'. The question is
answered today more in terms of what the great American business corporations want and is reflected in a policy of pre-
ventive control of 'subversion' (e.g. Guatemala 1956; Chile
1973)(6). Thus the assumption might well be that given an
alliance of interests between the United States and its
corporations and the internal economic groups in Latin America,
there will be a certain type of control over ideas, cultural
expressions, forms and structures of education within these
countries. The more complacent the political power to such
interests the greater the possibility of outside control.
This, of course, does not occur in a pure form. Even in the
regimes most closely aligned to international capitalism and
most severely repressive such as Chile there is some struggle
for the development of educational alternatives which run
counter to the imposed norms.(7) Developments do occur,
thinkers do appear, experiences get under way which challenge
prevailing modes and thus do not allow cultural invasion to
be totally triumphant. Popular theatre, literature, folk
music and art are other expressions of the capacity to
counteract domination. But the general picture of Latin
America is still one of cultural control. Neither individ-
ually as nations nor collectively as a region has Latin
America been able to achieve true independence. This is the
perspective that is reflected in what is to be discussed
below.

THE IDEOLOGY OF EDUCATIONAL CHANGE

The process of change in the educational systems of
Latin America in the past twenty five years or so has had a
fairly consistent direction throughout the region. This is
not necessarily the result of the analysis of a common reality
(there are vast differences between the countries)(8) but it
seems largely to be due to the influence of international
agencies both within and outside the United Nations' group.
Their criteria for change has largely been accepted throughout Latin America.
Several UNESCO meetings at the end of the forties, during
the fifties, and at the beginning of the sixties contributed
substantially to the framing of what might be called a

developmentalist approach to educational change (Cf. Solari
1977). A listing of these would include the Regional Educational Seminar (Caracas 1948), the Conference on Free and
Compulsory Education (sponsored by the OAS and UNESCO 1956)
and the Second Inter-American Meeting of Ministers of Education and Ministers responsible for Economic Planning in the
countries of Latin America and the Caribbean (Beunos Aires
1966), the Conference of Ministers of Education and Those
Responsible for the Promotion of Science and Technology in
Relation to Development (Caracas 1971), the Meeting of Experts
on the Implementation of the Recommendations of the Venezuela
Conference, Panama (1976) and the latest Conference of Ministers
of Education and Those Responsible for Economic Planning of
Member States in Latin America (Mexico City 1979). Papers
for all these meetings were prepared either by UNESCO teams
or by local experts including Latin Americans working in
organisations such as ECLA (UN Economic Commission for Latin
America). Receptivity to the ideas set forth was made
possible due to the increasing number of Latin Americans who
were either educated abroad (post-graduate studies) or were
acquainted with international views on education through
occupying policy positions and/or having travelled extensively
to international meetings.

The conferences referred to above jointly make up the
thinking about education and provide the directives for change
which were to permeate the years that followed the Santiago
UNESCO conference of 1962. Such meetings sponsored the
gathering of an enormous amount of data about the educational
systems of the countries involved which in fact allowed, as
stated by Lema and Marquez (1979) technical co-operation as
offered by UNESCO to be based on 'well-documented prior
knowledge of the state of education as a whole as well as of
the specific situations and the particular problems which had
to be solved'.

Which then were the dominant ideas of this period? In
the span between the fifties and the sixties it is difficult
to speak of a specific set of dominant ideas except for the
ntoion that to develop education in the poor countries it was
necessary to know about their real situation and to stimulate
the obviously crucial components of the system. Thus there
was support for diagnosis and mapping of the educational
area; there was scattered support for teacher training programmes, the running of certain institutes of a technical
vocational nature, and other educational pilot programmes
(Adiseshiah 1979). Towards the end of the fifties, however,
the consideration of education as linked to social and
economic development became part of the current discussion
and was fully endorsed at the Santiago Conference in 1962.
Together with the establishment of the First United Nations
Development Decade (1960-1970), educational change was seen
as a necessary factor to and an integral constitutent of

national development plans. The sociology of structural
functionalism and the 'Human Capital Theory' (Schultz 1961)
helped to define what might be called the ideology of educational modernisation as input to economic development. As has
been seen economic modernisation was geared in the early
sixties toward industrial growth and substitution of imports;
it assumed the development of a degree of local self-sufficiency
to be expressed in a growth for each country's GNP of 4%.
Within the scope of this target (for which there was to be
aid from the industrialised world amounting to 1% of their
combined GNP's or 0.7% of each country's GNP) education was
to serve the requirements of economic modernisation. With the
view that the educational system is part of the wider social
system it was assumed that changes occuring in the structure
and functions of both these systems would produce benefits to
the social whole. Thus with increased production, and a
greater movement of the economies from a strictly rural basis
to industrialisation (as measured by degree of urbanisation),
a wider distribution of income would accrue **benefitting the**
poor provided that they increased their participation in the
educational system. Furthermore, the 'Human Capital Theory'
assumed that investment in the development of human capacities
such as health, education, special training would enable the
individual to improve his contribution to the productive
process thus enabling better economic returns and a greater
equalisation of income amongst the various social groups.
Greater investment in education then should contribute to
economic development and to individual benefits translated
in higher personal income.
        It was in the light of the above theories that participants
of the meetings already mentioned formulated the targets for
educational modernisation and insisted that such changes be
incorporated into national development plans. The immediate
result of such ideas was the setting up of National Planning
Offices in almost all of the Latin American countries.
Farrell (1974) encountered planning offices in nineteen
countries of which fourteen had educational planning sections.
        The targets that were set for changes to take place were
of a quantitative and qualitative nature. The quantitative
changes reflected international recommendations on the
expansion of the educational systems and centred mostly on
the secondary and tertiary levels. Primary education was a
second priority and there was constant postponement of the
data in which universal primary education was to be achieved
(from 1965, to 1970, to 1975)(9). Development of rural primary
education was also considered a quantitative target as was
literacy (particularly by UNESCO); but as Solari (1976) asserts
although literacy was always stated as important it was seldom
presented as excluding the priority of secondary or higher
education. The assumptions behind such an expansion were
that the increase in production levels of economies striving

toward industrialisation required minimally educated manpower, while the political assumptions were that education might con- tribute to soothe social mobility aspirations of the middle classes and produce a favourable image of the status quo amongst the poorer sectors of the population. These assumptions re- quired of course that the content and quality of education be also controlled. Thus, an effective target of modernisation in terms of content, structure of the system, methods, materials and aids was also made part of the ideology of change. The main suggested reforms to the structure were the lengthening of primary education so as to make it a terminal stage. It was recommended that it should last for eight to nine years. The secondary system should move away from its French leanings (a stepping-stone into the University), and be structured so as to include a diversified cycle leading either to arts and sciences and preparation for Higher Education or to vocational studies as forming middle-level technical resources for indus- trial needs and the services. Concern with the efficiency of the system led to suggestions that promotion procedures be reformed so as to reduce the problem of repetition. It was also suggested that there should be changes in the content and methods of teaching and soon the Ralph Tyler model of curriculum change and the Taxonomy of Educational Objectives developed by Benjamin Bloom became a sort of blueprint for such changes.(10)

Educational reform in Latin America, especially the quantitative expansion of the system as outlined above, was a target of the Alliance for Progress Programme created in 1962 with the Charter of Punta del Este. The Alliance stressed the need for economic and social development in the Americas and multilateral co-operation and on that basis considered a programme of aid coming from the United States. A powerful support of the Alliance was the Interamerican Development Bank (IDB) which had been created in 1958 with help from the United States. The social targets of the Alliance had to do with reform of land tenure and taxation, expanded programmes of social welfare to benefit low income groups, and the promotion of universal primary education and the eradication of literacy. The Alliance for Progress was partly the effect of the liberalism and concern for social issues of the Kennedy administration and partly a way of ensuring that the Latin American nations remain within the sphere of influence of the United States. There were disturbing signs to be deflected such as the influence that Cuba's turn toward communism or the progressive government of Joao Goulart in Brazil might have over the region. The political target of the Alliance was to support economically those countries that agreed to some sort of social reforms but were not likely to alter substantially either the economic or the political system in the Americas. Thus, only after 1964 with the military take-over, did aid to Brazil take on a sustained developmental character, while the government of Eduardo Frei in Chile (well within the favoured developmentalist type of capitalist economy) was largely supported by Alliance for Progress funds. Direct aid to education however took the character of loans and was important only after 1966 when President Johnson of the United States announced that education, agriculture, and health were high priority objectives of the Alliance for Progress.

The end of the sixties witnessed the failure of the development targets that had been set. Aid was not channelled as recommended to the developing countries and the results of whatever growth took place in these tended to benefit the already privileged social groups. A 'malignant' style of development had taken place which did not result in the 'trickling-down' effects of investment and economic growth. The Latin American development style appeared 'concentrated and exclusive' (Cardoso 1977). Today the situation appears even worse as evidenced for example in the case of Brazil where it is estimated that at least 40 million Brazilians live below the poverty line while many executives earn 105 times more than the lowest wage earners (South 1980). In fact, Brazil was considered to be one of the greatest failures of the Alliance for Progress targets (Levinson and de Onis 1970).(11)

A closer examination of the characteristics of educational expansion in the sixties also leads to a questioning of the assumptions of developmentalist ideology. Noting the existence of four groups of Latin American countries, each one at different stages of economic and educational development, Filgueira (1978) looked into the relationship between education and social stratification. He observed that the greatest expansion in the sixties took place at the higher education level which increased by more than 70% in the period, while the relative decrease of illiteracy was only 15%. But each group of countries behaved differently. Those with a higher level of development had a more moderate growth (Argentina) but witnessed greater pressure for employment, consumer goods and a share of the income on the part of the educated population. At the other end of the scale countries such as Guatemala, El Salvador and Honduras with largely uneducated populations showed the fastest growth rate at the upper primary level though the number of uneducated people was diminished by only about 10%; secondary and higher education in these countries also experienced a relatively large growth but without altering very much the existing social stratification. No clear pattern emerged regarding the relationship between educational growth and the growth of gross per-capita income, but changes in the various educational levels produced increased aspirations and demands for more equitable distribution of the national product. These demands were not translated into redistributive policies owing to the existence of economic pressure groups and of bureaucratic and authoritarian regimes that had the power to curtail such desired response; this in fact contradicted the assumptions of the 'Human Capital' theory.

A case in point is Chile today. In the sixties the country underwent an extensive educational reform that achieved not only structural changes but a noteworthy expansion of the coverage of the system. By the mid-seventies a more educated population should have been able to partake increasingly in the national income. However, under the present authoritarian regime and its monetarist economic policies the reverse seems to be true(12). Filgueira (1978) concludes that in fact the expansion of education is the easiest process by which some fulfilment of hopes for social mobility can be achieved because it is the least rigid of the social institutions.

Judging from the data analysed for the decade the growth of education 'comes to be determined by the production structure, not because there is a growing demand for increasingly skilled manpower, as might be imagined under the 'manpower approach'; but precisely because of the rigidity of the economic structure, which has resulted in the educational system becoming the only means - or at least the most accessible means - of fulfilling hopes of social mobility'. (Filgueira 1978). A similar conclusion is reached by Carnoy after studying the cases of Brazil, Peru and Mexico when he suggests that equalising educational opportunities only produces greater equalisation of earnings if expansion of education goes together with a policy which tries to equalise 'the earnings of workers with lower levels of schooling in lower paying occupations, economic activities, and regions, and with less experience in the labour force to those in the higher paying categories of each of those variables'. (Carnoy 1979: 98).

The above discussion suggests that the reality of the Latin American nations and the structure of their economic and political development runs counter to the ideology of human capital and structural functionalism which permeated the developmentalist theory and modernisation attempts of the sixties' educational change. The results of such efforts though evident in a changed structure and content of the educational systems have not had, it seems, a bearing on the economy of the countries involved. As Solari (1977) indicates the ideas of the sixties, though still existing, had a short lived influence. Such notions as investment on human capital, educational planning, human resources planning, concentration on the formal system, etc. appeared around 1955 but the fashion was over by the close of the 1960s. What is important however, as Solari asserts, is that the basic reason for such a defeat was 'the evolution of ideas on educational policy in the central countries and the new power structures in Latin America'. The beginning of the seventies pointed to the need for alternative ways to formal schooling that might satisfy educational and manpower needs more efficiently and at a lower cost. Non-formal education and lifelong education were

enbodied in the recommendations of UNESCO's <u>Learning to Be</u>
(1972). It is still early to judge the effects of such
alternatives wherever they have been experimented - there has
not been sufficient research on them but they may well reflect
what Solari (1977) calls the 'new utopia'. The basic premise
is similar to the one supporting the expansion of formal
education, that is, that equal educational opportunities can
be provided through a variety of means whether formal or non-
formal within a society which is itself unequally constituted.
Radical sociologists of education in Latin America (Labarca
1977) deny that this is possible and though they praise some
partial effects of non-formal strategies(13), they urge that
education be seen in the light of needed economic and political
change.

Although it is true that educational change has been
largely the result of an 'agency' type of ideology it is also
true that Latin Americans have thought about education in their
own society. Their ideas however have limited influence
largely because they question the validity of development
economics and the possibilities of change through modernisation.

AUTOCHTHONOUS DEVELOPMENT

Perhaps the most well known views on education both in-
side Latin America and within other Third World countries
have been those of the Brazilian educator Paolo Freire.
Being a teacher in the poorest region of Brazil, the North
East, convinced him that exploitation of the peasants in the
area was enhanced by their own lack of awareness of the
injustice of their conditions and of the will to struggle for
a change. Human 'liberation' for human development includes
the capacity to act as a responsible agent in the process of
socio-economic change whereby the oppressed gain the possibility of living like free human beings. In Freire's view the
key to human liberation is awareness; this implies the understanding of the structure of oppression, the reasons why
poverty is an endemic condition for some while others never
know it. Education, especially literacy education, instead
of mechanically instructing the peasant in the techniques
of reading, writing and numeracy, should be a means whereby
the individual begins to examine his context critically and
acknowledges both his human dignity and the degradation imposed
by the conditions of his peasant life. Only through awakening
which is initiated by learning will the peasant understand his
role as participant and not mere observer of historical change.
These ideas of Freire fitted in the social and politically
progressive ideas that developed among some people in the
North East of Brazil in the early sixties; they were expressed
both in the actions of Miguel Arraes (later governor of
Recife) and of the Movement of Popular Culture that managed

to bring together radical intelligentsia of Recife and illiterate peasants of the rural interior. The Movement believed
in stimulating elements in the local culture by means of
popular theatre, folk art and education. They thought that
once people become literate they would be able to vote and
contribute to deciding the struggle between the rich and the
poor. Hence the importance of the literacy method that Freire
was to develop. (Freire 1974).

The extent to which Freire's ideas and the implications
of the Movement for Popular Culture ran counter to developmentalist ideology and to the political concerns of the United
States is illustrated in the following event. In 1962 and 1963
an agreement was signed whereby the United States Agency for
International Development (USAID) and the North East Regional
Development Agency in Brazil agreed to finance a programme on
adult basic education. Freire was asked by the Secretary of
State of Rio Grande do Norte to organise the programme. He
accepted under the condition that the work be done jointly with
the University of Recife and that students there participate
in the programme. Once launched the campaign was extremely
successful not only in its literacy aims but in contributing
to bridge the gap between the students' world and that of the
rural poor:

> A dynamic figure within the university, Freire attracted
> students and imbued them with a sense of personal involve-
> ment in the program. He believed that the students should
> not start a program unless the people clearly wanted it
> and considered it relevant to their needs. Before start-
> ing a literacy course in a community, a cadre of students
> would conduct a house-to-house inquiry and hold informal
> meetings to determine whether the community was receptive
> to the program. If it was, the students would catalog
> the words commonly used in the community, selecting the
> ones with the greatest emotional content. Returning to
> the university, they would draw up a basic vocabulary of
> about seventeen words designed for the particular locale.
> They also developed simple visual aids, charts, and slides
> to go along with the vocabulary. The process was time-
> consuming, painstaking, and clumsy. But the content had
> the great virtue of relevance to the living language and
> life situations of the community.
> Once the basic vocabulary and visual aids were developed,
> a student monitor would bring them back to the community
> and initiate a literacy class. But the meetings between
> the monitor and the participants were not 'classes' in
> the conventional sense, with an active teacher instructing
> passive students. The role of the student monitor was to
> provoke a dialogue with the participants to challenge
> them.
> (Levinson and de Onis 1970: 289-290).

In assessing the merits of this programme USAID's mission
in Recife became worried about two of its aspects: the lack
of written materials to accompany the verbal part of the
programme, but most important, the tone of the discussions
which inevitably led to dealing with the conflict between
peasants and landowners. As Levinson and de Onis (1970)
assess it the programme could be considered as subversive
insofar as it aimed at the development of a critical capacity
in the participants and led to individual and community
actions. The result of this assessment by USAID led to the
termination of its finance in January 1964 (three months before
the military coup that was to send people such as Freire into
exile). The meaning of this act was clear: the educational
changes being implemented had implications beyond mere learning on the part of the workers. There might result disruption
of the social and political order, not the harmonious participation within it as envisaged by structural-functionalists:

> Once the United States realised that social change
> taking place in the north eastern Brazil was inherently
> disorderly and even potentially revolutionary, it
> backed off and shifted its concentration to the
> society, hoping that by gradual expansion the core
> would eventually take in the marginals.
> (Levinson and de Onis 1970: 292)(14).

Freire's method of literacy training was later adopted
in Chile during the government of the Christian **Democrats**
(1964-1970) where it became an integral part of rural education
programmes linked to the process of land reform. The notions
of 'education for liberation' and of 'conscientisation' were
incorporated into the rhetoric of educational reforms in
Chile, Venezuela and Peru. They also received ecclesiastical
sanction at the Latin American's Bishops Conference in
Medellin (1968) when Christian education was seen as 'liberating
education' destined to help man by emphasising his critical
awareness and his role as an agent in social development.
But despite the popularity of the wording the thrust of the
theory with its revolutionary implications was never really
considered as an aim for restructuring education nor worthy
of financial assistance from the major agencies of development.
Adult education as general education for workers was not
a priority of the decade of the sixties; it became a voiced
need as movements of economic and social change took place in
countries such as Chile, Peru and Colombia and it was often
conducted by the trade unions themselves in an effort to
sustain the political awareness in their members (Cf. the case
of Chile, Gajardo 1976). It was only in the seventies, after
the movement from the base had emerged, that the Organisation
of American States (OAS) approved a Multinational Project on

Adult Education which included support (mostly technical) to local education projects in Peru, Haiti, and Chile. (OAS 1972).

The Peruvian educational reform was another example of a widespread effort to change the educational structure within the context of socio-economic changes (such as in Cuba). It was launched after the military take-over of General Velasoo Alvarado in 1968 and responded to the ideology of the Armed Forces movement: a nationalist, non-Marxist form of socialism. The aims of the Reform were to expand the system and equalise opportunities for the lower socio-economic groups and to provide a basis for integration of the indigenous population (mainly Quechua and Aymara speaking) which make up about 40% of the population. Concern for the underprivileged Indian groups was not new in Peru; it had been voiced in the thirties by among others, Jose Carlos Mariategue who represented one of the early voices decrying neocolonialism as a form of Europeanisation of Latin American culture:

> Not only through public instruction but through all other aspects of our life one can see the super-imposition of foreign elements. This problem has its roots in the situation of Peru after the Conquest. We are not a people who assimilates ideas and men from other nations impregnating them with our sentiments and our landscape. We are people that coexist without understanding each other, Indians and conquerors. Peru is the republic of conquerors more than of Indians. National education was born not from a national spirit but from a colonial spirit. When in public instruction programmes the State refers to the Indians it does not do so as if they were Peruvians. They are considered to be of inferior race. The Republic is no different from the Viceroyalty.

> ....The balance of the first century of the Republic closes with a general defficiency in public education; the problem of Indian illiteracy still remains. The State has not diffused education over the whole territory. The disproportion between material means the size of the problem is enormous. For the imple-mentation of a modest programme of popular education there is a great lack of teachers.

> ....The problem of Indian illiteracy is a huge one and its solution transcends the narrow concept of a pedagogical method. One can easily prove that the teaching of illiterates is not educational at all. The first real step towards their liberation must be the abolition of serfdom. (Mariategui 1965).

The ideological inspiration of the reform came from other Peruvian thinkers such as Salazar Bondy and Carlos Delgado equally concerned about the unity of the Peruvian nation and the need for socio-economic reforms that would radically alter the conditions of the dispossessed and the indigenous groups.

The reform was novel; much has been written about it (Avalos 1978; Bizot 1975) and it has been considered as an example of a radical change of the educational system to fit patterns of broader change. But the difficulties to implement it have also been enormous and not the least of these were of a financial order. Support from the World Bank was secured for the development of General Basic Education (a comprehensive school which integrates the primary and secondary levels), but the most original aspects of the reform, its bilingual policies and its literacy movement, are still largely under-financed and unable to achieve their targets.

Freire's notion of 'liberating education' was by no means novel. Not only was Mariategui in the thirties advocating a form of education geared toward freeing the most oppressed in society, but also in Bolivia there developed a schooling experience which in the thirties attempted to contribute to the liberation of the indigenous masses. Elizardo Perez one of the founders of the first Normal School in Bolivia (1906) was the originator of what has been called the Escuela-Ayllu of Warisata. The school was located in an indigenous Aymara community, the 'Ayllu' of Warisata. 'Ayllu' is a community linked by family relationships and a common set of economic, cultural, political, administrative activities that is located in a given geographical setting and structured into small plots of land. The experiment carried out by Perez establishe a central school in the Ayllu surrounded by a sectional school, what today is referred to as a nuclear type of organisation of schooling. The content of instruction was adapted to the cultural and socio-economic conditions of the Warisata community; the style of teaching was based on the participants style of the Indian community which included co-operation in productive activities. The children were to learn not only how to read, write and count but also about agricultural and livestock activities and craft and cottage industries. The school was financed by the community. The experience was later extended to other indigenous communities in Bolivia. It was however destined to failure.

As conceived by Elizardo Perez it responded very much to what is now the emphasis on rural education centred on the community, its methods and activities, and directly linked to productive activities. But it was an early experience that got buried in the later developments of Bolivia. After the War of Chaco with Paraguay (1936) the community of Warisata was deprived of most of its land which was turned over to big private ownership. The landowners pressed to have the school condemned as subversive, communist, and antinational and it

was finally closed by the government. New orientations were
to guide educational change removing it from its original
concern with an indigenous education based on Indian values
and way of life. Towards the end of 1944 educational ideas
coming from abroad were introduced and produced an agreement
between the government of Bolivia and the Interamerican
Educational Foundation. Bolivian educators were sent to the
United States and American experts were invited to contribute
their knowledge to developments in Bolivia, including,
health instruction and information on household crafts and
industries for the rural areas. The original Warisata
schools were subjected to modernisation through technical
assistance and ceased to be schools based on the indigenous
roots of their pupils as they once had been. (Huacani et al
1978).

The experiments of Freire in Brazil and the early steps
into rural-indigenous education in Bolivia show that they
were destined either to be stopped as in the case of Warisata
or to be deprived of financial assistance as in the programme
in the Brazilian North East. Original developments of this
sort which really try to put a wedge in the existing socio-
economic structure are unsuccessful; aid comes only when the
programmes are transformed into reputable technocratic programmes such as MOBRAL in Brazil (the present governments
Adult Literacy Movement) or the Integrated Rural Development
Project of Bolivia (financed with a World Bank loan to
contribute to indigenous rural education). Many of the
analysis of these experiences conclude that the conflictive
elements within them lie in their assumption that educational
innovation must rest on and contribute to very deep changes
in the socio-economic structure. (Huacani et al 1978;
Levinson and de Onis 1970; Vasconi 1977).

THE DIRECTION OF FOREIGN AID

It is generally assumed that foreign aid represents a
powerful instrument of neocolonialism insofar as it may
serve as a vehicle for transplanting ideas and for encouraging
developments that serve the interests of donor countries and
institutions (Altbach and Kelly 1978). The popular notion
that aid programmes represent a purely philanthropic pursuit
of the industrialised nations is clearly not real. Both in
terms of the trade benefits that accrue to the donor
countries (Pearson 1970) and of the political benefits to be
gained from assuring a climate similar to that of the donor
country (Levinson and de Onis 1970) aid is important to
industrialised nations. Aid to development according to Le
Thanh Koi (1976) 'consists mainly of a redistribution of the
public finances of the donor country (derived from taxation)
to the advantage of the private industries which is perfectly
in line with the capitalist system'. Nowhere is this more

clearly evident than in the aid policies that the United
States sought to pursue in Latin America especially after the
triumph of the Cuban revolution.

Foreign aid in Latin America in the late fifties and in
the sixties supported the general ideology of developmentalism
(analysed in the preceding section). Disenchantment with
developmentalism as evidenced in the Bellagio meeting in 1970
(Ward 1971) and the new orientations for education presented
in UNESCO's Learning to be (1972) served to reorient the aid
policies of major agencies such as expressed for example in
the latest Sector Policy Paper of the World Bank (1980).

At the end of the second World War the United States'
government initiated a programme of educational aid which was
incorporated in the Point Four Programme, an intergovernmental
scheme designed to assist poor countries in the achievement of
a better standard of living. The main form of this aid was
technical assistance and transfer of knowledge and technology
rather than funds for development. It was not until the late
fifties and early sixties that aid policies for education
became a more important concern for the American government.
Its influence then was exercised through various agencies:
the Organisation of American States (OAS), USAID and AID,
the Alliance for Progress, and private agencies such as the
Ford Foundation, the Rockefeller Foundation and governmental
agreements such as the Fulbright programme. One of the most
important sources of American influence has also been the
World Bank and the Bank of Interamerican Development both of
which initiated loan programmes to educational projects in
the sixties.

1. FOREIGN AID AND THE EDUCATIONAL SYSTEM

Secondary (general and diversified) and higher education
were the levels most benefited by aid. The following table
exemplifies how loans from the World Bank were distributed in
the period 1965-1979.

Table 8.1 World Bank Loans to Latin American Countries per Level of Educational System (Between 1966-1979)

Level	1966	1967	1968	1969	1970	1971	1973	1974	1975	1976	1977	1978	1979	Total
Basic Educ. Urban								1	2	2		2	1	8
Basic Educ. Rural								1			1		1	3
Secondary General	1	1	2	4	1	2	3	2	4	2	1			24
Secondary Technical			1	1	1	1				1		1		5
Post Secondary (Techn. and Agric.)	1			1		2	2	1	2				1	10
Vocational					1							4		5
Adult Training	1	1		1										3
Teacher Training	1	2	3	1	2		2	2	2	1		1		17

Source: World Bank, 'Education Sector Policy Paper'. Washington: April 1980.

It was only about 1974 that aid to Basic or Primary
education was considered. The same is true of non-formal
projects, rural community development and adult education
programmes. Also to be noticed in the data offered by the
World Bank is the fact that countries that did not offer
political security to the United States were not recipients
of loans. That was the case of Chile where the last loan
belongs to the fiscal year 1970 (the Marxist government there
was elected toward the end of the year) or of Brazil where
loans are interrupted between 1971 and 1975, the period in
which the left-oriented government of Joao Goulart was in
office. (World Bank 1980).

It is difficult to assess the extent to which the various
aid programmes contributed to the quantitative and qualitative
development of the systems or served to import alien models
and to produce cultural alienation at least in the middle and
upper classes that benefited most from this aid. It is
certainly true that whatever aid was channelled to Latin
America for the expansion of the secondary system was in fact
successful in its target.

Diversification of secondary education and the development of intermediate level manpower resources through the
vocational branch of the secondary school was institutionalised
in several of the reforms that took place in the late sixties
and seventies (e.g. Brazil, Venezuela, Chile, Bolivia, Peru).
How useful such a diversification has been is today a question
even for the Agencies that so enthusiastically supported the
notion:

> Yet, the success of diversified curricula and practical
> options in secondary schools has not met expectations.
> A review of 79 Bank-assisted projects that include
> diversified secondary schools with vocational, pre-
> vocational, or otherwise broadened curricula, tends
> to support the view presented elsewhere in this paper
> on diversified education ...Expensive facilities have
> often remained unused, or misused; the causes include
> lack of suitably trained teachers ...insufficient funds
> for the maintenance of equipment and the purchase of
> necessary consumables, and a lack of clarity of
> educational objectives of the diversified curricula.
> Project reviews show, ...that broad forecasts of
> needed manpower included in projects approved in the
> 1960s have usually not remained valid during their
> long cycles because of changes in the economic and
> educational situation.
> (The World Bank 1980).

2. HIGHER EDUCATION

A significant amount of the aid programmes to Latin

America were used for Technical assistance to Higher Education. These included scholarship programmes and the provision of experts or consultants for various areas of university training and research. Aid to the universities can be traced back to the mid-fifties when the Rockefeller Foundation provided grants-in-aid to improve instruction in selected institutions, mostly private, such as the Universidad de Los Andes (Colombia), Universidad del Valle (Cali, Colombia) and the Universidad de Concepcion (Chile). A decisive step in the university development programmes was President Kennedy's decision in 1961 to single out higher education as one of the avenues that could bring the Latin American nations closer to the United States. He thus requested the OAS to present a study on ways in which such co-operation might take place (Union Panamericana 1961). It was suggested that a similar organ- isation and content of teaching to that of United States' institutions might enhance co-operation as would also an openness of such institutions to Latin American issues and international development (Law of International Education 1966). The State Department, United States agencies such as AID and USAID, the Interamerican Development Bank and the World Bank as well as the United States' universities should all contribute to the modernisation of Higher Education in Latin America. With United States' sponsorship, as Renner (1974) suggests, the 'utilitarian' views of American univer- sities gained entrance in Latin America. The model for change which the agencies considered as acceptable was proposed in the Atcon Report (1963). Changes resulted in a restructuring of a number of universities into departments rather than Faculties or professional schools. This happened through different types of motivation in Argentina, Peru, Bolivia, Columbia, Costa Rica, Honduras, Venezuela (Tunnerman 1976). There was also some modernisation in procedures such as the introduction of a flexible curriculum and credit system.

The universities in Latin America, do not constitute an easy terrain for cultural and political domination due to a traditional strength of its student movement and to engrained notions of autonomy (academic and territorial). Of late, however, these notions and movements have been challenged by authoritarian political regimes. The process of university reform that took place in the late sixties in Latin America had different effects depending on the social and political context in which modernisation of the structure took place. Thus the Brazilian university, inserted as it is now in an authoritarian regime, was ideally attuned to the United States' technocractic model of universities (proposed by Atcon) and responded to the rationale of structural function- alism (Marini 1977). The universities in Uruguay and Chile on the other hand changed within the context of progressive political regimes (in the sixties) even though some of these changes were structurally similar to those in Brazil.(15)

However, when political conditions altered in these countries, governments intervened, as for example in the National University in Montevideo, the University of Buenos Aires, or the Chilean universities and both staff and students were subjected to harassment and repression. The universities in this context were thus expected to conform to an intellectual leadership not in conflict with existing political power and ideology. (Brunner 1980).

3. EDUCATIONAL RESEARCH

Another important area where foreign aid is noticeable (because most needed) is the field of educational research. Several conditions make it possible for research to develop: the existence of substantial research capacity by way of experienced scholars who are also sufficiently knowledgeable of the educational situation, support from an adequate institutional base, political conditions in which to operate with a certain degree of freedom, possibilities for communication among researchers and for diffusion of their results, and some degree of possibilities for implementation of research results. In Latin America until the early sixties few of these conditions existed. Most professional educators were dedicated to teacher training activities or employed as bureaucrats in the ministerial institutions; the universities had not yet recognised the need for developing their research functions especially as far as Education departments or Faculties were concerned. Few Latin Americans had been trained to higher levels in the fifties and those that had masters or doctorates had to yield to the pressure of teaching or administrative duties in the institutions that employed them. Thus whatever research was carried out about Latin American education was largely the work of foreign scholars.

With the developmentalist trends of the sixties governments became interested in analysing their systems and producing some information that would enable policy decisions to follow. As explained elsewhere in this paper, the techniques of manpower analysis imported from the OECD were used in Latin America to forecast the needs of the system; for the most part researchers were brought from abroad to direct these studies. The 'Human Capital' theoreticians also exported their experts to calculate rates of return to education within the scope of social and economic planning. At this time, on the other hand, the social sciences developed considerably in Latin America producing thinkers of influence upon education such as the Brazilians D'Arcy Ribeiro and Paulo Freire, the Argentinian, Tomas Vasconi, Uruguayans such as German Rama, and the group that formed part of the ECLA. The need to examine the educational system from a local perspective and not simply through the eyes of the foreign expert, planner or researcher, led to the establishment of research units in the ministries of education in Chile, Peru, Colombia and Venezuela. Much of the work done there however was linked to immediate needs such as diagnostic studies indicating feasibility of this or that type of policy. More seldom than not research interests were pushed aside due to pressures for preparation of material for new curricula or in-service teacher training such as occurred at the Chilean Centre for Educational Research, Experimentation and In-service Training.

The effect of technical assistance in the sixties was noticeable in the number of Latin Americans that went abroad to study. The vast majority of these went to the United States where they became familiar with the empirical-positivist method of research, and contributed on return to implementing this mode of research. However, though the model was brought over the rigour and sophistication used in the advanced centres of the United States and Europe were not found in local Latin American research (Garcia Huidobro and Ochoa 1978). A number of Latin Americans also went to Europe, mostly to France, Belgium and the United Kingdom. The influence of the French and Belgian studies was of a more theoretical kind thus leading some of the returning social scientists and educators to be closer to a structuralist-conflict analysis of society, basing their research on problems destined to point out the existing difficulties of dependent Latin American societies. Their research rarely had a bearing on educational practice or policy.

Educational research formally began to develop at the end of the sixties and in the seventies through the establish-ment of a series of research institutions, private, govern-mental, or university-linked which received substantial amounts of foreign funds for their projects. It is considered that the main sources of funding were the Ford Foundation, followed by the OAS, USAID, the Interamerican Foundation, the Inter-american Development Bank and the United Nations Development Programme(16).

The role of the Ford Foundation became particularly important when it decided to strengthen its research funding programme after a meeting held in Buenos Aires in 1969. Earlier, in 1967 at the meeting of Latin American presidents in Punta del Este major guidelines for inter-American co-operative action in the field of education, science, and technology were lain down that culminated in the establishment of the Interamerican Council for Education, Science, and Culture under the direction of the OAS in 1970 (Americas 1972). The Council recognised the importance of research and proceeded to set up a Multinational Plan for Research and Experimentation. It supported several national projects and centres in Buenos Aires, Costa Rica, Venezuela. Support from USAID has been directed for the most part to governments and has favoured

research and development projects. The Interamerican
Foundation has contributed since 1973 to an area of research
which is largely a Latin American development, not based on
positivist research models: action and evaluation research.
Later support has come from German, Swedish and Canadian
assistance agencies; especially noticeable at present is the
contribution of the International Development Research Centre,
a Canadian foundation oriented to research in developing
countries.
    It is difficult to assess the real effect of all these
contributions, but it does seem true to say that without such
participation educational research would have continued to be
non-existent in Latin America. The questions that really need
to be addressed are first, to what extent has support served
to increase dependency on foreign models and second, has it
served as a basis for generating an independent national
research capacity in the Latin American countries. Obviously,
the extent to which researchers have been trained in advanced
country centres is reflected in the characteristics of their
research. The work produced in institutions with strong
foreign links by way of funding and staff results in research
products that use the positivist model with a fairly good
degree of rigour and sophistication. (Garcia Huidobro and
Ochoa 1978). Studies that move away from this model tend to
be carried out in institutions not backed by external support
nor by foreign research groups or centres.
    There are two main modes of assistance which have a
different impact on the type of research that is carried out
and the building of local research capacity. These are
institutional support by way of grants that allow leeway to
the institution for deciding upon the nature of its projects
and for building local capacity and material resources for
such research. This mode of assistance was largely practised
by the Ford Foundation in the early stages of its research
aid programme. The other mode, the most common, is the support
which is project ear-marked. This leaves the institutions very
much at the mercy of what are the priorities set by the funding
agencies. In their analysis of research projects in Latin
America, Garcia Huidobro and Ochoa (1978) notice for example
a disproportionate number of projects which relate to higher
education and which were mostly done with external aid or by
external research institutions.
    An important consideration is the climate for research in
the Latin American countries as observed at the end of the
seventies. The increase of authoritarian regimes especially
in the southern part of the region, has severly limited the
contribution that educational research can make; this is
especially true when it results in either diagnosis or eval-
uations that criticise national policies or when it embarks
on projects which have an action component affecting the
behaviour of participants in some significant way. Thus in

assessing the direction of aid to the Latin American countries
it has been suggested that the building of local capacity
continues to be a priority area and that this cannot truly
take place unless the institutions have some possibility of
doing so. Moreover, the possibilities of attacking educational
problems from different perspectives and methodologies, and
thus avoid falling prey to the current fads requires greater
institutional self-sufficiency. In countries such as
Argentina and Chile practically all educational research takes
place outside the normally established institutions such as
the universities or governmental centres. The regimes of
these countries are likely to continue as authoritarian as up
to the present, with severe restrictions on the scope for
academic work, especially in the social sciences. Thus, the
independent institutions stand in dire need of support.
Paradoxically, the reversal of the trend of dependency on
foreign models and ideas which characterised the sixties might
only be achieved in the current political climate through a
commitment on the part of external organisations to back the
increasingly greater number of capable researchers in Latin
America who continue their work outside the scope of 'official'
institutions.

CONCLUSION

     This article has largely considered the problem of neo-
colonialism in Latin America from the point of view of the
region's continued economic and cultural dependency on the
United States. The first part of the article dealt with the
'open' attitude of Latin Americans since independence to
European and later to United States models of thought and
culture. This attitude resulted in the importation of
ideas and practices about education, and lately in the
acceptance of theories about society and education which
inspired reforms in the sixties and seventies. But neocolonialism is not simply the result of open attitudes to what
is offered from the outside. It is also the result of an
underlying economic dependency which operates between central
nations such as the United States and peripheral ones such
as the Latin American nations. As a result neocolonialism in
Latin American education is a necessary condition for the
maintenance of the United States' economic structure and
serves its concern for security as expressed in a policy of
political hegemony over the region.
     The most powerful means that the United States has of
establishing the conditions under which Latin America may
develop its education is through its aid programmes and
through the control it exerts over lending organisms such as
the World Bank and regional networks such as OAS. The changing
views in the United States about the appropriate directions
to secure its concern for economic returns and political

security also guide the directives by which educational change is induced from other international sources or generated within the Latin American community. But the degree of awareness or of acceptance of this dependency among the Latin Americans varies, so that when in need of aid a game is played. For those Latin Americans who are aware of what is happening, who know where change should go but lack the means to study or implement it - the question is to show how far aid agencies will allow space for such plans and support them. For the Latin Americans who have accepted the North American 'way of life' the task is to foretell constantly what is likely to be the trend in education that the donor country or institutions might appreciate and suggest it in advance. Both types co-exist in Latin America and that is why it is difficult to say that the neocolonialism by the United States is either totally effective or that it is a simple one-way movement. Latin Americans do manage to think about their reality and to be sufficiently concerned about improving the conditions of life for their country-men. Sometimes their proposals coincide with the political climate of their countries and are able to find some external support (such might prove to be the case in the coming years in Nicaragua); sometimes they grow in climates of repression and are only supported by the 'dissidents' within and among the Agencies. But many Latin Americans have also effectively been converted to the dominant system so that they want only the change that is supported by that system. It is in this sense that neocolonialism operates at its best.

This paper has not dealt with mass media as a means of cultural domination, but the media provides the most successful means of neocolonialism and in conclusion a brief mention must be made of the influence of the media. It can do this by transferring consumption and development styles 'which incorporate the peoples of the Third World, both psychologically and practically into the value system of the transnational power structure'. (Somavia 1977). In the measure of its success in presenting its views through films, journals, radio, and television programmes, as well as through its news agencies, the business corporations and the American politicians may ensure continued support from Latin Americans. In reviewing research on the impact of media, Beltran and de Cardona (1980) referred to a study by Nordenstreng and Varis covering many countries of the world in which they found that national TV programme structures 'were dominated in most countries by transnational procedures and that the international flow of television programme materials was essentially controlled by huge United States sales, of which one third corresponded to Latin America'. As long as children are able to characterise the 'goodies' and the 'baddies' in TV programmes as they did according to a Venezuelan study (Santoro 1975), the possibilities for cultural independence remain limited:

The 'goodies' are from the United States, while the
'baddies' are from other countries chiefly from
Germany and then from China.

The 'goodies' are whites who are rich and are usually
policemen, detectives or soldiers. The 'baddies' are
black and poor, and they work chiefly as labourers or
peasants, or in offices.

In conclusion then it may be said that from an educational
point of view such actions as overcoming cultural domination
through advertisements as documented by Roncagliolo and Janus
(1980) or of comics as documented by Dorman and Mattelart
(1975) or through textbooks or TV programmes remains a priority
area if a process of decolonisation is to take place.
Collective self-reliance seems to be one way of fostering such
change and as Oteiza (1979) indicates one of its most
important manifestations should be in the field of mass media
in order to sever the alienating dependency on news agencies
and radio and television programmes from the centre.

NOTES

1. 'Populist' governments emerged in several Latin
American countries that based their policies on the notion of
widening the popular base of support by enacting favourable
social legislation and gaining control of some national
resources. Some examples are Lazaro Cardenas' government in
Mexico (nationalised oil resources in 1936) and Getulio Vargas
in Brazil; also in the late thirties Jose David Toro in
Bolivia and Pedro Aguirre Cerda in Chile. Later in Bolivia,
after the revolution of 1952, tin mines were nationalised and
land reform was carried out. The trend toward nationalisation
continued in the sixties with the governments of Eduardo Frei
in Chile and General Velasco Alvarado in Peru.
2. See for example 'Covert Action in Chile, 1963-1973'
Staff Report of the Select Committee to Study Governmental
Operations with Respect to Intelligence Activities United
States Senate, U.S. Government Printing Office, December 18,
1975: 'Covert action has been a key element of U.S. foreign
policy toward Chile. The link between covert action and
foreign policy was obvious throughout the decade between 1964
and 1974. In 1964, the United States commitment to democratic
reform via the Alliance for Progress and overt foreign aid
was buttressed via covert support for the election of the
candidate of the Christian Democratic party, a candidate and
a party for which the Alliance seemed tailor made. During
1970 the U.S. Government tried, covertly, to prevent Allende
from becoming president of Chile. When that failed, covert
support to his opposition formed one of a triad of official
actions: covert aid to opposition forces, 'cool but correct'

diplomatic posture, and economic pressure. From support of what the United States considered to be democratic and pro-gressive forces in Chile we had moved finally to advocating and encouraging the overthrow of a democratically elected government'.

3. A recent publication by the Chilean sociologist Dahse (1979) has brought together data which indicates the following:

(a) Five economic groups now control 53% of the assets of 250 of the biggest private enterprises.

(b) Nine groups (including four of the above) control 32% of the assets of Banks.

(c) The same nine groups control 60% of bank credits and 64% of non-bank credit institutions.

(d) In a sample of 100 enterprises, the capital of those controlled by the five most important groups grew 97% between 1969 and 1978 while for the rest the growth rate was on only 14%.

This indicator of the situation is the increase in imports of consumer goods (not food) of a luxury type (alcohol, cig-arettes, photographic equipment, TV and radios, cars) which grew from 75.6 millions of dollars in 1970 to 1,258.8 million dollars in 1978 (1977 value of US dollar). Consumer patterns of essential goods (food, fuel and transportation) varied for the highest 20% income group betwen 1969 and 1978 in only 0.8%; while for the lowest 20% income group the variation was of -20.7%. (Foxley 1980).

4. Dependency theory constitutes if anything a rather original contribution by Latin American economists and socio-logists to the analysis of underdevelopment, to which is added the position of Andre Gunder Frank (1967). A good synthesis of the way in which the theory developed as linked to ECLA (UN Economic Commission for Latin America) is provided by Fernando Henrique Cardoso (1977); Chilcote (1974) has also provided a useful critical synthesis of the literature on dependency theory literature.

5. Weinberg (1977) quoting Roig (El Espiritualismo Argentino entre 1850 - 1900) underlines the sources of inspiration of Sarmiento's thought and his link to positivism through a feeling of communion with H. Spencer's ideas which Sarmiento expressed when he said: 'I understand him, because we walk the same road'. Roig's description asserts that Sarmiento's ideological development 'began under the influence of social romanticism, soon abandoned for liberalism with a background of moderate and almost vague deist rationalism. Though his apology of work in the style of Franklin, his phil-osophy of history which approximates Tocqueville's, an educat-ional philosophy inspired in Horace Mann, enthusiasm for the history of religions as suggested by Renan, an elevated interest in natural sciences, close contact with the eclectic doctrines of Burmeister, and finally through his acute socio-

logical sense Sarmiento anticipates the topics that will
later interest argentine positivism.
    6. Another way of expressing the situation is that the
United States in order to maintain political and economic
regimes in the region that are compatible with its own security
interests and those of its business corporations will utilise
alliances with friendly groups in the Latin American countries
either to destabilise a government or avoid a dangerous change.
This has been called the policy of 'preferential ally'.
(Silva Michelena 1976).
    7. The most important of these is the set of para-
academic institutions that exist under tne juridical umbrella
of the Catholic Cnurch: Centre for Economic Research (CIEPLAN),
the Latin American Faculty of Social Sciences (FLACSO), Centre
for Interdisciplinary Educational Research (PIIE), all of
which sponsor seminars and workshops well attended by university students and other interested people.
    8. The Latin American countries can be divided into
three groups depending on their GNP, percentage of literacy
and of urban population (Garcia Huidobro and Ochoa):
Group I: Argentina, Venezuela, Uruguay and Chile. These
countries have an urban population ranging from 83.2% to
74.7%; their literacy rate ranges from 92.6% to 77.1%, and
their GNP per capita for 1975 ranges from 1,486.2 dollars to
959.4 US dollars.
Group II: Panama, Brazil, Mexico, Costa Rica, Peru, Colombia
and Dominican Republic. Their urban population ranges from
68.2% to 47.9%; literacy rates go from 88.4% to 76.7%; and
GNP per capita from 1,085.5 to 618.0 US dollars.
Group III: Nicaragua (before its revolution), Ecuador, Paraguay,
El Salvador, Guatemala, Honduras, Bolivia, and Haiti. Urban
population ranges from 52.8% to 22.4%; literacy goes from
80.5% to 24.7%; and GNP per capita ranges from 643.1 to 150.2
US dollars.
    9. Solari (1977) points out that after it became clear
that the traditional educational model was not working Latin
Americans turned to a model 'offered by the common elements
of the present system in the developed countries'. Among
the common elements were the emphasis on the formal system
and the identification of its shortcomings, which in this case
meant development and diversification of secondary education
(to fit the requirements of economic development). Primary
education was not considered a priority and apart from UNESCO
it had hardly support from other agencies. The emphasis on
the present implied the Latin American approximation to the
actual state of education in developed countries with no
account of the historical process whereby such countries
arrived at their current situation. Solari adds that the
reasons for de-emphasising primary education were not hard to
understand. 'In the first place, economists and human resources
specialists rarely attached priority to elementary education;

secondly, if elementary education was so backward in Latin
America it was because the groups which might in theory have
supported firm priority for it had very little power; and
thirdly, the only external backing came from UNESCO. This
had two limitations: first, that it was not as exclusive as
the support given by the World Bank and IDB; and secondly,
that since UNESCO is not a Bank, its influence as regards the
possibilities of obtaining loans was very indirect, though
helped by the fact that AID assigned a certain priority to
primary education'.
     10. In at least two countries this was the model adopted
for the reform of their curriculum: Venezuela and Chile.
     11. For example, between 1960 and 1967 the out-of-school
population in Brazil (5 to 14 years old) decreased by 218,000
in Chile and increased by 600,000 in Brazil. The North East
of Brazil has the highest illiteracy rate in the country (60%).
     12. Unemployment in 1970 was 6.1% and at present it runs
over 13.8% (which rises to 18.4% if those partially employed
under the government's minimal employment programme are considered). Between 1969 and 1978 the difference in consumption
patterns of essential goods (food, fuel, transportation)
varied for the highest 20% income group in 0.8% and for the
lowest 20% income group it varied in -20.7%. (Foxley 1980).
     13. For a description of some such projects see Thomas
La Belle (1976).
     14. That this assumption has not been supported by facts
is illustrated by the current assessments of the situation in
the North East of Brazil. According to a study carried out
in 1976 (The Guardian Weekly 1980) in nine North East states
69% of the men earn twice or less of the minimum wage. The
monthly cost of feeding a family of five at the rate of
2,000 calories per member comes to three times the minimum
monthly wage which is 58 US dollars.
     15. In Chile for example as Graciarena (1972) indicates
what is sought is a university that can become 'a clear and
critical consciousness of the people', that is 'a democratic
university which is engaged, even militant in the eyes of some
and that participates intensely in a society that is
politically and socially mobilised, that is strongly national-
istic and in serious conflict with foreign investors'.
     16. I am indebted in this account to notes prepared by
R.G. Myers of Latin American Educational Research for a
publication by the International Development Research Centre
(Ottawa, Canada) on 'Connecting Worlds of Research'.

Chapter Nine

CO-OPERATION OR COLONIALISM? A PRELIMINARY CONSIDERATION OF
THE SCHEME OF CO-OPERATION BETWEEN NEW ZEALAND AND FIJI 1924-
1975

A.G. Hopkin

Fiji's education system is a well-established one. It
grew and developed steadily from the time that the Methodist
missionaries introduced schooling in the second quarter of the
nineteenth century. In 1916 the Colonial Government assumed
responsibility for the education system through an ordinance
passed that year, and it took over a pattern of schooling
that was well distributed throughout the archipelago. From
that time school places were provided through the co-operation
of the Education Department and non-government agencies, and
this continues to be the case. It is true that the indigenous
people of Fiji, the Fijians, whilst being profoundly conscious
of their cultural heritage and traditional way of life, also
accept schooling as a normal part of childhood. They have done
so for about a century so that schools are as much a part of
the social fabric as are the Christian churches and chapels.
Although schooling amongst the numerically most superior group
in the population, the Fiji Indians, has only developed in the
last seventy years, education is now more prized by that group
than by any other. A hundred years ago the first school for
Europeans and part-Europeans was established at Levuka and
another shortly after at Suva, and this has ensured that this
racial group has had adequate access to schooling for their
children. It must be borne in mind that for many years the
system of schooling in Fiji is both extensive and well entren-
ched compared with the systems of other developing countries.
     There are certain features in Fiji which justify it
being a case study. First is the multi-racial nature of Fiji
society. Partly as a result of local politics, the language
spoken, religious affiliations, and deliberate government
policy. A school system has developed which has a high
proportion of monoracial schools. Until 1960 the government
positively encouraged the development of schooling along racial
lines and, although the policy has since been abandoned, the
legacy is apparent through 'Fijian' and 'Indian' schools. A
second feature of the system is that the number of pupils enrolled in government controlled schools has never been more

than 7% of the total. The great majority of children have
attended schools controlled by non-government agencies -
missions, local committees, religio-political bodies and private
firms - and continue to do so. School places have been provided as a result of a partnership between the government and
the private agencies. The government, through a complex system
of legislation and control backed up by a system of grants in
aid, has been and is firmly established as the senior partner.
Such a partnership has resulted in variable standards as far
as the quality of educational provision is concerned, but the
standards in the best of the non-government schools have been
equal to and at times superior to those in the best Government
schools. By the end of the current seventh plan for education
the Fiji Government aims to provide over 90% of the children of
school age with ten years of schooling. This would not be
possible without the contribution of the other partners in the
educational enterprise. A third notable feature of education
in Fiji has been the presence of a significant number of non-
Fiji personnel as teachers and administrators in the system,
notably those recruited from New Zealand through the Scheme
of Co-operation between the Education Departments of the
respective countries. This paper will concern itself with a
description and evaluation of the part this group has played
in educational development in Fiji and the legacy that still
remains for independent Fiji.

       From the late nineteenth century the services of inspect-
ors and teachers from Victoria, Australia were used to establish and maintain standards in the Suva and Levuka European
schools. This system was useful but had lapsed by the start
of the first world war. By the early 'twenties the problem of
staffing these schools was critical: a regular source of supply
of competent teachers was essential if an adequate education
was to be provided for European children in these schools.
A committee was set up in 1922 to examine the issue of teacher
supply. Although the majority favoured a scheme with
Australia, the Acting-Director favoured New Zealand as a
source of supply. His opinion prevailed. Consequently, the
New Zealand Education Department was approached and negotiations
led to the Scheme being formally launched in 1924. (Fiji 1923).

       This decision was not taken lightly by the New Zealand
authorities. Whilst New Zealand had shown some imperial pre-
tensions in the first quarter of the twentieth century, Fiji
was certainly not on her agenda for annexation, and many
opposed the proposed Scheme of Co-operation. (Fiji 1928).
However legislation had already been enacted which made it
possible for New Zealand teachers to serve in Western Samoa
and still retain their superannuation rights, it was agreed
that this privilege should be extended to teachers who wished
to serve in Fiji under the Scheme of Co-operation.

       Controversy has frequently been associated with the
Scheme from the start. Initially relations between teachers

and citizens were strained but this passed as the Scheme became
established. In 1924 sixteen appointments were made to these
schools and these were about half of the total number of appointments in the Education Department. Fiji acknowledged that
there were three immediate benefits gained from the Scheme.
(Fiji 1925). The first was that New Zealand trained teachers
were available for service in Fiji schools. The next was that
regular annual visits of inspection would be made by New
Zealand inspectors to Fiji schools where Scheme teachers taught.
Linked with this benefit was the fact that New Zealand courses
of instruction were to be followed in the European schools at
Levuka and Suva, together with the usual New Zealand examinations.
The pattern was established whereby New Zealand criteria were
adopted for the inspection of the leading government schools
in Fiji. Furthermore, the number serving on the Scheme
increased: there were 38 by 1938, 58 new appointments were
made from 1938-1947, over 80 were serving in 1960, and there
were over 100 by 1970. These factors were partly instrumental
for the way the Scheme helped to orientate Fiji education to
the New Zealand system.

In practice the Scheme ensured that teachers from New
Zealand would find it relatively easy to fit into their new
teaching environment. The regular visits of inspection and
the paid leave after every three (later two) years, ensured
that teachers were able to keep in touch professionally and be
assessed for re-grading if they so wished. Periodic and necessary changes were made in the terms of service usually to
the benefit of the New Zealand personnel as the Fiji administration was usually anxious to keep their New Zealand teachers
happy. For example, in 1939 two Scheme teachers, acting on
behalf of their colleagues, applied for leave conditions and
medical benefits comparable with those enjoyed by Colonial
officers. (Fiji 1939). The Fiji Director did not concede
that the comparison was valid but the amendments were made as
requested. When a proposal was made that a branch of the New
Zealand Educational Institute (NZEI) should be formed in 1948,
the Director in Fiji welcomed the proposal and very good
relationahips were fostered between the Deparment, the NZEI
and other New Zealand teachers' organisations that were later
formed. Furthermore, in 1963 the Director approved of the
initiative of the NZEI when it proposed to help the local
teachers to develop along more professional lines. What was
also known was that Scheme teachers were able and willing to
take on extra responsibilities without extra remuneration,
for example as Associate Teachers and helping with student
teachers.

In the extrinsic sense teachers on the Scheme were well
looked after. Their teaching environment was also favourable
in that it was not too dissimilar to that of New Zealand.
From the start of the Scheme, one condition was that the Suva
and Levuka schools should be categorised in accord with New

Zealand standards and follow the same curricula as New Zealand
schools of the same category. This was written into the
Scheme. (Fiji 1935). A teacher in Levuka in the mid-1950s
commented on the small degree of difference in the work done
there and in New Zealand and that the school was very similar
to those of similar size in New Zealand. (Clark 1958). Not
all teachers on the Scheme taught at the Levuka and Suva
schools however and many were increasingly deployed in other
institutions.

External examinations have played a very important role
in both primary and secondary education in Fiji, notably after
1950 when secondary expansion increased rapidly. For a variety
of reasons the Director of Education decided that from 1949
the government secondary schools would take the New Zealand
School Certificate and that the Cambridge examinations would
be phased out. Before that time both were taken by students
in government schools. From the mid-sixties non-government
schools were also encouraged to take the New Zealand School
Certificate and University Entrance Examinations. By 1975 the
number of students being prepared for the Cambridge Syndicate
examinations were very few. Such policies, plus the increasing
presence of New Zealand Scheme personnel in administrative
posts after 1945, led to the secondary system being increasingly
dominated by New Zealand external examinations. With the
result that the curriculum in Fiji was not dissimilar from
that of New Zealand. From research undertaken by the author
it would appear that most New Zealanders who have taught on
the Scheme have found it relatively easy to adjust to the
curriculum that they had to follow.

The Scheme of Co-operation was not an aid scheme. New
Zealand recruited teachers on behalf of Fiji and Fiji paid
the costs of employing them. This included the salaries,
removal expenses, allowances, travel and superannuation pay-
ments. In addition Fiji shared the costs, with other island
countries, of the visits made by inspectors. The basic rates
of salary paid were the New Zealand rates but other allowances
ensured that teachers on the Scheme had a higher remuneration
than they would have had in New Zealand. That Fiji did not
find the cost of the Scheme excessive is reflected in the
increased number of teachers recruited. Furthermore, the
Scheme provided European teachers for Fiji at a rate cheaper
than they would have been if recruited from elsewhere. Before
and after the Second World War, it was officially acknowledged
that Fiji could not have imported Colonial Service teachers at
a comparable cost. One observer pointed out in 1949 that the
Scheme enabled Fiji to have the services of a greater number
of expatriate teachers than it would normally have been able
to afford on its pensionable establishment. (Gwilliam 1949).

An element of antagonism soured the relationship between
the two Education Departments when Fiji began to take the
Scheme for granted. This took place from about 1950 onwards

when new terms of service were drawn up without consultation
with the New Zealand Education Department. The Officer for
Island Education acted with scrupulous propriety and accepted
the change, but with reservations. (OIE 1949). A later more
serious controversy arose in 1958 when the dependency of Fiji
upon the Scheme became evident. The Scheme personnel were
appointed to the posts of Deputy Director and Chief Inspector
respectively and the charge was made that the Fiji Education
Department was exploiting the Scheme. This was, in fact, true
because at least fifteen New Zealand Scheme teachers were
occupying posts which should have been filled by Colonial
Officers. Dr. Beeby, the then Director of Education in New
Zealand, drew attention to the fact that New Zealand personnel
were being promoted and appointed to posts by methods which
were not in accord with those followed in New Zealand. (NZEDF
1949). Other carrots had been provided by Fiji one of which
was the agreement that long service of ten years or more on the
Scheme would be rewarded with paid leave to the United Kingdom.
One of the results of these and other inducements has been
that teachers trained in New Zealand, and with pensions paid
by the New Zealand Government, have spent virtually all their
working lives in Fiji and even retired outside New Zealand.
(NZEDF 1958).

The resolution of the above issue did reflect one of the
great strengths of the Scheme, that it was an informal arrangement between two Education Departments and not a formal one
between two governments. It was resolved amicably between the
two Directors on a personal basis and both Departments took
care to act scrupulously and with consideration for the other.
The Fiji Director agreed to run down the Scheme on the grounds
that it was not in Fiji's long term interests and also because
New Zealand was finding that the number seconded to Fiji was
a strain on her own resources.

Unfortunately this policy was not adopted and the number
of teachers, in spite of declining temporarily, rose subsequently.
This was because the Officer for Island Education - an ex-
Acting Director of Education in Fiji - acknowledged that Fiji
had made the right gesture but considered that too abrupt a
change of practice would cause difficulties for Fiji. (NZEDF
1960). A new Director was appointed in New Zealand and subsequently the number of New Zealand teachers rose to just over
a hundred at the time of independence in 1970. In a number of
respects this was inevitable and a consequence of the policy
adopted by Fiji. From 1960 the secondary and primary sectors
expanded rapidly and there was an increased demand for graduate
teachers and teacher trainers. More specialised services were
being provided by the Fiji Department and these required
specialised personnel not available in Fiji. The University
of the South Pacific opened in 1968 and specialist sixth form
teachers were needed to teach on the pre-degree programmes.
Once more the most convenient source of supply was the Scheme

of Co-operation with New Zealand and more teachers were
recruited for the diversifying system of education in Fiji.
It appeared that, just after independence, Fiji was as
dependent on the Scheme as she had been in the Colonial period,
and would continue to be so for some years to come.

It has been noted that the costs of the Scheme were borne
by Fiji and that before the mid 1960s the Scheme provided the
cheapest source of European teachers for the government schools.
However, this situation changed from about 1964 onwards and it
became obvious that Fiji was disadvantaged as a result of her
previous over-reliance upon the Scheme. A prophetic note was
struck in 1964 when a dispute arose concerning the salaries of
New Zealand teachers in Fiji. In making a comparison the
Director concluded that Scheme teachers were already significant
better off than other European officers and furthermore;

> ...I gather that New Zealand teachers' salaries are
> likely to be revised again in the near future, thus
> widening the gap which already exists between the
> salaries of Scheme of Co-operation teachers and
> teachers who have been designated. (NZEDF 1964).

The 'designated' teachers were those who were serving under the
British Overseas Aid Scheme whose Fiji salaries were supplemented by the British government. A number of attempts were
made by the Fiji Department to get Scheme teachers designated,
but the British authorities were not amenable to this. This
refusal was based partly on the grounds that the Scheme was an
informal one between the Education Departments of the respective
countries, and was not designed to help the United Kingdom fulfil her obligations to the Colonies. Fiji salary levels were
unattractive compared with those in other colonies and recruit-
ment of specialised personnel became increasingly difficult on
this and other grounds. Efforts to recruit specialist staff
had failed in 1965 so the Director was forced to '...fall back
again on New Zealand where salaries are very much higher'.
(Fiji 1965). Another difficulty was that there was a relatively
small pool of the specialised staff required in New Zealand.

The costs of employing Scheme teachers increased and
independent Fiji had to continue to leave one open and unspec-
ified vote in the annual budget to allow for anticipated
increases in the salary of New Zealand teachers. In 1970 the
costs to Fiji of employing the 90 Scheme teachers was about
$F5,255 each per annum whereas the total emoluments paid to
the teaching force of 4,517 teachers was $F4,212,684 or about
$F934 per head. (Fiji 1970). In 1971 there was an increase
in New Zealand salaries of up to 35% and Fiji had to pay this
increase to about a hundred teachers.

Another anomaly was that when the first local man was
appointed head of the Education Department, thirty-one New
Zealand teachers were being paid a higher salary than him and

the total cost was being borne by the Fiji government.
Finance was the principal reason for the decision to run down
the Schem and phase it out. In spite of some claims that it
could not be done, the Fiji Department did utilise other sources
and by the time of the introduction of the seventh plan for
education in 1976 there was only a handful of Scheme teachers
remaining in Fiji.

In the five years after independence considerable acrimony
was roused about the Scheme and the phrase was coined that
'New Zealand teachers do the scheming and Fiji does the co-op
erating'. This was unjust as the New Zealand teachers' organisations in Fiji pressed for the introduction of a supplement-
ation scheme and for New Zealand to offset the costs of the
Scheme to Fiji. What has to be borne in mind is that the
Scheme was an informal one and that Fiji was a British Colony
with no formal links with New Zealand, unlike the Cook Islands
and Western Samoa. When Fiji gained her independence, New
Zealand promptly and generously donated aid in a variety of
forms. However, there was no institutional provision for the
supplementing of salaries and so aid was offered which could
offset the cost of the Scheme to Fiji. Fiji was allowed to
present a 'shopping list' of aid projects, increased scholarships were awarded for Fiji citizens tenable in New Zealand,
experts and other personnel were supplied on aid terms to Fiji
and a positive response was shown to any Fiji initiative with
respect to educational development. In the subsequent half
decade after independence Fiji exploited the situation skil-
fully in the political sense, obtained extensive educational
and other aid from New Zealand, and reduced drastically the
number of Scheme personnel in Fiji. But it should be noted
that Fiji specified what was acceptable to her and also presented her list of priorities with respect to aid projects.
There was little to suggest that what was being given was only
on New Zealand terms.

There were, however, more subtle costs to pay. The
availability of Scheme teachers meant that the Colonial Government was able to pursue its policy of providing a European
type education for European children in the most prestigious
of the government schools. Whilst these schools set the
educational pattern for Fiji as a whole, their operation was a
tangible demonstration that the Government condoned that educational provision should be made along racial lines. Up to
1960, legislation supported this and even up to the time of
independence it was legal to give preference to applicants to
schools on the grounds of race or religion. New Zealand
teachers certainly taught in schools for all races but their
presence as a group facilitated racial policies in education
which meant that differential educational provision was made
for the different racial groups in Fiji, a situation that
still to a degree exists. The Scheme of Co-operation unwittingly made such racial policies possible.

Co-operation or Colonialism?

It has been noted that the upper secondary courses were dominated by New Zealand external examinations and that the presence of New Zealand teachers and administrators contributed to this. One unfortunate effect of this was that no advantage was taken of a number of moves by the Cambridge Syndicate to localise the content of their examinations. By 1975 few schools were preparing students for the Cambridge examinations. Yet when approached by the Fiji authorities on the matter, those responsible for the public examinations in New Zealand consistently made it clear that their examinations were for New Zealand children and that they did not have the resources to provide examinations in such areas as Fijian and Hindi or to orientate the content to individual island countries such as Fiji. Inevitably, at the upper secondary levels, the content of the external examinations taken was not relevant to Fiji and this had unfortunate effects upon the study of subjects lower down the age range, particularly the vernaculars. Since independence there has been a change and an appropriate lower secondary curriculum is being developed but the move to develop more appropriate examinations for South Pacific island students at the form 5 and 6 levels has been slow. This has been due to the inability of the island countries to agree amongst themselves and, partly, because the New Zealand authorities have insisted that the decisions with respect to such matters should come from the island countries themselves.

This has now changed. The New Zealand Education Department has dropped its stance that it is there to fulfil an advisory role only. It has initiated developments and is now prepared to offer alternative School Certificate papers in co-operation with any island country which wishes to avail itself of such a service. Fiji decided to do so in 1976 and currently students are being prepared for a limited number of alternative papers. This adherence to New Zealand and its standards may, to some, reflect the servility of the Fiji Education Department. To this writer, this is not so. It does reflect the concern of the Department, rightly or wrongly, with standards. Pupils, parents, teachers and administrators want a guarantee that any new development in external examinations will not lead to a devaluation of the award and they want it recognised by metropolitan countries. What must also be remembered is that the educational link between Fiji and New Zealand is unusually strong, stronger than those that exist between most other countries. Many of Fiji's educated elite received part of their education in New Zealand, frequently for extended periods, and these include the Head of State, the Prime Minister and numerous cabinet and other officials. For them to discount the validity of New Zealand educational standards would be for them to repudiate their own education. Also, the presence of the University of the South Pacific in Suva is another manifestation of New Zealand's educational system as Britain and New Zealand were the two major metropolitan contributors to this institution in its first decade.

Perhaps the principal criticism that may be levelled at
the Scheme of Co-operation was that the provision of such a
source of teachers was a disincentive for Fiji to develop her
own training facilities for secondary teachers. These were
virtually non-existent in the colonial period and reliance was
placed on recruiting from overseas. Expansion had taken place
in secondary education and the Director of Education was convinced in 1966 that the only real need for graduates in Fiji
was for secondary teaching. (East West Centre 1966). One
result of this was that too few graduates were trained and
those that were trained as teachers easily found jobs elsewhere.
This, plus the lack of trained secondary teachers, forced
independent Fiji to recruit teachers from diverse sources, who
were of varying standards. Inevitably this had its effect on
the teaching provided in schools. In 1976 the same official,
no longer Head of the Department, noted that '...The shortage
of trained teachers, particularly at the secondary levels, is
reflected in the examination results'. (Fiji 1976). This was
the case three years after the first graduates of the degree
and diploma programmes of the University of the South Pacific
began to teach in Fiji schools. Whilst those programmes, plus
other in-service programmes, had been drawn up to cater for
Fiji's needs at the secondary level, there is little doubt
that these steps were long overdue. That the steps had not
been taken earlier was the result of the short-sighted policy
of the Fiji Education Department which can be partly attributed
to the existence of the Scheme of Co-operation.

The 1959 Oxford Commonwealth Education Conference cited
the Scheme as a model of its kind. There are a number of
reasons for this which this writer believes should be incorporated into any scheme whereby teachers are to be supplied by
one country to another. The teachers recruited through the
Scheme were generally the type sought after by developing
countries. They were experienced teachers prepared to teach
for an effective period in the developing country. The terms
and conditions of service were good. Fiji was and is a reliable
employer. More important was the fact that those on the
Scheme remained within the New Zealand system, both from the
point of view of superannuation rights and career prospects.
Effective supportive services were provided to ensure that the
New Zealand teachers moved into a system that had features
similar to what they were used to and so could use their
experience to good effect. Any programme which provides con-
tract officers for fairly short terms must be more effective
if, as with the New Zealand scheme, those on it have a demonstrable degree of security, do not feel that their promotion
prospects are being undermined, and are reasonably familiar
with the system they enter. Teachers on such schemes are
more likely to be effective if they have good professional
and working relationships with their colleagues and with the

administration.

Another important element that needs to be built into such
a programme should be the one that was introduced into the
latter part of the Fiji one, namely that teachers should serve
for only a limited period. In the Fiji case, ten years was too
long; it should have been no more than five or six years. A
more effective contribution will also be made by teachers who
feel that they are welcome and who are willing to adapt to the
local cultural and social pattern. This was the case with the
New Zealand teachers and the Islands Office normally selected
the candidates for Fiji very carefully, and also later adopted
the practice of interviewing the spouse of an applicant. Any
scheme must have a built-in screening mechanism to ensure that
those sent are suitable, and this would normally mean that only
experienced teachers should be eligible.

It was sad that the last years of the Scheme were soured
by acrimony resulting from the high cost of the Scheme to Fiji.
In the event, the New Zealand pattern of granting aid was not
then flexible enough to adapt to the new circumstances.
Possibly the most reasonable model to follow with respect to
finance would be the British model whereby a system of supple-
mentation and allowances ensured that the cost of employing an
expatriate teacher or specialist would be no more than the
salary of a similarly qualified local person. Furthermore,
the recipient should be encouraged to live on the local salary,
thereby avoiding a living style which would demonstrate some of
the forms of conspicuous consumption for which highly paid
expatriate elites have been properly criticised. Lastly, the
general terms of service and control of personnel should be
entrusted to the recipient to deploy the aid in the way considered most appropriate. New Zealand has kept a very low profile
in Fiji in this respect and the strings attached to aid donated
have been minimal. This is the reason why Fiji still seeks the
advice and assistance of New Zealand in educational and other
matters.

Was the Scheme an example of colonialism or co-operation?
An aphorism coined in Fiji not long after independence was that
Australia ruled the economy, New Zealand the education system,
but that Britannia still ruled. There was and is a kernel of
truth in this but New Zealand, whilst still being a major
presence in the education system, takes its cue from the Fiji
Department as to the assistance and advice that it should give.
As far as the Scheme was concerned, the Fiji Government did
exploit it to a degree, as did certain individual New Zealanders
but this was generally with the full knowledge and acquiescence
of the New Zealand Department. In matters pertaining to the
Scheme of Co-operation between the Departments, the initiative
always lay with the Fiji Department. If the Scheme is an
example of colonialism, then New Zealand is an extraordinarily
naive colonialist - or a profoundly subtle one.

Chapter Ten

EDUCATIONAL NEOCOLONIALISM - THE CONTINUING COLONIAL LEGACY

Keith Watson

It can be seen from several of the previous chapters in
this book that they are concerned with colonial practice beyond
the classical colonial period, that they show that colonialism
is an ongoing process, and that the relationships between
Third World countries and the industrial world - can be ones
of dependency(1).
    Not surprisingly, the concept of dependency is used most
forcefully in this volume by Brock and Avalos since it originated in Latin America in the late 1960s/early 1970s and was
later used to apply to the plantation economies of the Caribbean. The concept was coined to describe the economic dependency of Latin America and the Caribbean countries on the industrial world of the North, especially the USA; to show that in
so many aspects the Latin American and Caribbean economies are
interlinked with the capitalism of Western Europe and North
America; and that however much these countries might like to
break away and develop along independent, or even radical
lines (e.g. Chile), they are unable to do so. (Beckford 1972;
Cardoso 1972; Cardoso and Faletto 1979; Cockroft J.D. et al
1972; Frank 1967; Galtung 1972; Lall 1975; Palma 1978). Above
all, dependency is concerned with the influence of external
forces on a network of internal relationships, structures,
political and economic decisions in individual Third World
countries. As Cardoso and Faletto argue dependency implies:
    a situation that structually entails a link with the
    outside in such a way that what happens internally in
    a dependent country cannot be fully explained without
    taking into consideration the links that internal
    groups have with external ones. Dependence should no
    longer be considered an 'external variable': its
    analysis should be based on the relations between the
    different social classes within the dependent nations
    themselves. (1979: 22).

    Closely associated with dependency theory is that of
centre-periphery relationships, whereby economic developments

181

at the periphery help sustain and build up the economies at
the centre. (Galtung 1972). This occurs at several levels,
both national and international. In individual countries the
development of regional capitals or cities depends upon the
economic growth and exploitation of the regional hinterland.
In all developing countries the capital city or the major port,
if there is one, and if it is distinctive from the capital
city - has grown out of all proportion to the economic growth
in the rest of the country, in population, industrial development, job creation, wealth, economic infrastructure and
political power. As a result the bigger the city grows the
more it absorbs economic investment and the more economic
investment that is put into the city the larger it grows, with
the result that the rest of the country, the periphery, is
usually underdeveloped economically and neglected politically(2)
Because the centres, the capital or regional cities were usually
developed by the colonial powers initially - all the cities of
South East Asia for example, with the exception of Bangkok,
are colonial cities (Ginsberg 1955) - because they are seats
of political power, they are also usually centres of major
educational investment, containing the majority of the most
prestigious institutions of secondary, tertiary and specialised
education. The result is that those who do not have access to
wealth, power or education, that is the bulk of the population,
are disadvantaged.

In international terms, economic developments at the periphery of the global economy, that is in the poor countries of
the Third and Fourth Worlds(3), help to sustain the economies
of the rich industrial North. This view is widely accepted
and the evidence to support it is overwhelming. (Cockroft et
al; Mende 1973; Brandt 1980). However, it also applies in
educational and intellectual terms. Not only is the most
economic and industrial power and wealth concentrated in the
North - Europe, North America, Japan, the Soviet Union and
Australia - but the majority of intellectual and educational
power is also concentrated there. The majority of the world's
leading universities, research institutions, academics,
academic journals, publishing houses, library and research
facilities are also concentrated in the developed countries so
that developing countries seeking to develop any of these
particular areas must look to the developed countries for
leadership and assistance. As such they become more subservien
than ever during the colonial period, especially when it is
considered that the speed of developments in research and
publishing activities increasingly places the North ahead of
the South. The countries on the periphery, the South, are
thus disadvantaged, but because the relations between the
metropolitan powers and the developing countries tend to be on
a government to government basis, i.e. from elites in one
centre to elites in another centre, those people on the periphe
of the poorest countries are even more acutely disadvantaged

in economic and educational terms.

While recognising that both the dependency theory and the centre-periphery theory, both of which are essentially economic analyses, have a contribution to make to an understanding of educational relationships, and while there are writers like Memmi (1968) and Carnoy (1974), who argues that 'imperialism colonises everyone but those who make the decisions at the centre of the metropole' (p.69), the term neocolonialism is possibly more apposite when considering the post - colonial educational relationships and problems facing developing countries during the last two decades of the twentieth century, since it is the means by which existing educational institutions and patterns are subtly, and not so subtly, preserved, or even controlled by external powers, usually the former colonial authorities. It is at the same time more difficult to 'prove' or quantify educational neocolonialism than it is trade or economic relationships because the educational relationship between the metropolitan powers and the developing countries simply because it is often very subtle; because aid to education is often couched in terms of the highest altruism; and because the educational and political elites of Third World countries acquiesce in this relationship either because of inertia, because they can see no way round it or because it suits their interests by helping to maintain them in power.

Several definitions have been offered for the term 'neo-colonialism': 'the continued post-colonial impact of the advanced industrial countries on the educational systems and policies as well as the intellectual life of the developing areas' (Altbach 1971, p.237); 'the persistence of foreign control despite seeming national independence' (Altbach and Kelly 1978, p.29); 'the continuation of the educational system erected by the colonial regime is by far the most powerful instrument for perpetuating the concepts, the outlook, and the value on which the privileged classes' power is built'. (Mende 1973, p.99). The implications of this control and influence are serious, not only because as Myrdal (1970, p.95), points out 'the monopoly of education is the most fundamental basis of inequality and it retains its hold more strongly in the poorer countries', but because it is not always deliberately planned and because, as Thompson points out, 'the international networks of constraint make it almost impossible for developing countries to develop systems of education tailored to their own individual needs'. (Thompson 1977). The result, as Mende scathingly, though not entirely accurately observes, is that:

> much of the education now dispersed in poor countries is not only irrelevant to the solution of the problems they face, but tends to be positively harmful. It perpetuates contempt for menial tasks, and widens the gulf between the privileged minorities and the uneducated or illiterate masses. Sometimes, with substantial foreign help in the form of technical assistance it stamps alien attitudes

and values on minorities who, because of their foreign
education are destined to become members of the ruling
groups. It fails to provide any vocational training,
elements of modern science, useful technology, or knowledge about modern agriculture to confront real problems
impeding material progress. And while it usually produces
a few highly qualified scientists and specialists likely
to flatter national pride, it almost universally fails to
provide the required number of foremen or even of trained
mechanics capable of repairing and maintaining valuable
imported equipment in proper condition'. (Mende, pp.101-2)

In this chapter and in the light of the preceding chapters
therefore, it is worth examining in what ways there is a legacy
of colonial control and influence on education systems which
persists and even distorts educational and economic development.
As has been shown one of the most enduring features of the
colonial legacy has been <u>the formal school system</u>, Western in
concept and linear in application in so far as children must
progress from one grade to another systemmatically and during
a given age span, while at the same time there has been an
almost total disregard for non-formal approaches to education,
especially for adults. Indeed many of the existing non-formal
arrangements were destroyed, or at the least severely weakened,
as a result of colonial involvement. One striking aspect of
this situation is not that the school systems which exist
throughout the Third World, derive from European or American
models and are divided into primary, secondary, vocational,
teacher training and tertiary levels, but that they have been
left largely untouched and uncriticised from within the countries
concerned. Critics have generally been a radical minority or
Western academics concerned that if education should have a
vital role to play in national, social and economic development,
it needs to be reformed quite drastically so that it takes into
account local needs and indigenous cultures and so that it is
far more concerned with local situations and with the realities
of the employment market. Instead of aiming at producing
numerous clerks, lawyers and administrators greater emphasis
should be placed on training better farmers, engineers, entre-
preneurs, agronomists, scientists and so forth. In fact far
from being drastically overhauled school systems in developing
countries have been expanded dramatically to cope with increasing
demand and rising birth rates in spite of the costs involved
in this exercise.
It has also been far easier to increase school enrolments
than to initiate fundamental reforms. A study of the enrolment increases in say the Philippines, Indonesia, Bangladesh,
India, Nigeria, Kenya or Morocco show the dimension of this
vast linear expansion. The fact that these education systems
were built for a different purpose, for the selection of an
elite to fulfil a leadership role in society (initially a sub-

servient one to the colonial rulers) has been immaterial. Indeed only recently has the extension of an elitist school system for mass consumption been called into question in the Western world, at least by a non-radical (Husen 1979), but to
challenge this extension in India, Sri Lanka or Nigeria would
be almost treasonable. Expansion without questioning the
purpose or orientation of schooling might have kept millions
of children off the streets and introduced them to a modicum
of literacy and numeracy, but the cost in financial and human
terms has been colossal, and one only needs to examine dropout
and wastage rates, still as high as 60% or 70% in some countries
(World Bank 1980) to see that the impact on attitudes towards
social and economic development has been minimal. Indeed, the
1974 World Bank Education Sector Review commented that the
social conservatism, inertia and resistance to change in the
majority of developing countries was far greater than had
originally been realised.

The expansion of formal school systems came about partly
because of the United Nations Declaration of Human Rights that
placed education fairly and squarely as a human right, partly
because of the UNESCO Regional Plans at the beginning of the
1960s(4), which advocated expansion across the board, but
largely because politicians, development economists and educationists believed that education was essential for social and
economic development. (Adams and Bjork 1971; Coleman 1965;
Harbison and Myers 1964). 'Education' meant the formal school
system. There were only a few sceptics at the time (Anderson
1969; Anderson and Bowman 1965). Thus national goals were
established for educational expansion in the vain belief that
it would lead to rapid modernisation and structural changes.
Only as costs increased, the enrolments increased and economies
did not progress as expected has there begun to be a requestion-
ing, (Illich 1971; Weiler 1976; Watson 1981b) but it is easier
to diagnose the problem than to change course, especially because of popular demand.

Where reform has taken place it has been marginal and un-
systematic and it has often followed on similar developments in
the Western powers. Indeed, there has been a tendency for
institutional changes that have taken place in the developed
world to be copied in the LDCs. Thus three of the most enduring
features of educational development in Western Europe since the
early 1960s, roughly co-inciding with independence for so many
nations of the Third World, have been automatic promotion from
grade to grade, the development of comprehensive secondary
schooling and the raising of the school leaving age. These
patterns have been followed by numerous developing countries.
Many countries that ought to have considered reducing the
length of schooling in order to cover costs and population
increase have felt obliged to increase the length of schooling
because this has been the pattern pursued in the developed
nations(5). Many have introduced automatic promotion from

grade to grade and Iran, Thailand, Malaya, Vietnam are amongst many LDCs that have developed some form of comprehensive educ- ation. Local reasons for the changes may have varied, from a means of providing greater opportunities for children in rural areas, to postponing selection until as late as possible, to ensuring that some vocational/technical education is taught alongside academic subjects to all secondary children. Whatever the reasons that have been given one cannot help but wonder how far policy decisions have been taken as a result of emulation of Western developments and how far transplants have really been suited to the new situations.

The picture can be enlarged upon with other illustrations. The 1960s in Britain especially saw the development of teachers centres, open plan primary schools, curriculum development, diversified higher education including the Open University, though curriculum developments and changes in higher education were also common features throughout Western Europe. Hundreds of visitors were brought over from Third World countries by the British Council, the Ministry of Overseas Development, UNESCO and allied organisations to study these developments. Numerous reports were written extolling their virtues and numerous specialist visitors went overseas advocating similar develop- ments in Third World countries, whether or not they were suit- able to local needs. Comparative education has always been to some extent concerned with cultural borrowing but this situation got out of hand as teachers' centres were advocated for Sierre Leone, Ghana, Nigeria, Botswana, India and Bangladesh, curriculum development centres were established in Kuala Lumpur, Delhi, Bombay, Bangkok, Nairobi and Lagos, the Open University was copied in Iran, Pakistan, Singapore, Colombia and the Ivory Coast regardless of its suitability, the administrative capabil- ities and the financial resources of the countries concerned.

Some of these institutional and structural changes have been advocated by international agencies, especially UNESCO and the World Bank, through numerous reports and international conferences, and as such they have had a profound influence on the thinking of politicians and educationists in the Third World. Yet interestingly enough the more radical proposals from UNESCO on lifelong education, rural development and non- formal educational programmes (Faure 1970; Lengrand 1970; Coombs and Ahmed 1973; World Bank 1974) have been heralded with fanfares and press releases and yet have had remarkably little impact. Lipservice has been paid to non-formal education and community education and rural development departments within Ministries of Education have been set up especially to deal with non-formal educational developments, yet only a small percentage of the educational budget in the majority of countries has been allocated to developments in these areas. When the British government produced a new aid strategy of 'More Help for the Poorest' (ODM 1975), following publication of the 1974 World Bank Education Sector Paper advocating the allocation of an

186

increasing proportion of aid to the poorest, usually rural, parts of the poorest nations of the world, the British Ministry of Overseas Development found it could not spend its aid allocations because it could not find sufficient projects worthy of support and because it could not find sufficient interest in the governments of Third World countries.

WHY SHOULD THIS BE?

There would appear to be at least four reasons. The _first_ is linked with job structures and qualifications. As Dore (1976, 1980) and Oxenham (1980) have amply shown, because schooling in the West is concerned with qualifications, diplomas and certificates, employment opportunities are also bound up with these qualifications and vice versa, the situation in most developing countries is even more chronically inter-related:- Iredale (1978) has shown in the Indian context that NFE programmes were only accepted in Tamil Nadhu after agreement had been reached with government officials that those completing NFE courses would receive a paper qualification equivalent to that given to students in full-time schooling; while Lewin (1975) has shown that extra years spent in the education system in Sri Lanka and Malaysia - and hence a higher educational qualification - bring financial rewards out of all proportion to the extra period of education. Thus unless the rich countries break the link between education, qualification and employment the LDCs are unlikely to follow suit. In the present circumstances therefore, unless NFE brings its own certificate rewards it is likely to prove relatively unpopular.

A _second_ reason is that with the exceptions of the Scandinavian countries, especially Sweden and Denmark, with their generous adult education, NFE programmes (Paulston 1980) and France, which levies a tax on all large companies in order to provide adult education programmes, most European countries have played down lifelong education and NFE. Programmes are highly developed in Canada and the USA but only _after_ adequate formal school provision. In the eyes of many leaders in Third World countries, therefore, because NFE and community lifelong education are not highly regarded or developed or adequately funded in European countries they are regarded as second best and inferior in their own countries. Moreover, in spite of pleas. to the contrary by Coombs and Ahmed (1974), costs can be as high, if not higher than formal schooling (Simmons 1980). In the Western world education, and especially the peripheral non-formal aspects of it, is always cut in times of economic crisis. Because it is an unknown quantity and because there is a constant economic crisis NFE therefore gets played down in most developing countries.

A _third_ reason is the attitude of educationists and politicians as well as the ordinary citizens, in the former colonies. The elite groups are unwilling to modify the existing

school system radically because it helped them to reach power,
because it is familiar and because it can help to sustain them
in power by producing similar types for the leadership. Ordinary citizens and young men (and women) aspiring for elite status
are not very eager to see changes because they view the school
system as an avenue of upward social mobility. For many indigenous leaders the education system they went through divorced
them from the rural and frequently the linguistic and cultural
background of the majority of their countrymen, especially those
living in the rural areas. As such therefore, they are afraid
to reform it radically. Above all, however, the existing school
system exists because it was left by the colonial rulers and
because a similar pattern exists in the metropolitan powers.
Even where there have been attempts at radical change and at
breaking from the familiar pattern of Western type education
as for example in Cambodia, Laos, China, Tanzania, Cuba and
Mozambique, there has eventually been a reversal back to a
formal pattern of schooling. It is significant also that in
all the countries mentioned above there have also been attempts
at a radical restructuring of the society and the economy in
the hope that this would lessen their political and economic
dependence on the industrial nations of the North. Only writers
like **Illich**   (1971) and Reimer (1971) have advocated the
complete abolition of formal schooling. Even Carnoy in his
solutions to the educational problems of under-development does
not dispense with formal schooling: he simply re-focuses its
purpose and the content of the curriculum for he writes:

> According to the encroachment strategy, the struggle
> for control is based on the continued operation of the
> plant. The school would continue to graduate students,
> but students with a different kind of knowledge: it
> would continue to employ teachers, but teachers who
> play a different role in the educational process -
> participants instead of managers. (Carnoy 1975: 400).

A _fourth_ and inter-related reason is that of resistance
to change. Partly because of the very success of educational
expansion there are enormous sums of money tied up in plant,
personnel and administrative structures. These arrangements
are not easy to unscramble. There is also a reluctance to
develop something significantly different from what is internationally acceptable and which might be regarded as inferior.
This applies as much to new approaches to schooling as to vernacular language instruction and localised or agriculturally
biassed curricula. Colonial governments found themselves unable
to make much headway in these areas. Governments of newly
independent territories find themselves faced with even stronger
opposition. Even in revolutionary societies like China, Cuba
and Tanzania there has been considerable opposition to the
changes which has never been adequately curbed.
This leads onto another aspect of the colonial legacy

which has neocolonial overtones. The curricula and syllabuses
used in many former colonial territories still remain largely
unchanged in many of their essential ingredients, either because
of inertia or as a direct result of overseas assistance in the
form of personnel and textbooks. This was to a great extent
inevitable in the years immediately following independence when
school systems, the administrative framework, the curriculum
and textbooks were often continued by expatriate administrators,
advisers and teachers who stayed on to help with the administration of newly independent territories. It was also to some
extent inevitable because with educational expansion and book
shortages in individual countries charitable organisations like
the Ranfurley Trust in the United Kingdom and political/cultural
organisations like the United States Information Service (USIS),
the East West Centre and the British Council made presentations
of large quantities of surplus textbooks and reading books from
the metropolitan countries. Inevitably it was easier and more
prudent to accept these, and be influenced by their thought
patterns and values, than to go without. Lack of change was
also understandable and to some extent inevitable because it
was usually regarded as more important to expand school provision than to change the curriculum or syllabuses, and because
coming to grips with managing 'a new country' was often more
important than being concerned with what was taught. Changes
have come but these have often only been peripheral.

     Moreover in the early years following independence as
school systems expanded rapidly expatriate staff were required
to continue to run the schools. Even now some countries are
still dependent on expatriate staff while others, with growing
concern that academic and linguistic standards have declined
since they ceased recruiting some years ago, are now recruiting
specialised staff, especially in science subjects. With the
best will in the world expatriate staff cannot be dissociated
from their own past experiences, perceptions and cultural
blinkers. The approaches they bring to their work were and are
therefore, bound to be biassed.

     The whole idea of an academic curriculum taught in school,
divorced from much of the everyday life of pupils outside the
school, is European in origin. This was transferred to the
developing countries at the height of the colonial period and
has remained more or less intact since. There have been experiments with agricultural and vocational/craft courses, as there
were during the colonial period, but the concept of separate
subject areas/disciplines taught for so many hours per week is
European(6). Individual syllabuses might have changed. History
and geography now have a different perspective, are more related
to the local situation and are not studies of developments as
perceived through European eyes. Civics is related much more
to the local and national needs of independent countries and to
the responsibilities of her citizens. Language, where the
language of instruction is a European language, can have a pro-

found impact on patterns of thinking, especially if there is little indigenous literature available in any of the European languages. Inevitably much of the literature and poetry that is studied is Western, with all that that implies in re-inforcement of cultural values and attitudes. There is a growing body of modern literature in the Caribbean, West Africa and the Indian sub-continent written in English and West African and South East Asian literature written in French, yet while some of this is studied in schools(7) the tendency is still to study Shakespeare or Racine or the great European literature(8).

The whole issue of language is an important one and has generated a voluminous literature on the subject. As Wong Hoy Kee has pointed out:

> Language is an essential means of communication and when the language in question is also the mother tongue, it is one of the most important formative influences in moulding the intellect as well as the character of the child. Indeed, it is a powerful instrument by which not only individuals may express their personality, but groups may also identify their collective consciousness. (1973).

Language can be a barrier to integration in multi-ethnic, multi-lingual societies just as much as for example in America and Australia it can be a means of developing a sense of national identity. Yet surprisingly few developing countries have tried to break away from the metropolitan language of their colonial masters to develop a national language. Bangladesh, Indonesia, India, Tanzania, Vietnam and Malaysia are a few countries that have attempted to make the break, at considerable cost in terms of finance and administration and in the restructuring of syllabuses and textbooks. There are many countries like Botswana, Lesotho, Kenya, Malawi, Ghana, Senegal and the Ivory Coast, to name but a few, that have deliberately maintained English or French as the National language, the language of communications, law and administration as the most neutral language to bind together the disparate linguistic and ethnic groups within their territories. Indonesia has possibly been the most successful LDC and certainly the most successful plural society to use its national language Bahasa Indonesia, as a means of welding together over 136 million people in over 3000 scattered islands into a nation. (Nicherlein 1974; Wong Hoy Kee 1971). Although the mother tongue or local vernacular is used as the medium of instruction for the first three years of schooling, if it is widely spoken or is so requested by a sufficient number of parents, Bahasa Indonesia is used throughout the rest of the system and as such gives the Indonesian education system a national character.

The first Prime Minister of the Federation of Malaysia, Tungku Abdul Rahman, perhaps most effectively summed up the idea of a national language being synonymous with national

development when he said:
> It is only right that as a developing nation we should
> want to have a language of our own....If the national
> language is not introduced our country will be devoid
> of a unified character and personality - as I would put
> it, a nation without a soul and without life.(9)

Hence in Malaysia a National Language and Literature Agency,
the Dewan Bahasa dan Pustaka, was opened in 1959 with the purpose of translating thousands of scientific and technical words
into Malay and of developing Malaysian textbooks for use in
school. Gradually, Bahasa Malaysia has been introduced as the
national language and as the medium of instruction in the
education system. (Watson 1980e). In India a similar Language
Agency was opened in New Delhi soon after independence to develop Hindi as the national language, but the impact of the
national language in non-Hindi speaking areas, especially in
the South of India, has been limited and at university level
and in many specialist scientific and research institutes, as
well as in the press, English still predominates.

Where the language of instruction is a metropolitan language it is far easier for aid agencies and Western governments
to make inputs in the form of personnel equipment or textbooks.
For this reason much Western aid has gone to build up secondary
and tertiary level institutions in Third World countries, in
the form of buildings, equipment, materials, etc. with the
result that educational development has been frequently distorted: secondary and higher education has expanded at rates far
faster than at primary level with the result that UPE has not
yet been achieved in many countries. (Fredericksen 1981;
Simmons 1980). Knowledge of a metropolitan language, especially
English, is considered essential for higher education because
of the access to an international network of research and
academic contacts and because in the fields of science, medicine
and engineering Western knowledge is all important.

The point is it is not simply a question of language, but
of thought forms, values and ideas, access to materials,
journals and research that is also important. The leaders of
so many developing countries not only still use European languages for international conferences and diplomacy, but often
also for pleasure and in reading, for discussion amongst themselves, and because a metropolitan language provides them with
a degree of power over - and separation from - the masses. In
a country like India, as Altbach (1975) has shown this has an
impact out of all proportion to the numbers who speak and use
English, because the majority of national papers and journals
are produced in English, though only about 2% of the population
are literate in the language, thereby sustaining the thinking
and cultural patterns, as well as the language of the elite.

Closely linked with language is the whole area of publishing.
Here again strong neocolonial influences are still to be found.

191

Educational Neocolonialism - The Continuing Colonial Legacy

Not only do the major industrial nations, especially the USA,
Britain, France, the Soviet Union and West Germany, have a
major slice of the world's publishing and therefore control of
learned journals and scientific texts, but they have a disproportionate influence in Third World countries, because they can
to a great extent influence what books or knowlede is disseminated in these countries and they can if necessary handout obso-
lete or unwanted textbooks or produce works not necessarily the
most relevant to national needs. In India for example, according
to Altbach (1975) barely 10% of the books published are concerned
with scientific subjects compared with 25% in the USA and 54%
in the USSR. More important however, is the fact that the
majority of books, even Soviet books for overseas consumption,
are published in a European language. We have seen that over
50% of all books published in India are in English while barely
2% of the population is literate in English, while in Francophobe
and Anglophobe Africa virtually all books are published in
French or English yet between 80% and 95% of the population are
illiterate in those languages. The result is that the vast
majority of the populations are prevented from exploring new
avenues of knowledge through ignorance of a metropolitan language, and are thus condemned to a second-class intellectual
citizenship. This is not necessarily deliberate policy, but
commercial publishing houses need markets and need access to
these markets. If because of the generally low level of the
education system markets far away from the urban educated
elite are unprofitable they will not be catered for.
     Even in a country like Malaysia which has changed the
language media to a national language, foreign publishing
houses still help produce textbooks for use in schools, colleges
and universities. In many of the larger and more important
former colonial territories commercial publishing houses that
were established during the colonial period are still operating
with international interests and on a commercial basis. Many
of the books produced are written by Europeans or Americans.
Many are textbooks used in other situations, often European,
that are slightly modified to suit new markets. As such, they
are based on alien ideas and premisses. A good example would
be the English Language Book Scheme (ELBS), often administered
by the British Council, whereby basic textbooks in engineering,
mathematics, law, literature and history which are used in
Britain are made available at a fraction of the cost to Third
World countries. The scheme was conceived with the highest of
motives, as a quick and relatively cheap means of meeting a
student market in countries like India, Pakistan and Bangladesh
and there was no deliberate intention of inhibiting the development of local textbook writing and production: although this
is in fact what has resulted. Certain reading and language
schemes and mathematics textbooks developed for say West Africa,
have had names and situations changed to suit an East African
context though they are essentially the same books.(10) Even

science materials developed for use in Scotland or England have been transferred to developing countries with only a few modifications.

Surprisingly it would be thought that science was neutral and would not be used as a form of colonial control but Alam (1974) has shown that far from being neutral science is yet another form of colonialism since most recent developments and knowledge are those conceived of in Western terms, the great scientists referred to are those from Western traditions while indigenous scientists, small scale local skills and techniques, as for example in herbal medicine and animal husbandry, have been glossed over, or, as more frequently is the case, despised. In terms of curriculum development no subject has been more open to change and innovation than science education. As a UNESCO Report on developments in Asia observed: 'all the countries in Asia, without exception, have chosen the curriculum as a focal point of their programmes for the renovation of science education'. (UNESCO 1977). Yet one of the difficulties has been that because science has been fragmented into separate disciplines (in spite of recent attempted changes) - physics, chemistry, biology, mathematics - it has led to fragmentation and factual ignorance regarding scientific knowledge and the whole approach to scientific thinking, so that it has not been conceived as multi-disciplinary.

Curriculum developments in the Third World countries generally have tended to be adaptations of or the adoption of curriculum developments from the developed countries. Curriculum Development Centres established in many parts of the Third World, often funded by UNESCO or World Bank money, have often been modelled on their European counterparts and, in the early stages at least, have often been manned by Europeans. The structures and approaches to curriculum development are thus very European or North American - with very few exceptions the aspect of curriculum development that has relied most heavily on outside inputs and influences has been that of science education. This has been so largely because the importance of science education for Third World countries has been recognised as essential if attitudes towards development are to be changed, if there is to be understanding of the causes of water pollution and soil erosion and disease, whether of cattle, crops or humans, and because most apparent breakthroughs in this field have come from the West. The four schemes that have especially found their way around the world have been the Scottish Integrated Science scheme, the Nuffield Combined Science and Nuffield Mathematics Programmes and the Harvard Integrated Science Project. Commenting on the introduction of American devised science curricula into Latin America it has been observed that however high the motives in introducing these curricula overseas, transplantation is bound to take place through the use of foreign textbooks and materials, foreign teachers and/or the training of indigenous teachers by foreign staff often in the USA. The advisers involved have been frequently selected because of their political reliability. (Altbach 1971). In a paper on the introduction of a modified version of the Scottish Integrated Science programme into peninsular Malaysia (Watson 1980c) has shown that considerable neocolonial contraints have been involved. Not only were British advisers sent out to conduct orientation courses, develop materials and help train personnel, using their own inevitable biases and perceptions which were not necessarily remotely related to the real needs of the rural Malay peasants and only marginally related to those in the urban areas, but the scheme was introduced hurriedly and without adequate planning and foresight. Apart from inadequately trained teachers, few of whom could conceive of <u>integrated</u> science, having been used to a separate subject approach, there were insufficient laboratory technicians and inadequate supplies of equipment so that in the first instance, much of the equipment had to be imported at considerable expense to the Malaysian government and at commercial benefit to the manufacturers concerned. Above all, however, a two year non-examinable subject was modified to a three year examinable one because this suited the existing school structure, itself a direct legacy of the colonial era as Watson shows in his chapter in this volume.

A Chinese Malaysian (Sim 1977) has criticised 'the prevailing pernicious pre-occupation with examinations, which seems to permeate pedagogical practices in Malaysian schools' and Lewin (1975) has shown that a 45% increase in formal education, i.e. to the end of university instead of leaving after Grade XII is likely to lead to a 400% increase in starting salary. These comments could equally apply in any one of several dozen countries because the very structure of the school system and the status of examinations not only reinforce a European style curriculum but ensure longterm external involvement. Although the London University and Cambridge Overseas Examinations Syndicates may have been replaced by local examination boards, e.g. the Caribbean Examinations Council, the West African Examinations Board, the Tanzanian National Examinations Council, the Federation of Malaysia Examinations Syndicate, and although certain subjects have been modified to suit local conditions, the format of examinations, their role as mechanisms of selection and the use of Europeans as external assessors and advisers to help guarantee the status of the qualifications, imply that the decolonising process still has a long way to go. Brock points this out in relation to the Caribbean but it is undoubtedly true in many other societies as well.

The status of qualifications from Third World countries is important for those going overseas to study in foreign universities, especially under technical assistance agreements, because however good the local university maybe, however much its teachers may be concerned for and its courses related to local

needs and conditions, thousands of students still hope to gain
a qualification from a university in Australia, New Zealand,
Canada, North America or Europe. Why? Because of the international prestige attached to these institutions: because 90%
of the world's research is conducted in them (or in related
research institutes); because most of the world's academic
journals emanate from them or are edited by Western academics;
because even where research links are established with Third
World countries they are normally on terms set by Western
universities and on terms most likely to bring kudos to Western
academics, rather than necessarily being of relevance or value
to the Third World countries; and because many 'students' from
the Third World hope to find better paid, more attractive employment in the rich world after gaining their qualification.

Technical assistance training thus helps the neocolonial
hold, not only because of financial investment in the host
country, not only because of the attitudes and values taught
in the West, but because of the 'brain drain' of talented personnel from the poor world to the rich world(11). Because of
shortages of indigenous personnel many Third World governments
have been only too pleased to send staff overseas for training
in order to reduce the number of expatriates in their country
and in order to provide trained indigenous personnel. Unfortunately, training in North America or Europe is not necessarily
the most suitable for local conditions in the tropical and semi-
tropical countries. By encouraging more and more students to
go abroad both the metropolitan powers and the LDCs have delayed
the development of local courses. The diplomas and qualifications awarded by overseas institutions tended to be regarded not
only as essential but as the pattern to be followed when local
institutions were eventually developed. A further irony is
that because of the minimum entry requirements demanded by
European universities especially, education systems in the
former colonial countries became geared to preparing for the
necessary qualifications or their equivalent. Even when local
examination boards were established, as we have seen they were
based on the models of their European counterparts.

Technical assistance is a two-way process which need not
necessarily involve academic training. Thus, educationists
may visit Britain from Sabah, Fiji, Bangladesh, Sierre Leone
or Cyprus, or France from Senegal, Benin, Chad or Morocco to
study aspects of educational provision. This may be open plan
primary schools or team teaching in England or school inspection
in France. Educational administrators may come from Kuwait,
Nigeria, Pakistan and Malaysia to study English local education
authorities: while school principals from Sudan or Sri Lanka
may come to study comprehensive secondary schools in the belief
that something can be learnt or transferred from a study of
these institutions. Similarly, specialist advisers may be sent
from the metropolitan powers to advise on community education
in Thailand or the Philippines, educational administration in

Singapore, new approaches to mathematics teaching in Jamaica, Barbados, Ghana, Pakistan or Kenya. In both the inward and outward flow of personnel and ideas there are inevitably biases and prejudices.

Mende (1973) has shown that most French or British or Dutch aid, in general terms, goes to former colonial territorie even though in effect the benefits accrue to the economy of the donor country, while the USA tends to support only those countries regarded as politically favourable to their cause in the cold war against the Soviet Union. While educational aid is part of the general aid programme it can have a multiplier effect and be of considerable importance, because of its long term influence, beyond the actual sums of money involved, which are usually small as Beatrice Ayalos has shown in the context of Latin America. Apart from educational aid in the form of curriculum development projects, teaching and training personne teaching materials, overseas aid has also had a strong influence in shaping the policy and budgets in a number of countries Provision of language laboratories in schools in tropical countries has often helped sales of language laboratories in rich countries but has been a drain on over-stretched budgets in the recipient countries and has also led to frustration if they have broken down either because of a shortage of adequatel trained technicians or because of a shortage of spare parts. Capital aid programmes that have helped with the building costs of luxurious university campuses in Malawi, Kenya, Jamaica or Thailand, or with lavish hospitals in Dakar in Senegal or Saigon in Vietnam, or with the establishment of expensive educational television networks in the Ivory Coast or Colombia or Pakistan have also distorted indigenous educational budgets because the cost of maintaining and staffing these lavish institutions has frequently absorbed a disproportionate amount of the educational budget. One teaching hospital in Senegal for example, built with French money, absorbs over 90% of the total medical budget for the entire country!!

During the heady and optimistic days of <u>university expansi</u> in the 1960s - a global phenomenon incidentally - many American and European advisers found themselves swept along by the euphoric belief that universities were essential for national development and that they would provide the trained manpower which was so desperately needed in the Third World that they had not the heart or the inclination - to urge newly independen governments to prune down demands for replicas of models that were then in existence in the USA, France or England. As Ashby (1966) has written of the post war development of universities in British colonies there was a massive assumption 'that the pattern of university appropriate for Manchester, Exeter, and Hull was <u>ipso facto</u> appropriate for Ibadan, Kampala and Singapore'. Where advisers did urge caution, as in Malawi, they were severely rebuked. (Michael 1981). The countries of Africa, Asia and the Middle East were not going to be content with anything less than that which existed in developed nations. The result was a series of transplants of developed nation institutions to beautiful campuses in Third World countries. Thus there were American technological transplants to Latin America and American style Land Grant Colleges to India, Nigeria, Indonesia and Latin America. There were British style universities developed in Nigeria, India, Malaya, the Pacific region and the Caribbean. Only gradually was it realised that many of the countries (e.g. Lesotho or Mauritius) hardly had sufficient populations to sustain a viable university; that an excess of lawyers, social scientists, humanists and administrators was being produced while doctors, engineers, agronomists and scientists were being produced in insufficient numbers; while the costs of sustaining the edifice of higher education with its Western style academic 'standards', between one hundred and two hundred times those of primary education, were preventing the possibility of ever achieving universal primary education. A further weakness has been that so often these new universities have lacked library and research facilities and because of heavy teaching loads, little research work has been undertaken into local needs and problems. As such, many universities are symbols of ill-conceived aid programmes.

THE WAY AHEAD

Given the neocolonial constraints and influences on developments in the Third World, imposed wittingly or unwittingly by the industrial countries of the North is there any way short of revolution - or even radical reform of the socio-economic infrastructure of society - that can bring about the development of education systems that are more adapted to local needs than the Western models currently in existence? While it is probably more realistic to believe that radical educational change is only likely to come about as a result of overall social, political and economic revolution nevertheless, different approaches have been attempted during the 1960s and 1970s, (Watson 1981b), and the time has probably now come for all Third World governments concerned with mounting costs, financial crises, unemployment and slow economic growth to consider certain important steps. These are by no means exhaustive but are offered as a realistic way of making progress.

1. There should be greater problem-oriented research into socio-economic linkages; into inertia and psychological barriers to change; into the best form of education (not necessarily schooling) most suited to a particular country; into whether parental education - especially maternity and pre-school education, new approaches to health and hygiene are more suitable than formal schooling beginning at the age of six or seven; into whether literacy is best achieved in schools; and into whether examinations can be dispensed with. So often research

has been conducted by expatriate individuals or organisations, has been prejudiced and often rather erudite - academically interesting maybe, but not exactly what is going to be of the greatest practical value to the country concerned. So often research has been linked to overseas universities or research institutes because of the shortages of finance in the local country, indicating that it is lowly regarded. There is a need therefore, to increase the financial commitment to research, to set about some fundamental rethinking and to question whether or not the existing pattern of educational provision is the most suitable for the needs of that society or parts of that society. In some cases it may be; in others it may be far from being suitable.

2. Another area for reform would be the breaking of the link between school or university qualification and employment opportunities and the salary structures offered. There has to be some form of selection for all employment, but qualifications modelled on Western ones are not necessarily the most suitable for the job or the most appropriate means of selection. The application of other more practical on-the-job means of selection - personality and ability tests, can somebody actually do the job - would be a fairer means of assessing potential. It would also lead to the introduction of more practical skills on the curriculum.

3. Curriculum reform is essential. There is a place for formal teaching; there is a place for academic subject matter formally taught and learnt, but there are only a limited number of hours in a school day and with 80% of the world's population for the remainder of this century living in villages and the rural areas of Third World countries, having no more than basic primary education being available, one questions the wisdom of schooling modelled on metropolitan lines and preparing for the next stage of schooling. Schools should be encouraged to do what they can do best - the teaching of certain knowledge and skills that will be of value whatever the society and wherever one lives. They should be encouraged to drop what could best be taught by skilled craftsmen or villagers or community leaders. Aspects of non-formal and community education outside the school should have a greater role to play.

4. Higher education. Because higher education is so expensive, funding should be made available only on condition that those in the institution carry out problem-oriented research linked to national or regional needs rather than research programmes linked to international networks. Students should be discouraged from semi-automatic promotion from secondary to tertiary level education (as for example, in China, Tanzania and Botswana partly because this will act as a filtering device, partly because students would be better motivated and therefore of

greater value, and partly because higher education will not
encourage wrong attitudes and expectations at the secondary
level. Moreover, the state could then insist that in return
for the privilege of higher education students should undertake some form of national service for the state. This may be
attacked as an infringement of personal liberty but it is
successfully done in some countries and it could at least
guarantee the service of some of the best brains in the country
for the use of their fellow citizens. If there could only be
a break from the pattern and belief that all universities have
to be modelled on Western ones, and if there could be a recognition that academic standards are less important than that new
developments or research related to local needs are undertaken,
this could be a major step forward. It is recognised that
while academic standards might be important, they are not the
be-all and end-all and there is a danger that they are distorting
indigenous developments by _not_ allowing or encouraging research
and assistance to those areas of greatest need. The new universities in the Third World must recognise the need to change
as they face different and difficult needs and situations.

Many of the problems facing the poorer countries of the
world can be blamed on to the colonial heritage and the neocolonial links - but not all. The time has come in the 1980s
for individual countries to recognise and, if possible, break
those neocolonial links that hamper their national educational
development; and to recognise their own weaknesses and failures
of which maladministration and distorted economic development,
inertia and psychological barriers to change are amongst the
most acute. Above all, the time has come to take stock and to
recognise that not all the blame for educational and economic
failures can be laid at the doors of the colonial powers, and
that many of the solutions must rest within the former colonies
themselves.

NOTES

1. The Bulletin of the Institute for Development Studies
at Sussex University, Vol. 12, 1 December 1980, entitled 'Is
Dependency Dead?' has some useful papers on the centre-periphery
and dependency theory debate.
2. See Dwyer, D.F. (1974): The City in the Third World,
London; Macmillan for discussion of the role of urban centres
in development.
3. During the 1970s, there has been a growing awareness
that a Fourth World exists, a world made up of the poorest 30
to 40 countries.
4. The International Journal of Educational Development,
1. 1 1981, discusses the impact of the UNESCO Regional Plans
on educational growth in the Third World.
5. Thailand is an exception to this. During the current

Fourth National Educational Development Plan the length of compulsory schooling is being reduced from seven to six years.

6. Although the Buddhist monastic schools of South East Asia had a 'timetable', hours were flexible and much of what was taught was related to local crafts and the local environment See for example, Watson, J.K.P. (1973): The monastic tradition of education in Thailand. Paedagogica Historica, XIII, 2, 1973.

7. In recent years there has been a substantial growth of West Indian creole literature and African English literature, some of which is being used in schools in England where there is a considerable multi-racial mixture amongst pupils.

8. This author's experience of teaching in Bangladesh and Thailand would indicate that textbooks used and literature taught in British schools are still widely used in schools and colleges in these two countries.

9. Quoted in Noss, R. (1967), Language policy and higher education, Higher Education and Development in South East Asia. Vol. 3, part 2, p.12. Paris: UNESCO and IAU.

10. One reputable publishing company modified its highly successful English language course for West Africa for use in East Africa simply by changing a few names. Illustrations were hardly altered at all.

11. Mende, T. (1973), From Aid to Recolonisation, London, Harrap, has some very startling figures about the Brain Drain from the Third World to the industrialised nations and shows for example, that over 90% of Filipino students trained in the USA remain there and that there are twice as many Iranian doctors working in the USA, Germany, France and England as there are in Iran.

SELECTED BIBLIOGRAPHY ON COLONIALISM AND EDUCATIONAL
DEVELOPMENT

The literature on the educational aspects of colonialism
is considerable especially if all the unpublished M.A., M.Ed.
and Ph.D. theses from British, American, Australian and New
Zealand universities are included. However, only published
materials appear in this bibliography. Readers seeking more
specialised materials written for advanced degrees in British
universities are advised to consult British Education Theses
Index 1950-1980, (Librarians of Institutes and Schools of
Education), or the Register of Educational Research in the
U.K. (NFER), published annually.
    The following bibliography mainly concerned with British,
French and American policies, is divided into (I) the main
publications dealing with general aspects of education and
colonialism and neocolonialism and (II) publications related
to colonial education in the major geographical regions of
the world. Within it are included the majority of references
used in the text of this book. Miscellaneous references from
the text are to be found in section (III).

(I) GENERAL

Adiseshiah, Malcolm S. (1979): 'From International Aid to
    International Co-operation: Some Thoughts in Retrospect'.
    International Review of Education, v. XXV, 2-3, pp.213-230.

Alam, M.A. (1978): 'Science and Imperialism'. Race and Class.
    Winter. XIX 3.

Altbach, P.G. (1971): 'Education and Neocolonialism: a Note'.
    Comparative Education Review XV 2 June, pp.237-239.

Altbach, P.G. (1971): 'Education and Neocolonialism. Teachers
    College Record. 72, 4, pp.543-558.

Altbach, P.G. (1975): 'Literary Colonialism: Books in the Third
    World'. Harvard Educational Review. 45, 2, pp.226-236.

Altbach, P.G. (1977): Servitude of the Mind? Education, Dependency and Neocolonialism. Teachers College Record. 79, 2, pp.187-204.

Altbach, P.G. and Kelly, G.P. (1978): Education and Colonialism. New York: Longmans.

Ashby, E. (1966): Universities: British, Indian, African: A Study in the Ecology of Higher Education. London: Weidenfeld and Nicolson.

Beckford, G.L. (1972): Persistent poverty: underdevelopment in plantation economies in the Third World. New York: Oxford University Press.

Beltran, Luis Ramiro and Elizabeth Fox de Cardona (1980): 'Mass Media and Cultural Domination'. Prospects, v. X, No. 1. pp.76-89.

Betts, R.F. (1961): Assimilation and Association in French Colonial Theory 1890-1914. New York: Columbia University Press.

Bolt, Christine (1971): 'Victorian Attitudes to Race'. London: Routledge and Kegan Paul.

Bolton, G. (1973): Britain's Legacy Overseas. London: Oxford.

Brandt, W. (1980): North-South: A programme for survival. A Report of the Independent Commission on International Development Issues under the Chairmanship of Willy Brandt. London: Pan Books.

Brown, M.B. (1963): After Imperialism. London: Heinemann.

Brown, M.B. (1974): The Economics of Imperialism. Harmondsworth: Penguin.

Brunschwig, H. (1966): French Colonialism, 1871-1914: Myths and Realities. New York: Praeger.

Cambridge History of the British Empire. 8 Volumes. 1929-1963. London: Cambridge University Press.

Carnoy, M. (1974): Education as Cultural Imperialism. New York: David McKay.

Carrington, C.E. (1950): The British Overseas. Cambridge: Cambridge University Press.

Cerych, L. (1965): Problems of Aid to Education in Developing Countries. New York: Praeger.

Chamberlain, M.E. (1970): The New Imperialism. London: The Historical Association.

Clatworthy, F.C. (1971): The Formulation of British Colonial Education Policy, 1923-48. University of Michigan, Comparative Education Dissertation Series No. 3. Michigan: Ann Arboa.

Clight, R. (1971): Damned if you do, damned if you don't: the dilemmas of coloniser-colonised relationships. Comparative Education Review 15, 3, pp.296-313.

Clignet, R. (1980): Education and employment after independence in Simmons, J. ed. The Education Dilemma: policy issues for the developing countries in the 1980s. Oxford: Pergamon Press.

Comparative Education Review. June 1971 - devoted to Colonialism and Education.

Cross, C. (1970): The Fall of the British Empire, 1918-1968. London: Paladin.

Crouzet, P. (1931): Education in the French Colonies. Education Yearbook, pp.267-566.

Dore, R. (1976): The Diploma Disease: Education, qualifications and development. London: George Allen and Unwin.

Education Yearbook (1931): devoted to Education in the Colonies. New York: Columbia Teachers College.

Education Yearbook (1933): devoted to Missions and Education. New York: Columbia Teachers College.

Eisenstadt, S.N. (1978): European expansion and the civilisation of modernity in Wesselling, H.L. ed. Expansion and Reaction. Comparative Studies in Overseas History. 1. Leiden: Leiden University Press.

Emerson, R. (1960): From Empire to Nation - the Rise in Self-Assertion of Asian and African Peoples. Cambridge, Mass: Harvard University Press.

Epstein, E.H. (1978): Social control thesis and educational reform in dependent nations. Theory and Society, 5. pp.255-276.

Evans, D. (1971): Decolonisation: does the teacher have a role? Comparative Education Review. 15, 3, pp.276-287.

Fanon, F. (1967): Black skins, white masks: the experiences of a black man in a white world. New York: Grove Press.

Fanon, F. (1969): The Wretched of the Earth. Harmondsworth: Penguin.

Fieldhouse, K.K. (1973): Economics and Empire 1830-1914. London.

Fletcher, B.A. (1936): Education and Colonial development. London: Methuen.

Freire, P. (1971): Pedagogy of the oppressed. London: Penguin.

Freire, P. (1972): Education for Critical Consciousness. London: Sheed and Ward.

Galtung, J. (1972): A structural theory of imperialism. African Affairs. I, i, pp.93-138.

Girardet, R. (1972): L'idee coloniale en France, 1871-1962. Paris: La Table Ronde.

Hayter, T. (1971): Aid as Imperialism. Harmondsworth: Penguin.

Hensman, C.R. (1975): Rich Against Poor: the Reality of Aid. Harmondsworth: Penguin.

Holmes, B. (ed)(1967): Educational Policy and the Mission Schools. London: Routledge and Kegan Paul.

Johnson, D. (ed) (1973): The World of Empires. Tha Making of the Modern World. Vol. 2. London: Ernest Benn.

Khoi, Le Thanh (1976): 'Aid to Education - Co-operation or Domination?', Prospects. v. VI, No. 4, pp.583-594.

Labouret, H. (1928): L'education des indigenes: methods brittaniques et francaises. L'Afrique Francaises. 38. October. pp.404-411.

Lall, S. (1975): Is dependence a useful concept in analysing underdevelopment? World Development, 3, 11.

Latourette, K.S. (1947): A History of the Expansion of Christianity. 7 Vols. London.

Lauwerys, J.A. (1967): Preface in Holmes, B. ed: <u>Educational Policy and the Mission Schools</u>. London: Routledge and Kegan Paul.

Lee, J.M. (1967): <u>Colonial Development and Good Government</u>. Oxford: Clarendon Press.

Lema, Vicente and Angel D. Marquez (1978): 'What Kind of Development and Which Education', <u>Prospects</u>, v. VIII, No. 3, pp.295-305.

Lewis, L.J. (1954): <u>Educational policy and practice in British Tropical Areas</u>. London: Nelson.

Mair, L.P. (1944): <u>Welfare in the British Colonies</u>. London: Royal Institute of International Affairs.

Magdoff, H. (1969): <u>The Age of Imperialism: The Economics of U.S. Foreign Policy</u>. New York: Monthly Review Press.

Marshall, D.B. (1973): <u>The French Colonial Myth and Constitutional Making in the Fourth Republic</u>. New Haven, Connecticut: Yale University Press.

Mannoni, O. (1956): <u>Prospero and Caliban: The Psychology of Colonialism</u>. London: Methuen.

Mayhew, A. (1938): <u>Education in the Colonial Empire</u>. London: Longmans.

McIntyre, W.D. (1974): <u>Colonies into Commonwealth</u>. London: Blandford Press.

Memmi, A. (1965): <u>The Coloniser and the Colonised</u>. Boston: Beacon Press.

Memmi, A. (1968): <u>The Dominated Man</u>. Boston: Beacon Press.

Mende, T. (1973): <u>From Aid to Recolonisation: Lessons of a Failure</u>. London: Harrap.

Neill, A.S. (1965): <u>A History of Christian Missions</u>. Harmondworth: Penguin.

Nkrumah, K. (1965): <u>Neo-Colonialism: The Last Stage of Imperialism</u>. New York: International Publishers.

Perham, M. (1961): <u>The Colonial Reckoning</u>. London: Oxford University Press.

Peterson, P.M. (1971): Colonialism and Education: The Case of the Afro-American. Comparative Education Review. 15. 2. pp.146-157.

Roberts, S. (1929): The History of French Colonial Policy 1870-1925. 2 Vols. London: P.S. King.

Robinson, K. (1965): The Dilemmas of Trusteeship: Aspects of British Colonial Policy Between the Wars. London: Oxford University Press.

Roncagliolo, R. and N.Z. Janus (1980): 'Transnational Advertising, the Media and Education in the Developing Countries'. Prospects, v. X, No. 1, pp.68-75.

Scott, H.S. (1937): Educational Policy in the British Colonial Empire. Yearbook of Education, pp.411-438. London: Evans.

Shils, E. (1968): The Implantation of Universities: Reflections on a Theme of Ashby. Universities Quarterly. 22 March, pp.142-166.

Shils, E. (1972): The Intellectuals and the Powers and other essays. Chicago: University of Chicago Press.

Sutton, W. (1965): Education and the making of modern nations. London: Ward Lock.

Thomas, R. (1966): Colonialism: Classic and Internal. New University Thought. 4. pp.37-44.

Thompson, A.R. (1977): How far free? International Networks of Constraint Upon National Education Policy in the Third World. Comparative Education. 13. 3, pp.155-168.

Thornton, A.P. (1959): The Imperial Idea and Its Enemies. London: MacMillan.

Ward, F.C. (ed) (1974): Education and Development Reconsidered. New York: Praeger.

Watson, J.K.P. (1979): The Colonial Legacy in Education: a Review. Compare. 9, 1. pp.86-92.

Wesseling, H.L. (ed) (1978): Expansion and Reaction. Comparative Studies in Overseas History, 1. Leiden: Leiden University Press.

Whyte, W.F. (1969): The role of the U.S. professor in developing countries. American Sociologist. 4, February, pp.19-28

(II) (i) AFRICA

Adams, B.N. (1972): Africanisation and Academic Imperialism:
    A study in planned change and inertia. East African
    Journal, May. pp.23-27.

Ajayi, J.F.A. (1965): Christian Missions in Africa 1841-1941.
    London: Longmans.

Aknyemi, A.B. (1974): The Organisation of African Unity -
    Perception of Neo-Colonialism. Africa Quarterly. 14,
    1-2, pp.32-52.

Anderson, J. (1970): 'The Struggle for the School'. Nairobi:
    Longmans.

Ankomah, K. (1970): The Colonial Legacy and African Unrest.
    Science and Society, 34, pp.129-145.

Asiwaju, A.I. (1975): Formal Education in Western Yerubaland
    1889-1960: A Comparison of the French and British Colonial
    Systems. Comparative Education Review, 19, 3. pp.434-450.

Ayandale, E.A. (1977): The missionary impact on Modern Nigeria:
    1842-1914 - A political and social analysis. London:
    Longmans.

Barrington, J.M. (1979): American and African Education,
    Compare, 9, 2. pp.179-182.

Battle, V.J. and Lyons, C.H. (1971): Essays in the History of
    African Education. New York: Teachers'College Press.

Beck, A. (1966): Colonial Policy and Education in British East
    Africa. The Journal of British Studies, 5, 11. pp.115-138.

Bennet, G. (1963): 'A Political History - the Colonial Period'.
    Oxford University Press.

Benson, T.G. (1936): The Jeanes Schools and the Education of
    the East African Native. Journal of the Royal African
    Society, 35, October. pp.418-431.

Berman, E.H. (1971): American Influence on African Education:
    the role of the Phelps-Stokes Fund's Education Commissions.
    Comparative Education Review, 15, 2, pp.132-145.

Berman, E.H. (1975): African Reactions to Missionary Education.
    New York: Teachers' College Press.

Bittinger, D.W. (1940): <u>Black and White in the Sudan: An
Educational Experiment in its Cultural Setting.</u>
Illinois: Brethren Press.

Brett, E.A. (1972): <u>Colonialism and Underdevelopment in East
Africa.</u> London: Heinemann.

Brown, G. (1964): 'British Educational Policy in West and
Central Africa', <u>Journal of Modern African Studies</u>, 2.
3. pp.365-377.

Brown, G.N. (1975): An educational strategy for reducing conflict between the traditional and the West in African
education in Brown, G.N. and Heskett, M. (1975): <u>Conflict
and harmony in education in tropical Africa.</u> London:
Allen and Unwin.

Brown, G.N. and Heskett, M. (1975): <u>Conflict and harmony in
education in tropical Africa.</u> London: Allen and Unwin.

Brownstein, L. (1972): <u>Education and Development in Rural
Kenya.</u> New York: Praeger.

Bunche, R.J. (1934): French educational policy in Togo and
Dahomey. <u>Journal of Negro Education</u>, <u>3</u>. pp.69-97.

Burns, D.G. (1965): <u>African Education: An Introductory Survey
of Education in Commonwealth Countries.</u> London: Oxford
University Press.

Cameron, J. (1975): Traditional and Western education in
Mainland Tanzania: an attempt at synthesis? in Brown.
G.N. and Heskett, M: <u>Conflict and harmony in education
in Tropical Africa.</u> London: Allen and Unwin, pp.350-362.

Cameron, J. and Dodd, W.A. (1970): <u>Society, schools and progress
in Tanzania.</u> Oxford: Pergamon Press.

Capelle, J. (1949): Education in French West Africa. <u>Overseas
Education</u>, 21, October. pp.956-972.

Chinweizu (1974): <u>The West and the rest of us: White Predators,
Black Slaves and the African Elite.</u> New York: Random House

Clarke, J.D. (1937): <u>Omu: an African experiment in education.</u>
London: Longmans Green.

Clignet, R. (1968): The Legacy of Assimilation in West African
Educational System. Its meaning and ambiguities.
<u>Comparative Education Review</u>, XII, 1. pp.62-67.

Clignet, R. and Foster, P.J. (1964): French and British Colonial Education in Africa. <u>Comparative Education Review</u>, 8, 3. pp.191-198.

Clignet, R. and Foster, P.J. (1966): <u>The Fortunate Few: A Study of Secondary School Students in the Ivory Coast.</u> Evanston: North Western University Press.

Cohen, Sir Andrew (1959): <u>British Policy in Changing Africa.</u> London: Routledge and Kegan Paul.

Cowan, L.G., O'Connell, J. and Scanlon, D.G. (1965): <u>Education and Nation Building in Africa.</u> New York: Praeger.

Cox, Sir Christopher (1965): 'The Impact of British Education on the Indigenous Peoples of the Overseas Territories', <u>Advancement of Science</u>, XIII, 50. September 1965.

Crowder, M. (1964): Indirect rule: French and British style. <u>Africa</u>, <u>34</u>. pp.197-205.

Crowder, M. (1964): Colonial rule in West Africa: Factor for Division or Unity. <u>Civilisations</u>, 4.

Crowder, M. (1968): <u>West Africa under Colonial Rule.</u> London.

Denne, A. (1961): <u>Africa and the Victorians: The Climax of Imperialism.</u> New York: St. Martin's Press.

Dickson, K.B. (1971): <u>A Historical Geography of Ghana.</u> Cambridge: Cambridge University Press.

Dougall, J.W.C. (1939): The Case for and against Mission Schools. <u>Journal of the Royal African Society.</u> January.

D'Souza, D.H. (1975): External influences on the development of educational policy in British Tropical Africa from 1923 to 1939. <u>African Studies Report</u>, <u>17</u>. pp.35-44.

Dumont, R. (1966): <u>False Start in Africa.</u> New York: Praeger.

Ekechi, F.K. (1972): <u>Missionary Enterprise and Rivalry in Igboland.</u> London: Frank Cass.

Farine, A. (1969): Society and Education: The Content of Education in the French African School, <u>Comparative Education</u>, <u>5</u>, 1. pp.51-66.

Foster, P.J. (1965): <u>Education and Social Change in Ghana.</u> London: Routledge and Kegan Paul.

Gann, L.H. and Duignan, P. (1970): <u>Colonialism in Africa</u>
    <u>1870-1960</u>. Cambridge: Cambridge University Press.

Gillett, M. (1963): Western academic role concepts in an
    Ethiopian University. <u>Comparative Education Review</u>, <u>7</u>,
    3. pp.149-162.

Gifford, P. and Weiskel, T. (1971): <u>African Education in the</u>
    <u>Colonial Context: the French and British Styles</u>, in
    Gifford, P. and Louis, W.R. (eds) (1971): <u>France and</u>
    <u>Britain in Africa</u>. Yale: Yale University Press.

Gold Coast (1942): Report of the Gold Coast Education
    Committee 1937-1941. Accra: Government Printer.

Griffiths, V.L. (1953): <u>An Experiment in Education</u>. London:
    Longmans.

Hailey, Lord (1938): <u>An African Survey</u>. London: Oxford
    University Press.

Hargreaves, J.D. (1967): <u>West Africa: The Former French States</u>.
    Englewood Cliffs: Prentice Hall.

Hargreaves, J.D. (1976): <u>The End of Colonial Rule in Africa</u>.
    London: The Historical Association.

H.M.S.O. (1925): <u>Educational Policy in British Tropical</u>
    <u>Africa</u>. Cmd. 2374. London: H.M.S.O.

H.M.S.O. (1933): Advisory Committee on Education in the
    Colonies, Memorandum on Educational Grants in Aid.
    <u>Parliamentary Papers</u>. Col. No. 54.

H.M.S.O. (1935): <u>Memorandum on the Education of African</u>
    <u>Communities</u>. Col. No. 103. London.

H.M.S.O. (1937): <u>Higher Education in East Africa</u>. Col. No.
    142. London: H.M.S.O.

H.M.S.O. (1944): <u>Mass Education in African Society</u>. Col. No.
    186. London: H.M.S.O.

Horton, R. (1971): 'African Conversion', <u>Africa. XLI. 2.</u>

Huxley, Julian (1932): <u>Africa View</u>. London: Chatto and Windus.

Ikejiani, O. (1964): Education for Efficiency, Chapter 6 in
    O. Ikejiani (ed) <u>Nigerian Education</u>. London: Longmans.

Ingham, K. (1959): The making of modern Uganda. London: Oxford University Press.

Jones, T.J. (1922): Education in Africa: A Study of West, South and Equatorial Africa by the African Education Commission 1920-21. London: Edinburgh House Press.

Jones, T.J. (1925): Education in East Africa: A Study of East, Central and South Africa by the Second African Education Commission under the auspices of the Phelps-Stokes Fund, in co-operation with the International Education Board. London: Edinburgh House Press.

Jones, V. (1965): Content of History syllabuses in Northern Nigeria in the early colonial period. West African Journal of Education, 9 October. pp.145-148.

Kaniki, M.H.Y. (ed) (1980): Tanzania Under Colonial Rule. Historical Association of Tanzania. Dar-es-Salaam: Longmans.

Kay, S. and Nystrom, B. (1971): Education and Colonialism in Africa: An annotated bibliography. Comparative Education Review, 15, 2. pp.240-259.

Kenya (1960): Education Commission Report, Nairobi.

Kilson, M. (1970): The emergent elites of Black Africa, 1900-1960 in Duigan, P. and Gann, L.G. (eds) (1970): Colonialism in Africa, 1870-1960. Vol. 2. Cambridge: Cambridge University Press. pp.368-370.

King, K.J. (1975): Nationalism, Education and Imperialism in Southern Sudan (1920-70) in Brown, G.M. and Heskett, M. (1975): Conflict and harmony in education in tropical Africa. Studies in Modern Asia and Africa 10. London: Allen and Unwin.

Kinsey, D.C. (1971): Efforts for Educational Synthesis Under Colonial Rule: Egypt and Tunisia. Comparative Education Review, 15, 2. pp.172-187.

Kinwanuka, M.S. (1970): Colonial Policies and Administrations in Africa: The Myths of the Contrasts. African Historical Studies. III, 2. pp.295-315.

Kitchen, H. (ed) (1962): The Educated African. New York: Praeger.

Knight, E.G. (1955): Education in French North Africa. Islamic Quarterly 2, 4 December, pp.294-308.

Kunene, D.P. (1970): African Vernacular Writing: an essay on
    self-devaluation. African Social Research, 9, pp.639-59.

Lewis, L.J. (1962): Education and Political Independence in
    Africa. London: Nelson.

Lewis, L.J. (ed) (1962): Phelps-Stokes Reports on Education
    in Africa. London: Oxford University Press.

Leys, C. (1975): Underdevelopment in Kenya: The Political
    Economy of Neocolonialism. London: Heinemann.

Linden, I. (1974): Catholics, Peasants and Chewa Resistance.
    London: Heinemann.

Lugard, Sir F.D. (1925): Education in Tropical Africa.
    Edinburgh Review. Vol. C. July.

Lugard, Sir F.D. (1929): The Dual Mandate in British Tropical
    Africa. London: Blackward.

Manuwuike, W. (1978): Disfunctionalism in African Education.
    New York: Vantage Press.

Mason, R.J. (1959): British Education in Africa. London:
    Oxford University Press.

Mathews, Z.K. (1963): Christian Education in Africa. (All
    African Churches Conference). London: Oxford University
    Press.

McWilliam, H.O.A. and Kwamena-Poh M.A. (1959): The Development
    of Education in Ghana.

Moumouni, A. (1968): Education in Africa. London: Andre
    Deutsch.

Mumford, W.B. (1927): Native Schools in Central Africa,
    Journal of the African Society. XXVI. April.

Mumford, W.B. (1929): Memorandum on Education and the Social
    Adjustment of the Primitive People of Africa to
    European Culture. Africa II, 2. April.

Mumford, W.B. (1930): Malangali School, Africa. III, 3 July.
    pp.265-290.

Mumford, W.B. (1932): Malangali School, a typescript and
    illustrated account of the school dated 1.1.32.
    University of London Institute of Education Library.

212

Mumford, W.B. (1933): Some Problems in Native Economic Development and a possible solution in Co-operative Societies, Africa, VI. 1 January.

Murray, A.V. (1929): School in the Bush. London: Longmans Green.

Nuffield Foundation (1953): African Education: A Study of Educational Policy and Practice in British Tropical Africa. Oxford: Nuffield Foundation.

Nyerere, J.K. (1967): Education for Self Reliance. Dar-es-Salaam: Government Printer.

Oliver, R. (1953): The Missionary Factor in East Africa. London.

Ormsby-Gore, W.G.A. (1924): Visit to West Africa. Cmd. 2744. London: H.M.S.O.

Ormsby-Gore, W.G.A. (1925): Education Policy in British Tropical Africa. Parliamentary Papers (1924-25). XXI.

Perham, M. (1974): in the foreword to Robertson, Sir James (1974): Transition in Africa. London: Hurst & Co.

Peshkin, A. (1965): Educational Reform in Colonial and Independent Africa. African Affairs, 64, July. pp.110-216.

Ranger, T.O. (1965): African Attempts to Control Education in East and Central Africa: 1900-1939. Past and Present, December, pp.57-85.

Ranger, T. and Kimambo, I. (1975): Themes in the Christian History of Central Africa. London: Heinemann.

Robinson, R., Gallagher, J. and Denny, A. (1961): Africa and the Victorians: The Climax of Imperialism. New York: St. Martin's Press.

Rodney, W. (1972): How Europe Underdeveloped Africa. Dar-es-Salaam: East African Publishing House.

Scanlon, D.G. (ed) (2966): Church, State and Education in Africa. New York: Teachers' College Press.

Shepherd, R.M.W. (1941): Lovedale South Africa: The Story of a Century 1841-1941. Lovedale Press.

Smith, E.W. (1926): The Christian Mission in Africa, a study
    based on the proceedings of the International conference
    at Le Zoute, Belgium, 1924. London: Edinburgh House.

Smith, K. (1975): Who Controls Book Publishing in Anglophone,
    Middle Africa? Annals of the American Academy of
    Political and Social Science, 421, September. pp.140-150.

Snelson, P.D. (1970): Educational Development in Northern
    Rhodesia. Lusaka: Oxford University Press.

Stabler, E. (1969): Education Since Uhuru: Kenya's Schools.
    Middletown, Connecticut: Wesleyan University Press.

Summer, D.C. (1963): Education in Sierra Leone. Freetown:
    Government Printer.

Tignor, R.L. (1976): The Colonial Transformation of Kenya.
    Princeton: Princeton University Press.

Van Den Berghe, P. (1968): European Languages and Black
    Mandarins. Transition, 7, pp.19-23.

Van Den Berghe, P. (1973): Power and Privilege in an African
    University. Middletown, Connecticut: Wesleyan University
    Press.

Village Education in Africa. Report of the Inter-Territorial
    Jeanes Conference. Salisbury, Southern Rhodesia.
    Salisbury: Lovedale Press.

Ward, J.C. (1970): The Expatriate Academic and the African
    University. African Journal 7, October pp.12-16.

Whitley, S. (1971): English Language as a Tool of British
    Neocolonialism. East Africa Journal 8, December. pp.4-6.

Wise, C.G. (1956): A History of Education in British West
    Africa. London: Longmans.

Yates, B. (1976): The Triumph and Failure of Mission Vocational
    Education in Zaire, 1879-1908. Comparative Education
    Review, 20, 2. pp.183-208.

(ii)   ASIA AND THE PACIFIC

Allen, J. de V. (1970): 'The Malayan Civil Service 1874-1941:
    Colonial Bureaucracy/Malayan Elite'. Comparative Studies
    in Society and History. 12.1.

Altbach, P.G. (1975): _Indian Publishing: An Analysis_. New
York and Delhi: Oxford University Press.

Arasaratnam, S. (1970): _Indians in Malaysia and Singapore_.
Kuala Lumpur: Oxford University Press for the Institute
of Race Relations.

Attygale, R.C.L. (1961): Social Change and the idea of
excellence in tropical Asian society. _World Yearbook
of Education_. London: Evans. pp.181-188.

Bastin, J. and Benda, H.J. (1968): _A History of Modern South
East Asia_. Englewood Cliffs: Prentice Hall.

Basu, A. (1974): _The Growth of Education and Political
Development in India, 1918-1920_. Delhi: Oxford University Press.

Benda, H.J. (1965): Political Elites in Colonial South East
Asia. _Comparative Studies in Society and History_. _XII_.
April.

Cady, J.F. (1964): _South East Asia: Its Historical Development_.
New York: Macmillan.

Chai Hon-Chan (1964): _The Development of British Malaya 1896-
1909_. Kuala Lumpur: Oxford University Press.

Chai Hon-Chan (1977): _Education and Nation Building in Plural
Societies: the West Malaysian Experience_. Development
Studies Centre Monograph No. 6. Canberra: Australian
National University.

Cheeseman, H.R. (1948): _Education in Malaya_. Kuala Lumpur:
Oxford University Press.

Chelliah, D.D. (1940): _A Short History of the Education Policy
in the Straits Settlements_. Singapore.

Chesneaux, J. (1966): Trans. Salmon, M., _The Vietnamese
Nation_. Sydney: Current Book Distributors.

Clifford, H. (1898/9):'Malaya: as it is and as it was'.
Proceedings of the Royal Commonwealth Institute, _XXX_.

Cooke, D.F. (1966): 'The Mission Schools of Malaya, 1815-1942'.
Pedagogica Historica. 6. pp.364-399.

Collis, M. (1966): _Raffles_. London: Faber and Faber.

De Silva, K.M. (1965): <u>Social Policy and Missionary Organis-</u><u>ation in Ceylon 1840-1855</u>. London: Oxford University Press.

Doraisamy, T.R. (ed) (1969): <u>150 Years of Education in</u> <u>Singapore</u>. Singapore: T.T.C. Publications.

Duke, B.C. (1966): Dualism in Asian Education. <u>Comparative</u> <u>Education</u>, 3. 1. pp.41-48.

Edwards, M. (1926): <u>British India</u>. New York: Taplinger.

Elder, J.W. (1971): The Decolonisation of Educational Culture: The Case of India. <u>Comparative Education Review</u>, 15, 3. pp.288-295.

Emerson, R. (1937): <u>Malaysia: A Study in Direct and Indirect</u> <u>Rule</u>. New York: Macmillan.

Ennis, T.E. (1936): <u>French policy and developments in Indo-</u><u>China</u>. Chicago: University of Chicago Press.

Fall, B. (1960): <u>La republique democratique du Vietnam 1945-</u><u>1960</u>. Paris: Armand Colin.

Federation of Malaya (1954): Education Report of the Federation of Malaya. Kuala Lumpur: Government Printer.

Federation of Malaya (1956): Report of the Education Committee. (Razak Report). Kuala Lumpur: Government Printer.

Fernando, C.N.V. (1963): Christian Missionary Enterprise in the early British period. <u>Ceylon University Review</u> VII.

Fifield, R.H.: The thirty years' war in Indochina: a conceptual framework, <u>Asian Survey</u>, 17, 9, 1977. pp.857-79.

Fisher, C.A. (1964): <u>South East Asia: A Social, Economic and</u> <u>Political Geography</u>. London: Methuen.

Freedman, M. (1960): The Growth of a Plural Society in Malaya. <u>Pacific Affairs</u>, <u>30</u>.

Furnivall, J.S. (1943): <u>Educational Progress in South East</u> <u>Asia</u>. New York: Institute of Pacific Relations.

Furnivall, J.S. (1956): <u>Colonial Policy and Practice</u>. New York: New York University Press.

Gilbert, J. (1972): The Indian Academic Profession in the Origins of a Tradition of Subordination. Minerva, 10, July. pp.384-411.

Hall, D.G.E. (1955): A History of South East Asia. London: Macmillan.

Hartog, Sir P. (1939): Some Aspects of Indian Education Past and Present. London: Oxford University Press.

H.M.S.O. (1940): Report on Higher Education in Malaya. Col. No. 173. London: H.M.S.O.

Hoang Van Chi: From Colonialism to Communism. New York: Popular Library, 1964.

Hough, G.G. (1933): The Education Policy of Sir Stamford Raffles. Journal of the Malayan Branch of the Royal Asiatic Society. XI, 2.

Hunter, G. (1966): South East Asia: Race, Culture and Nation. London: Oxford University Press for Institute of Race Relations.

Jayasuriya, J.E. (1978): Educational Policies and Progress during British Rule in Ceylon (Sri Lanka) 1796-1948. Colombo: Associated Educational Publishers.

Kelly, G.P. (1971): Education and Participation in Nationalist Groups: An Exploratory Study of the Indo-Chinese Communist Party and the V.N.D.D. 1929-31. Comparative Education Review. 15, 2. pp.227-236.

Kelly, G.P. (1978): Colonial Schools in Vietnam: Policy and Practice in Altbach, P.G. and Kelly, G.P. (eds): Education and Colonialism. New York: Longmans. pp.96-121.

Kiernan, V.G. (1956): Britain, Siam and Malaya, 1875-1885. Journal of Modern History, 28.

Loh Fook Seng, P. (1970): The Nineteenth Century British Approach to Malay Education. Journal Pendidekan 1. 1.

Loh Fook Seng, P. (1975): Seeds of Separatism: Educational Policy in Malaya 1874-1940. Kuala Lumpur: Oxford University Press.

Marr, D.G: Vietnamese anticolonialism. Berkeley: University of California Press, 1971.

Mason, F. (1953): The Schools of Malaya. Singapore: Donald Moore.

Masson, A: Histoire du Vietnam. Paris: Presses universitaires de France, 1960.

Mayhew, A. (1926): The Education of India. London: Faber and Gwyer.

Mayhew, A.I. (1929): Memorandum on Education in Malaya. Colonial Office Papers. Vol. 67.

Maxwell, Sir George (1932): Memorandum on the Educational Policy of the Straits Settlements and Federated Malay States. 31 December. Co. 273. Vol. 585.

McCully, B. (1943): English Education and the Origins of Indian Nationalism. New York: Colombia University Press.

McVey, R.T. (1967): Taman Siswa and the Indonesian National Awakening. Indonesia, 4. pp.128-49.

Mills, L.A. (1942): British Rule in East Asia. London: Oxford.

Nairn, R.C. (1966): International Aid to Thailand: The New Colonialism? New Haven, Connecticut: Yale University Press.

Neilson, J.B. (1934): Education in British Malaya. Yearbook of Education. London: Evans.

Nguyen Khac Vien (ed) (1969): Le Vietnam traditionnel, Etudes vietnamiennes; 21, Hanoi.

Nguyen Khac Vien (ed) (1971): L'enseignement general en R.D.V.N Hanoi: Tran Hung Dao.

Nguyen Khac Vien (ed) (1975): U.S. Neocolonialism in South Vietnam: the vietnamisation of the war. Vietnamese Studies, 42, Hanoi.

Nguyen Khac Vien (1975): Tradition and revolution in Vietnam. Berkeley: Indochina Resources Centre.

Osborne, M.E. (1969): The French presence in Cochinchina and Cambodia: Rule and Response (1859-1905). Ithaca: Cornell University Press.

Osborne, M.E. (1971): Region of Revolt, Focus on South East Asia. Harmondsworth: Penguin.

The Oxford History of India (1958). London: Oxford University
    Press.

Pannikar, K.M. (1959): <u>Asian and Western Dominance: A survey</u>
    <u>of the Vasco da Gama epoch of Asian history 1498-1945</u>.
    London: Allen and Unwin.

Pannikar, K.M. (1964): <u>A survey of Indian history</u>. 4th edition.
    London: Allen and Unwin.

Parkinson, C.N. (1959): <u>British Intervention in Malaya (1867-</u>
    <u>1877</u>). London: Oxford University Press.

Paton, D.M. (1965): Christian Missions in Asia in Wint, G. (ed):
    <u>Asia: a handbook</u>. London: Antony Blond.

Pearn, B.R. (1963): <u>A Short Introduction to the History of</u>
    <u>South East Asia</u>. Kuala Lumpur: Longmans of Malaya.

Purcell, V. (1953): <u>The Colonial Period in South East Asia</u>.
    New York: Oxford University Press.

Raffles, Lady (1830): <u>Memoir of the Life and Public Services</u>
    <u>of Sir T.S. Raffles</u>. London.

Report of the Special Committee on Education in Ceylon (1943).
    Colombo: Government Press.

Roff, W.R. (1967): <u>The Origins of Malay Nationalism</u>. New
    Haven, Connecticut: Yale University Press.

Romain, J.R. (1962): <u>The Asian Century: a history of modern</u>
    <u>nationalism in Asia</u>. Translated by J.E. and R.T. Clark.
    Berkely: University of California Press.

Rubern, R. (1961): <u>Education in Colonial Ceylon</u>. Kandy.

Ryan, N.J. (1964): 'The Malay College 1905-1963'. <u>Malaysian</u>
    <u>History</u>. <u>VIII</u> 2. April, pp.26-32.

Sadaka, E. (1968): <u>The Protected Malay States 1873-1895</u>.
    Kuala Lumpur: Oxford University Press.

Salvaratnam, V. (1974): Decolonisation, the Ruling Elite and
    Ethnic Relations in Peninsular Malaysia. IDS Discussion
    Paper No. 44. March. Institute of Development Studies.
    University of Sussex.

Sargent, Sir J. (196): <u>Schools, Society and Progress in</u>
    <u>India</u>. Oxford: Pergamon Press.

Schwartz, K. (1971): Filipino Education and Spanish Colonialism: Toward an Autonomous Perspective. <u>Comparative Education Review</u>, <u>15</u>, 2. pp.202-218.

Shils, E.A. (1965): The Asian Intellectual in Wint, G. (ed): <u>Asia: a handbook</u>. London: Antony Blond.

Stevenson, R. (1975): <u>Cultivators and Administrators. British Educational Policy Towards the Malays 1875-1906</u>. Kuala Lumpur: Oxford University Press.

Swettenham, Sir F.A. (1948): <u>British Malaya: An Account of the Origin and Progress of British Influence in Malaya</u>. London: Allen and Unwin.

Van Der Droef, J.M. (1968): Asia's Brain Drain. <u>Journal of Higher Education</u>, <u>39</u>.

Van Neil, R. (1960): <u>The Emergence of the Modern Indonesian Elite</u>. The Hague: W. Van Hoeve.

Vella, W.F. (1955): <u>The Impact of the West on the Government of Siam</u>. Berkeley: University of California Press.

Vella, W.F. (1973): <u>Aspects of Vietnamese History</u>. Honolulu: Asian Studies at Hawaii, 8.

Von Der Mehden, F.R. (1974): <u>South East Asia, 1930-1970: The Legacy of Colonialism and Nationalism</u>. London: Thames and Hudson.

Watson, J.K.P. (1973a): The Problem of Chinese education in Malaysia and Singapore. <u>Journal of Asian and African Studies</u>, <u>VIII</u>, 1-2. pp.77-87.

Watson, J.K.P. (1973b): A Comparative Study of educational development in Thailand, Malaya and Singapore. <u>Education in the Commonwealth</u>, No. 6: Education in Developing Countries of the Commonwealth. London: The Commonwealth Secretariat. pp.57-62.

Watson, J.K.P. (1976): The Education of Racial Minorities in South East Asia with special reference to the Chinese. <u>Compare</u>, <u>6</u>, 2. pp.14-21.

Watson, J.K.P. (1979): Education, Cultural Pluralism and National Unity in Peninsula Malaysia. <u>The First International Symposium on Asian Studies</u>. Hong Kong: Asian Research. Service. pp.733-750.

Watson, J.K.P. (1980a): Missionary Education in Asia: Lessons from the past - Challenge for the Future. Spectrum, 12, 3. pp.4-9.

Watson, J.K.P. (1980b): Education and Cultural Pluralism in South East Asia, with special Reference to Peninsular Malaysia. Comparative Education, 16, 2. pp.139-158.

Watson, J.K.P. (1980c): Influences and Constraints on Curriculum Development in the Third World (with reference to the Integrated Science Programme in Malaysia). Canadian and International Review of Education, 9, 2. pp.28-42.

Watson, J.K.P. (1980d): Missionary Influence on Education in Thailand, c. 1660-1970. Pedagogica Historica, XXI, 2. (in print).

Watson, J.K.P. (1980e): Cultural Pluralism, Nation Building and Educational Policies in Peninsular Malaysia. Journal of Multi-lingual and Multi-cultural Development, 1, 2. pp.155-174.

Weld, Sir F. (1883/4): 'The Straits Settlements and British Malaya'. Proceedings of the Royal Commonwealth Institute XV.

Wong Hoy Kee, F. (1966): An Investigation into the work of the De La Salle Brothers in the Far East. Pedagogica Historica, 6, pp.440-504.

Wong Hoy Kee, F. (1971): The development of a national language in Indonesia and Malaysia. Comparative Education, 7, 2. pp.73-80.

Wong Hoy Kee, F. and E.E. Tiang Hong (1971): Education in Malaysia. Hong Kong: Heinemann Education Books (Asia) Ltd.

Woodruff, P. (1963): The Men Who Ruled India. 2 Vols. London: Jonathan Cape.

(iii)   LATIN AMERICA AND THE CARIBBEAN

Altschuler, L.R. (1976): Satellization and Stagnation in Latin America. International Studies Quarterly, 20, 1. pp.39-82.

Avalos, B. (1978): Educational Change in Latin America. The Case of Peru. Cardiff: University College Cardiff Press.

Barbados (1945): <u>Evaluation of Education in Barbados</u>.
    Barbados: Department of Education.

Bodenheimer, S.J. (1971): <u>The Ideology of Developmentalism</u>:
    <u>The American Paradigm - Surrogate for Latin American</u>
    <u>Studies</u>. Beverly Hills: Sage.

Braithwaite, L.E. (1965): The Role of the University in the
    Developing Society of the British West Indies. <u>Social</u>
    <u>and Economic Studies</u>, <u>14</u>, 1. pp.75-96.

Brock, C. (1978): Education and Multi-culturalism in the
    Caribbean Region, in Corner, T. (ed): <u>Education in</u>
    <u>Multi-cultural Societies</u>. Proceedings of the Thirteenth
    Annual Conference of the Comparative Education Society
    in Europe (British Section). Edinburgh University.
    pp.87-119.

Cardoso, F.H. (1970): Dependency and Development in Latin
    America. <u>New Left Review</u>, 74. July - August.

Cardoso, F.H. and Faletto, E. (1979): <u>Dependency and Develop-</u>
    <u>ment in Latin America</u>. Berkeley and London: University
    of California Press.

Carnoy, Martin <u>et al</u>. (1979): <u>Can Educational Policy Equalise</u>
    <u>Income Distribution in Latin America</u>. Guildford, Surrey:
    Biddles Limited.

Chilcote, Ronald H. (1974): 'Dependency: A Critical Synthesis
    of the Literature'. <u>Latin American Perspectives</u>, v. I,
    No. 1, Spring. pp.4-29.

Cockroft, J.D., Frank, A.G. and Johnson, D.L. (eds) (1972):
    <u>Dependence and Underdevelopment: Latin America's</u>
    <u>Political Economy</u>. Garden City, New York: Anchor Books.

Crozier, B. (1973): Soviet Pressures in the Caribbean: The
    Satellisation of Cuba. <u>Conflict Study</u>, 35. London:
    Institute for the Study of Conflict.

Education in the West Indies, 1931-32. Report of the
    Education Commissioners. West Indian. No. 221. 1932.

Farrell, J.P. (1967): Education and Pluralism in Selected
    Caribbean Societies. <u>Comparative Education Review</u>, XI,
    2. pp.160-181.

Figueroa, P.M.E. (1971): <u>Schools, Society and Progress in the</u>
    <u>West Indies</u>. Oxford: Pergamon.

Frank, A.G. (1967): <u>Capitalism and underdevelopment in Latin America: Historical studies of Chile and Brazil</u>. New York and London: Monthly Review Press.

Frank, A.G. (1969): <u>Latin America: Underdevelopment or Revolution</u>. New York: Monthly Review Press.

Furtado, Celso (1969): 'U.S. Hegemony and the Future of Latin America' in Irving Louis Horowitz, Josue de Castro and John Gervassi, (eds): <u>Latin American Radicalism: A Documentary Report on Left and Nationalist Movements</u>. New York: Vintage Books.

Goertzel, T. (1974): American Imperialism and the Brazilian Student Movement, <u>Youth and Society</u>, <u>6</u>, December. pp.123-50.

Gordon, S.C. (1963): <u>A Century of West Indian Education</u>. London: Longmans.

Gordon, S.C. (1968): <u>Reports and Repercussions in West Indian Education, 1835-1939</u>. London: Ginn & Co. Ltd.

H.M.S.O. (1933): Report on the Problems of Secondary and Primary Education in Trinidad, Barbados, Leeward and Windward Islands, 1931-32, Col. No. 79. London: H.M.S.O.

H.M.S.O. (1939): Education in the Leeward and Windward Islands. Col. No. 164. London: H.M.S.O.

H.M.S.O. (1945): Report on the West Indies Committee of the Commission on Higher Education in the Colonies. Cmnd. 6654. London: H.M.S.O.

Jamaica (1952): Report of the Education Department of Jamaica for 1950. Kingston: Government Printer.

Jervier, W.S. (1977): <u>Educational Change in Post-Colonial Jamaica</u>. New York: Vantage Press.

Kandel Report (1943): <u>Secondary Education in Jamaica</u>. Kingston: Government Printer.

Miller, E. (1976): Education and Society in Jamaica, in Figueroa, P.M.A. and Peraud, G: <u>Sociology of Education: A Caribbean Reader</u>. London: Oxford University Press. pp.47-66.

Murray, D.J. (1965): <u>The West Indies and the Development of Colonial Government 1801-36</u>. London: Oxford University Press.

Parry, S.H. and Sherlock, P.M. (1956): A short history of the West Indies. London: Oxford University Press.

Paulston, R.G. (1971): United States Educational Intervention on Peru. Pedagogica Historica, 11, 2. pp.426-451.

Renner, R. (ed) (1973): Universities in Transition: The U.S. Influence in Latin American Education. Gainesvill, Flo: University of Florida, Centre for Latin American Studies.

Renner, R. (1974): U.S. Aid to Latin American Universities: A Case of Cultural Transfer. Intellect, V. 102. pp.385-386.

Roberts, G.W. and Abdullah, N. (1965): Some observations on the Educational Position of the British Caribbean. Social and Economic Studies, 14, 1. pp.144-154.

Sandoval, R.P. (1973): Dependency and Education in Colombian Underdevelopment. Madison. Wisconsin: Land Tenure Centre, University of Wisconsin.

Solari, Aldo (1977): 'Development and Educational Policy in Latin America'. CEPAL Review (first half 1977). pp.59-91.

Smith, M.G. (1965): The Plural Society in the British West Indies. Berkeley: University of California Press.

Sunkel, O. (1971): Underdevelopment, the Transfer of Science and Technology and the Latin American University. Human Relations, 24, February. pp.1-18.

Williams, E. (1951): Education in the British West Indies. New York: University Place Bookshop.

(III)   MISCELLANEOUS AND SPECIALISED REFERENCES USED IN THE TEXT

The references listed below are additional miscellaneous references used in the text and are not necessarily related to colonialism. They are listed under the chapters in which they appear.

Chapter One

Coleman, J.S. (1965): Education and Political Development. Princeton, N.J. Princeton University Press.

Coombs, P.H. and Ahmad, M. (1974): Attacking Rural Poverty: How non-formal education can help. Baltimore: Johns Hopkins: University Press.

D'aeth, R. (1978): <u>Education and Development in the Third World</u>. Farnborough: Saxon House.

Paulston, R.G. (1975): Strategies for Non-formal Education. <u>Teachers' College Record</u>, 76, 4. Spring. pp.569-597.

Purcell, V. (1966): <u>The Chinese in South East Asia</u>. London: Oxford University Press and Royal Institute for International Affairs.

Reimer, E. (1971): <u>School is Dead: Alternatives in Education: An Indictment of the System and a strategy of resolution</u>. Harmondsworth: Penguin.

Simmons, J. (ed) (1980): <u>The Education Dilemma: policy issues for developing countries in the 1980s</u>. Oxford: Pergamon Press.

Watson, J.K.P. (1973c): The Monastic tradition of education in Thailand. <u>Paedagogica Historica</u>, XIII, 2. pp.515-529.

Watson, J.K.P. (1974): Primary education in Thailand: plans, problems and possibilities. <u>Comparative Education</u>, 10, 1. pp.35-47.

World Bank (1980): Education Sector Policy Paper.

Chapter Two

Broomfield, Canon (1927): 'The Education of African Women and Girls in Tanganyika'. Typescript memo., June 1927. Box 258, Joint International Missionary Council/Conference of British Missionary Societies Archives.

Fiji Department of Education (1943): Director of Education's Comments on the Governor's Note, 12 April 1943, File 24/22/22.

Harvey, R.J. (1929): 'Modern Education and Tribal Life'. Typescript memo., Box 258, Joint International Missionary Council/Conference of British Missionary Societies Archives.

H.M.S.O. (1926): <u>Imperial Conference 1926</u>. Appendices to the Summary of Proceedings. Cmd. 2769. London.

Chapter Three

Garvey, B. (1974): The Development of the White Fathers Mission Among the Bemba Speaking Peoples. Unpublished Ph.D thesis, University of London.

Mbiti, J.S. (1969): <u>African Religion and Philosophy</u>. London: Heinemann.

Palmer, R. and Parsons, N. (eds) (1977): <u>The Roots of Rural Poverty in Central and Southern Africa</u>. London: Longmans.

Parrinder, G. (1962): <u>African Traditional Religion</u>. London: Longmans.

Weiler, H.N. (ed) (1964): <u>Education and Politics in Nigeria</u>. Freiburg: Verlag Rombach.

Zanelli, N.B. (1971): <u>Education Towards Development in Tanzania</u>. Basle: Phenos-Verlag.

Chapter Four

American Methodist Mission (1894): Minutes of Malaya Annual Conference of the Methodist Church.

Backus, M. (1884): <u>Siam and Laos as seen by our own American Missionaries</u>. Philadelphia.

Brown, W.A. (1933): The problem of education and religious purposes in <u>Educational Yearbook</u>. New York: Columbia Teachers' College. pp.227-256.

Bruce, R. (1968): King Mongkut of Siam 1851-68. <u>History Today</u>, XVIII, 10.

Casey, E. (1976): The contrubiton of the mission schools to education in Malaysia. <u>Studies in Educational Administration</u>. Commonwealth Council for Educational Administration. 8. December. pp.1-8.

Chaplin, J. (1937): Education in Siam. <u>Yearbook of Education</u>. London: Evans.

Cobb, D.J. (1966): Relations between religion and state in Thai education. <u>World Yearbook of Education</u>. London: Evans.

Collis, M. (1965): <u>Siamese White</u>. London: Faber and Faber.

Downs, R.C. (1968): Thailand: A struggling church in a stable land in Anderson, G.H. (ed): <u>Christ and Crisis in South East Asia</u>. Singapore: Friendship Press.

Federated Malay States (1902): Code of regulations for government and grant aided schools. Kuala Lumpur.

Federated Malay States (1937): Annual Report. London: H.M.S.O.

Hutchinson, E.W. (1933): The French Foreign Mission in Siam during the Seventeenth Century. _Journal of the Siam Society_, 26, April.

Jumsai, M.L. Panich (1951): _Compulsory Education in Thailand._ Paris: UNESCO.

Leonowens, A. (1870): _The English Governess at the Siamese Court._ London: Arthur Baker Ltd. (New edition (1970): Cedric Chivers Ltd.

Lord, D.C. (1969): _Mo Bradley and Thailand._ Michigan: Wm. B. Erdmans.

Ryan, N.J. (1967): _The making of modern Malaysia._ Kuala Lumpur: Oxford University Press.

Straits Settlements (1924): Annual Education Report.

Straits Settlements (1926): Annual Education Report.

The Straits Times, 22 June 1964.

Sukontarangsi, S. (1966): The development of government control of public education in Thailand. _Paedagogica Historica._ 6. pp.416-439.

Thomas, M.M. (1966): _The Christian response to the Asian Revolution._ London: S.C.M. Press.

Thompson, V. (1941): _Thailand, the new Siam._ New York: Macmillan.

Watson, J.K.P. (1980d): _Educational development in Thailand._ Hong Kong: Heinemann Education (Asia) Ltd.

Waugh, A. (1970): _Bangkok, the story of a city._ London: W.H. Allen.

Wong Hoy Kee, F. (1971): Education and Christian missions: Malaysia and Singapore in Wong Hoy Kee, F. (1971): _Comparative Studies in South East Asian Education._ Hong Kong: Heinemann Education (Asia) Ltd.

Wyatt, D.K. (1969): _The politics of reform in Thailand: Education in the reign of King Chulalongkorn._ New Haven: Yale University Press.

Chapter Five

Alatas, Syed Hussein (1971): The Rukenagara and the return to
    democracy in Malaysia. *Pacific Community*, 2, 4.

Aziz Report (1968): Report of the Royal Commission on the
    Teaching Services. Kuala Lumpur: Government Printer.

Barnes Report (1951): Report of the Committee on Malay
    Education. Kuala Lumpur: Government Printer.

Council Paper No. 53. (1946).

F.M.S. (1898): Annual Report of the Resident-General of the
    Federated Malay States for 1898.

F.M.S. (1902): Special Report on Education in the Federated
    Malay States.

F.M.S. (1920): Chief Secretary's Report, Federated Malay States.

Fenn-Wu Report (1951): Chinese Schools and the Education of
    Chinese Malayans: the Report of a Mission Invited by the
    Federation Government to Study the Problem of the Chinese
    in Malaya. Kuala Lumpur: Government Printer.

Gungwu, Wang (ed) (1964): *Malaysia: A Survey*. London: Pall
    Mall.

Lewin, K. (1975): Science Education in Malaysian and Sri Lanka.
    IDS Discussion Paper No. 74. Institute of Development
    Studies, University of Sussex.

McGee, T.G. (1964): 'Population: A preliminary analysis in
    Malaysia' in Wang Gungwu (ed): *Malaysia: A Survey*.
    London: Pall Mall.

Majid Report (1971): Report of the Committee appointed by the
    National Operations Council to study campus life of
    students in the University of Malaya. Kuala Lumpur:
    Government Printer.

Milne, R.S. (1970): National Ideology and Nation Building in
    Malaysia. *Asian Survey*. July.

Ministry of Education (1950): Report of the Central Advisory
    Committee on Education. Kuala Lumpur.

Parliamentary Papers: c. 6566, 1888; c. 6222, 1890; c. 6576,
    1892; c. 4276, 1932.

Perak Annual Report (1890).

Purcell, V. (1936): _Problems of Chinese Education._ London: Kegan Paul, Trench, Truber.

Purcell, V. (1966): _The Chinese in South East Asia._ London: Royal Institute of International Affairs and Oxford University Press.

Razak Report (1956): Report of the Education Committee. Kuala Lumpur: Government Printer.

Rudner, M. (1977): 'Education, Development and Change in Malaysia'. _South East Asian Studies._ 15. 1 June.

Sidhu, M.S. (1976): Chinese dominance of West Malaysian towns 1921-1970. _Geography 61._ 1 January. pp.17-23.

Silcock, T.H. (1964): _South East Asian Universities: A Comparative Account of Some Development Problems._ North Carolina: Duke University Press.

Sim Wong Kooi (1977): The Evolution of Integrated Science Teaching in Malaysia. _New Trends in Integrated Science Teaching._ IV. Paris: UNESCO.

Straits Settlements (1883): Annual Report for the Straits Settlements 1883. Appendix 13.

Straits Settlements (1901): Proceedings of the Straits Settlements Legislative Council. 19 October.

Straits Settlements (1921): Annual Report on Education.

Watson, J.K.P. (1973c): Educational Development in South East Asia. Unpublished Ph.D. thesis, Reading University.

Wilkinson, R.J. (1957): 'Malay customs and beliefs'. _Journal of the Malayan Branch of the Royal Asiatic Society._ XXX. 4 November.

Wooley Report (1870): Report of the Select Committee of the Legislative Council.

Wong, J. (1979): _ASEAN Economies in Perspective. A Comparative Study of Indonesia, Malaysia, the Philippines, Singapore and Thailand._ London: Macmillan.

World Bank (1981): World Development Report 1981.

Chapter Six

Devereux, R. (1968): South Vietnam's new constitutional
    structure. _Asian Survey_, 6, 6. pp.627-645.

Donnell, J.C. (1976): South Vietnam in 1975: the year of
    communist victory. _Asian Survey_, 16, 1. pp.1-13.

Fitzgerald, F. (1973): _Fire in the lake_. New York: Random
    House.

Foreign Languages Publishing House (1968): _Vietnamese and_
    teaching in Vietnamese in DRVN universities. Hanoi:
    Foreign Languages Publishing House.

Foreign Languages Publishing House (1975): _The Democratic_
    Republic of Vietnam. Hanoi: Foreign Languages Publishing
    House.

Horn, R.C. (1979): Soviet-Vietnamese relations and the future
    of south-east Asia. _Pacific Affairs_, 51, 4. pp.585-605.

Kahin, G.M. (1972): Minorities in the Democratic Republic of
    Vietnam. _Asian Survey_, 12, 7. pp.580-586.

Lindholm, R.W. (ed) (1959): _Vietnam: the first five years_.
    Michigan: Michigan State University Press.

Naughton, P.W. (1979): Some comparisons of higher education
    in Vietnam. _Canadian and International Education_, 2, 8.
    pp.100-116.

Nguyen Khac Vien (ed) (1977): _Cultural problems_. Vietnamese
    Studies, 49. Hanoi.

Scigliano, R. (1963): _South Vietnam: Nation under stress_.
    Boston: Houghton Mifflin.

Thai Quang-Nam (1979): Education et travail productif au
    Vietnam. _Canadian and International Education_, 8, 2.
    pp.92-98.

Winston, J.S. (1970): What will happen to Vietnamese education
    when the war is over? _Adult Leadership_, 19, 1. pp.2-4,
    31-33.

Woodside, A.B. (1971): _Vietnam and the Chinese Model_.
    Cambridge, Massachusetts: Harvard University Press.

Woodside, A.B. (1977): Problems of education in the Chinese
    and Vietnamese revolutions. _Pacific Affairs_, 49,4. 648-66.

Vietnam, 222,6. 1977.

Vietnam Courier, 63, 8. 1977.

Vietnam Courier, 70, 3. 1978.

Vietnam Courier, 77, 10. 1978.

Chapter Seven

Barrett, L.E. (1977): The Rastafarians. Kingston, Jamaica,
    Sangster's and Heinemann.

Brock, C. (1980): 'Problems of Education and Human Ecology in
    Small Tropical Island Nations', in Brock, C. and Ryba, R:
    A Volume of Essays for Elizabeth Halsall: Aspects of
    Education 22.   University of Hull Institute of Education,
    pp.71-83.

Caribbean Examinations Council (1978): Fact Sheet.   Bridgetown.

Clarke, C.G. (1976): Insularity and Identity in the Caribbean.
    Geography, 61, 1.   pp.8-16.

Clarke, C.G. and Lowenthal, D. (1981): 'Barbados Alone', The
    Geographical Magazine, LIII, 7.   pp.465-470.

Cross, M. (1979): Urbanisation and Urban Growth in the
    Caribbean. Cambridge: Cambridge University Press.

Demas, W.G. (1975): 'Change and Renewal in the Caribbean',
    Mitchell, D.I. (ed): Challenges in the New Caribbean, 2.
    Barbados, C.C.C. Publishing House.

Edwards, V.K. (1979): The West Indian language issue in
    British Schools: challenges and responses. London:
    Routledge and Kegan Paul.

Foner, N. (1973): Status and Power in Rival Jamaica. New York
    and London: Teachers' College Press, Columbia University.

Moss, R. (ed) (1973): The Stability of the Caribbean. London:
    Institute for the Study of Conflict.

Naipaul, V.S. (1969): The Middle Passage. Harmondsworth:
    Penguin.

Spate, O.H.K. (1963): 'Islands and Men', Fosberg, F.R. (ed):
    Man's Place in the Island Ecosystem. Honolulu, Bishop
    Museum Press. pp.253-264.

Chapter Eight

Beltran, Luis Ramiro and Elizabeth Fox de Cardona (1980): 'Mass
    Media and Cultural Domination'. Prospects, v. X, No. 1.
    pp.76-89.

Bizot, Judith (1975): 'Educational Reform in Peru: A Study
    Prepared for the International Educational Reporting
    Service'. Paris: UNESCO.

Brunner, J.J. (1980): 'La Universidad y la Formacion de
    Intelectuales'. Mensaje (Santiago, Chile), No. 242.
    September. pp.494-499.

Cardoso, Fernando H. (1977): 'The Originality of a Copy:
    CEPAL and the Idea of Development'. CEPAL Review,
    Second half of 1977. pp.7-40.

Dahse, Fernando (1979): El Mapa de la Extrema Riqueza.
    Santiago (Chile): Editorial Aconcagua.

Dorfman, Ariel and Armand Mattlart (1975): How to Read Donald
    Duck. Imperialist Ideology in the Disney Comic. New
    York: International General.

Farrell, Joseph (1974): 'National Planning Systems in Latin
    America: Their Environment and Their Impact'. Educational
    Planning, vol. I, No. 1. (May). pp.20-33.

Filgueira, Carlos (1978): 'Educational Development and Social
    Stratification in Latin America (1960-1970). Prospects,
    V. VIII, No. 3. pp.222-243.

Foxley, Alejandro (1980): 'Hacia una Economia de Libre Mercado:
    Chile 1974-1979'. Paper presented at the Workshop 'Six
    Years of Military Rule in Chile, sponsored by the Latin
    American Program of the Woodrow Wilson International
    Center for Scholars, Smithsonial Institution, Washington
    D.C. (May 15-17).

Frank, Andre Gunder (1972): Lumpen-Bourgeoisie and Lumpen-
    Development: Dependence, Class and Politics in Latin
    America. New York: Monthly Review Press.

Freire, Paolo (1972): Education for Critical Consciousness.
    London: Sheed and Ward.

Gajardo, Marcela (1976): 'Educacion Campesina y Cambio Cultural:
    Una Experiencia Piloto'. Educacion Hoy, v. VI, No. 32.
    (September-October). pp.41-75.

Garcia Huidobro, J.E. and Jorge Ochoa (1978): 'Tendencias de la Investigacion en Educacion en America Latina'. Santiago (Chile): Centro de Investigacion y Desarrollo de la Educacion (Manuscript Report).

Graciarena, Horge (1972): 'Los Procesos de Reforma Universitaria y el Cambio Social en America Latina' in P. Dooner and Ivan Lavados (1979) (eds): La Universidad Latin americana: Vision de una Decade. Santiago (Chile): Corporacion de Promocion Universitaria CPU.

Guardian Weekly (1980), November 2.

Huacani, C., Mamani, E. and Subriats, J. (1978): 'Warisata "Escuela-Ayllu". El Por que de un Fracaso'. La Paz (Bolivia): Centro Boliviano de Investigacionny Accion Educativas (Manuscript Report).

Juarez, Benit (1971): Documentos, Discursos y Correspondencia. Selected and edited by Jorge L. Tamayo. Mexico: Secretaria del Patrimonio Nacional.

La Belle, Thomas (1976): Non Formal Education and Social Change in Latin America. Los Angeles: UCLA Latin American Center Publications.

Labarca, Guillermo et al (1977): La Educacion Burguesa. Mexico: Editorial Nueva Imagen, S.A.

Lagos, Gustavo and Horacio H. Godoy (1977): Revolution of Being. A Latin American View of the Future. New York: The Free Press.

Lema, Vicente and Angel D. Marquez (1978): 'What Kind of Development and Which Education'. Prospects, v. VIII, No. 3. pp.295-305.

Levinson, J. and J. de Onis (1970): The Alliance that Lost Its Way. A Critical Report on the Alliance for Progress. Chicago: Quadrangle Books.

Mariategui, Jose Carlos (1965): Siete Ensayos de la Realidad Peruana. Lima (Peru): Editorial Amanta.

OAS (1972): 'Co-operative Action in the Late 1960s'. Americas (April).

Oteiza, Enrique (1979): 'Collective Self-Reliance: Some Old and New Issues' in Jose J. Villamil, (ed): Transnational Capitalism and National Development. New Perspectives on Dependence. Hassocks, Sussex: The Harvester Press.

Marini, Ru Mauro et al (1977): 'The Brazilian University'.
    Brazilian Studies. Toronto: Latin American Research
    Unit (LARU), Working Paper.

Pearson, Lester B. (1970): Why Aid: Partners in Development.
    Report of the Commission on International Development.
    New York: Praeger.

Santos, Theotonio dos (1970): Depenencia Economica y Cambio
    Revolucionario. Caracas: Nueva Izquierda.

Schultz, Theodore (1961): 'Investment in Human Capital'.
    American Economic Review 51 (March).

Silva Michelena, Jose A. (1976): Politica y Bloques de Poder.
    Mexico: Siglo Veintiuno.

Somavia, Juan (1978): 'The Transnational Power Structure and
    International Information'. LARU Studies, v. II, No. 3.
    (June). pp.6-15.

Stavenhagen, Rodolfo (1969): 'Seven Erroneous Theses About
    Latin America' in Irving Louis Horowits, Josue de Castro
    and John Gervasi, (eds): Latin American Radicalism. A
    Documentary Report on Left and Nationalist Movements.
    New York: Vintage Books.

South. The Third World Magazine, (1980), No. 1. (October).

Tunnerman, C. (1976): 'Diagnostico y Tendencias Innovatives de
    la Educacion Postsecundaria en Latinoamericana y del
    Caribe sobre Nuevas Formas de Educacion Postsecundaria.
    Caracas.

UNESCO: International Commission on the Development of
    Education (1972). Learning to Be. Paris: Harrap.

Union Panamericana (1961): 'La Educacion Superior en America
    Latina y la Co-operacion Internacional'. Washington D.C.

Vasconi, Tomas (1977): Aportes para una Teoria de la
    Educacion. Sobre la Imagen Pequeno Burguesa de la
    Escuela, la 'Piramide Escolar' y la 'Democratisacion'
    en G. Labarca et al. La Educacion Burguesa. Mexico:
    Editorial Nueva Imagen, S.A.

Ward, F. Champion (ed) (1974): Education and Development
    Reconsidered. The Bellagio Conference Papers. New York:
    Praeger.

Weinberg, Gregorio (1977): 'Modelos Educativos en el Desarrollo Historico de America Latina'. Manuscript publication of the <u>Desarrollo y Educacion en America Latina y el Caribe</u>, an international project sponsored by UNESCO, ECLA and PNUD.

World Bank, The (1980): <u>Education Sector Policy Paper</u>. Washington D.C: World Bank.

Chapter Nine

Anon (1961): 'Welcome for Mr. Chips'. Fiji Times and Herald 5.8.61.

Clarke, Joy W.K. (1958): Levuka Public School, Ovalau, Fiji. A Comparison with a District High School in New Zealand. Diploma in Education Essay, Auckland University.

East West Centre (1966): Correspondence, Director of Education, Fiji to Vice-Chancellor, Institute for Student Exchange, East West Centre, Hawaii. 19.10.66.

Fiji (1923): Journal of the Legislative Council. Annexure to Message No. 3 of 1923 Council Paper No. 15.

Fiji (1925): Journal of the Legislative Council, 1925. Council Paper No. 2.

Fiji (1928): Journal of the Legislative Council, 1928. Council Paper No. 87.

Fiji (1935): Journal of the Legislative Council, 1935. Council Paper No. 8.

Fiji (1939): Correspondence - Messrs. Swinton and Usher to Director of Education, Wellington. 31.1.39. Fiji Education Department Files.

Fiji (1945): Correspondence - Ban, M. et al to Members of Board of Education. 5.1.45. Fiji Education Department Files.

Fiji (1963): Correspondence - Director of Education, Fiji to Officer for Islands Education. 24.4.63. Fiji Education Department Files.

Fiji (1964): Correspondence - Director of Education, Fiji to Officer for Islands Education, New Zealand. 24.11.64. Fiji Education Department Files.

Fiji (1965): Memorandum, Director of Education, Fiji to
    Financial Secretary, Fiji. 23.11.65. Fiji Education
    Department Files.

Fiji (1969): Correspondence - Officer for Island Eduction to
    Secretary, Association of New Zealand Teachers - Fiji.
    14.4.69. Fiji Education Department Files.

Fiji (1970): Correspondence - Director of Education, Fiji, to
    Secretary for Foreign affairs, Fiji. 22.10.70. Fiji
    Education Department Files.

Fiji (1976): Ministry of Education, Youth and Sport. Achieve-
    ments - 1965 to 1975. Suva: Ministry of Education, Youth
    and Sport.

Gwilliam, F. (1949): Report from Fiji. Undated. Fiji Education
    Department Files.

New Zealand Education Department (1958): Correspondence -
    Director of Education, New Zealand to Director of Educ-
    ation, Fiji. 26.5.58.

New Zealand Education Department (1958): Correspondence -
    Officer for Islands Education, New Zealand to Director
    of Education, New Zealand. 31.3.58.

New Zealand Education Department (1959): Correspondence -
    Director of Education, New Zealand to Director of
    Education, Fiji. 8.6.59.

New Zealand Education Department (1960): Correspondence -
    Officer for Islands Education, New Zealand to Director
    of Education, Fiji. 7.11.60.

Office for Islands Education (1949): Comments by Officer for
    Islands Education, 1949.

Chapter Ten

Adams, D. and Bjork, R.M. (1971): Education in Developing
    Areas. New York: Longmans.

Anderson, C.A. and Bowman, M.J. (eds) (1965): Education and
    Economic Development. Chicago, Aldine.

Anderson, C.A. (1969): Some heretical views on educational
    planning. Comparative Education Review, 13, 3. pp.260-75

Coleman, J.S. (1965): Education and Political Development.
    Princeton: Princeton University Press.

Coombs, P.H. and Ahmed, M. (1974): Attacking Rural Poverty: How non-formal education can help. Baltimore: Johns Hopkins U.P.

Dore, R. (1980): The Future of Formal Education in Developing countries in Simmons, J. (ed): The Education Dilemma: Policy issues for developing countries in the 1980s. Oxford: Pergamon Press.

Faure, E. et al (1972): Learning to Be. Paris: UNESCO.

Fredriksen, B. (1981): Progress Towards Regional Targets for Universal Primary Education: A Statistical Review. International Journal of Educational Development, 1, 1, in print.

Ginsberg, N.S. (1955): The Great City in South East Asia. American Journal of Sociology, 40.

Harbison, F. and Myers, C.A. (1964): Education, Manpower and Economic Growth. New York: Holt, Rinehart-Winston.

Husen, T. (1979): The School in Question. London: Oxford University Press.

Illich, I. (1971): De-schooling Society. Harmondsworth: Penguin.

Iredale, R. (1978): Non-formal education in India: dilemmas and initiatives. Comparative Education, 14, 3. pp.267-275.

Lengrand, P. (1972): An introduction to lifelong learning. Paris: UNESCO.

Lewin, K. (1975): Science education in Malaysia and Sri Lanka. Institute of Development Studies Discussion Paper 74, July. University of Sussex.

Michael, I. (1981): The Role of the University in Development, Education and Development. Proceedings of the Education Study Group of the Development Studies Association, 2, 1, in print.

Myrdal, G. (1970): The Challenge of World Poverty. New York: Pantheon Books.

Nichterlein, S. (1974): Languages and Values in Indonesia, in Murray-Smith, S. (ed): Melbourne Studies in Education. Melbourne: Melbourne University Press. pp.222-240.

237

Overseas Development Ministry (1975): Overseas Development.
    The Changing Emphasis in British Aid Policies. More
    Help to the Poorest. Cmnd. 6270. London: H.M.S.O.

Oxenham, J. (1980): Employers and Qualifications. IDS Bulletin.
    University of Sussex, 11, 2, May 6-12.

Palma, G. (1978): Dependency: a formal theory of underdevelop-
    ment on a methodology for the analysis of concrete
    situations of underdevelopment. World Development, 6,7-8.

Paulston, R.G. (1980): Other Dreams, Other Schools: Folk
    Colleges in Social and Ethnic Movements. Pittsburg:
    University Centre for International Studies.

UNESCO (1977): Bulletin of Education in the Asian Region.
    Bangkok.

Watson, J.K.P. (1981b): Alternative Strategies for Educational
    Development: an overview. Education and Development:
    Proceedings of the Education Study Group of the Develop-
    ment Studies Association. 1, 1.

Watson, J.K.P. (1981c): The impact of the Karachi Plan on
    educational development in Asia. International Journal
    of Educational Development, 1, 1. pp.32-49.

Weiler, H. (1976): Education and Development: from the age of
    innocence to the age of scepticism. Comparative Education.
    14, 3. pp.179-198.

World Bank (1974): Education Sector, Policy Working Paper.

World Bank (1975): Rural Development Sector Policy Paper.

World Bank (1980): Education Sector Policy Paper.

Wong Hoy Kee, F. (1973): Comparative Studies in South East
    Asian Education. Hong Kong: Heinemann.